WOODCHIPS & BEANS

LIFE in the EARLY LUMBER WOODS of NOVA SCOTIA

MIKE PARKER

NIMBUS
PUBLISHING

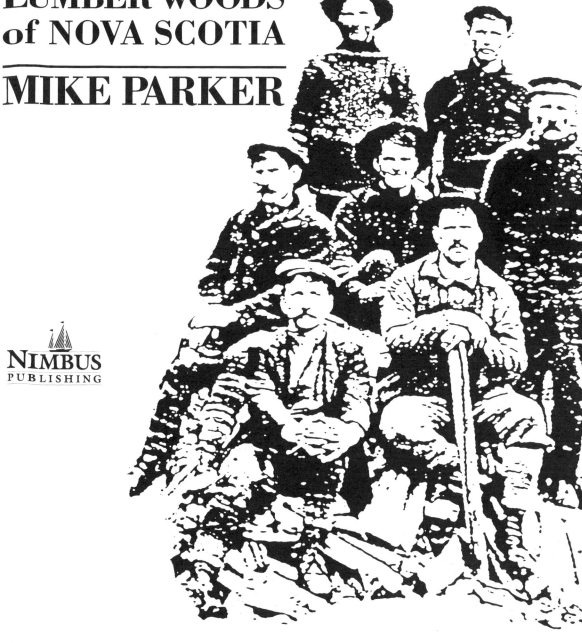

Nimbus Publishing Limited
P.O. Box 9301, Station A
Halifax, N.S. B3K 5N5
(902) 455-4286

Design: Kathy Kaulbach, Halifax
Cover photograph: Lumber camp and crew near Bear River. Donated by Harold Porter.
Printed and bound in Canada by Hignell Printing Limited

Canadian Cataloguing in Publication Data

Parker, Mike.

  Woodchips and beans

  Includes bibliographical references.
  ISBN 1-55109-023-6

1. Lumbermen—Nova Scotia—Biography. 2. Lumbering—Nova Scotia—
History—20th century. 3. Logging—Nova Scotia—History—20th century.
4. Forests and forestry—Nova Scotia—History—20th century. I. Title.

SD146.N6P37 1992   634.9'8'092   C92-098650-1

For my wife Helen, whose patience and
support made this book possible.

CONTENTS

CREDITS

Nova Scotia Department of Tourism & Culture for their financial assistance; Nimbus Publishing, especially Dorothy Blythe; Paul Collins and Scott Robson of the Nova Scotia Museum; Don Cruickshank and staff of Sherbrooke Village; Bear River Historical Society; Nova Scotia Public Archives; Rick Swain; Douglas Beall; Dan Harmer; Chuck Edgren; Tom Kennedy; Ralph Stopps; Wallace MacRae; Lillian Scott Perry; Gary & Barb MacDonald; Fred Ellis; Orrin Pulley; Hilton Scott; Wilbur Parker; George Volans; Parker Cruickshank; Charles Noonan; Roy Harrison; Peter Breen; Art Mattix; Ralph Burgoyne; Harris Lewis; Stanley Scott; Lee Keating; Arron Darris; Charlie Kelly; Robert Kincaid; Willis Forrest; Duncan John MacAskill; Alan Hunt; John Taul; Irene Jones; Henry Young; Gerald Day; James Moore; Maggie Graham; Jack Anderson; Melvin Bower; Herbert Harris; Paul Armstrong; Creighton Balcomb; Clinton Miller; Joe MacLean; Jimmy McKinnon; John Nicholson; Walter MacDougall; Harry McCurdy; Dorothy Bayers; Vern Crockett; Clarance Archibald; John Scott; Myrtle Whittemore; Fred Power; Frank Burns; Leonard Taylor; Howard Coady; George MacRae; Ralph Baker; Harold Trenholm; Ernie Coates; Arnold Smith; Layton Smith; Harry Carter.

INTRODUCTION

"The traveller among Nova Scotian backwoods settlements, with an observant eye for fresh 'types' of humanity, is sure to have his attention arrested by little knots of men with weather-roughened features who gather about front steps of village stores, the doors of the hotels, and the clandestine bar-rooms, masquerading as eating saloons. These men are not farmers; they are not hunters or trappers; nor are they village loafers; their athletic appearance, their bright blue and scarlet blouses, their neat leggings laced with tasselled cords, their jaunty hats proclaim them to be a class apart. They are 'loggers' or 'lumberers,' men not quite of the forest nor quite of the farm. Their summers are occupied by the rude cultivation of some rugged patch, by courtesy called a 'farm,' where a few acres of clearing fall apart from the dark shadows of the coniferous woods. Winter finds them deep in the heart of the forest primeval, in a log camp crowded with their mates. Here they go on all winter long in spite of cold and snows and the ravings of wild winds among the tops of the pines and hemlocks, cutting down the giants of the forest, and piling up the trunks on the frozen river. Should the traveller during the weeks of early autumn go canoeing up any Canadian forest stream...he will be sure to encounter groups of 'axemen' passing up river to their winter exile."

Arthur P. Silver, *Farm Cottage, Camp & Canoe in Maritime Canada*, 1907.

What follows is an oral history of the lumber and pulpwood camps, river drives, sawmills, and the people who worked them. It covers approximately a thirty-year period, from the 1920s to the 1940s, a time when camp life and work methods remained for the most part unchanged from the turn of the century and groups of axemen still passed upriver to their winter exile.

Lumbering in Nova Scotia has a long and storied history, dating back nearly four centuries to the arrival of the French explorers De Monts and Champlain and their establishment of Canada's oldest permanent settlement in 1605 at Port Royal. In 1612, North America's first sawmill was built at nearby Lequille, and by 1632, French trader Nicholas Denys was exporting whipsawed timbers from the LaHave River, a first for commercial lumber trade in the New World. According to Denys, who travelled extensively throughout the province, Nova Scotia's forests of 1600 were made up predominantly of red oak, white cedar, white and red pine, spruce, fir, hemlock, white and yellow birch, beech, aspen, maple, and ash.

Following a century and a half of conflict between England and France over possession of Canada, all the spoils of war were ceded to Britain in 1763 with the Treaty of Paris. A vigorous campaign to settle Britain's new acquisitions was soon undertaken, enticing would-be colonists with land grants, often huge tracts to be divided among a group of proprietors. Most early grants in Nova Scotia were along the coast or river courses, as these were the only means of transportation, and roads were virtually nondescript until the 1790s. A Broad Arrow Policy instituted in 1728 in the province reserved all white pine twenty-four inches in diameter at a distance of twelve inches from the ground for ships' masts of the Royal Navy. Failure to heed the mark of the blazed arrow would see one's land grant forfeited to the crown.

Thirty-one sawmills were at work in Nova Scotia by 1761, and in 1762 the first laws respecting forests and what constituted marketable timber products were passed by the Nova Scotia Legislative Assembly. Being a maritime colony surrounded by the sea, shipbuilding was well under way by the mid-1700s, providing vessels for fishing, commerce, transportation, and war. To meet these demands, and others placed upon the forests by the influx of settlers, the government offered building incentives of £20 for every new sawmill. Sixty-five mills were running in 1783, 90 in 1785, and 112 by 1787.

Trade with the West Indies began in the mid-1780s, and this market remained valuable to the Nova Scotian economy for more than a hundred years. Timber products, fish, and whale oil were shipped down in exchange for rum, molasses, sugar, salt, and coffee. Other trading partners of that era included Bermuda, South America, Newfoundland, and England. Coupled with the Napoleonic Wars in 1793 which closed Britain's primary source of timber and wood products in the Baltics, an increased demand for Nova Scotian ships and lumber ushered in the nineteenth century.

In 1800, 565 loads of fir were exported to England; by 1812, this had increased to 25,203 loads, or roughly fifteen million board feet. In 1804, forty-nine vessels carried exports to the West Indies; by 1814, 181 ships were plying their trade; and from 1835 to 1875, the West Indies was Nova Scotia's primary trading partner. The ship-building industry flourished: virtually any port along our two thousand miles of coastline had some form of shipyard, often in the close vicinity of a sawmill, and as early as 1831 at least forty of these seafaring communities were carrying on an export trade. By 1864, Yarmouth town was the richest port in North America. Sometime around 1870, three thousand vessels were built in one year in Nova Scotia, giving the province the world's third-largest merchant marine fleet, preceded only by England and France.

The proliferation of timber exports and shipbuilding put tremendous demands upon the forest resources. By the very early 1800s, virtually all timber of any significance along the coast had been cut, and the search for new stands turned to the interior. River drives were in full swing by 1810 and men had begun their "winter exiles" in lumber camps. As Arthur P. Silver wrote, "The shelter for the horses and the long-horned mild-eyed oxen, which patiently tug at the logs all winter, is hardly distinguished from the men's camp, except that it is over-hung by no wreaths of smoke." By mid-century various counties had become well known for their specific products: Cumberland for its deal, Queens for pine boards, Lunenburg for spruce and hemlock lumber, and Pictou, Colchester, and Halifax for their squared timber.

Water was *the* prime factor in early operations. A dry steam bed leaving logs miles away and water wheels silent was a lumberman's worst nightmare, causing financial ruin on more than one occasion. In 1871, 1,144 sawmills were operating in Nova Scotia, of which all but eighteen were water-driven. Even as late as the mid-1930s, sawmills were dependent for over thirty percent of their power on water. In 1930, 838 mills could be found in the province.

Early on, lumber production was tediously slow and labour-intensive. Two men on a whipsaw could only put up one or two hundred board feet of lumber a day. But with the advent of the single up and down water-driven saw, production increased to as much as one thousand feet a day. And this was improved upon considerably with the gang saw, a group of up and down saws working in unison. Circular saws, cutting more than thirty thousand feet a day with less wastage, were common by the 1880s, and within ten years, band saws were producing forty thousand feet and more a day.

Until the late nineteenth century, sawmills were stationary, built advantageously at the mouth of a river or at the confluence of its tributaries. Many were small family operations that cut a hundred thousand board feet or less and operated no more than six months of the year. Larger mills, some much larger, were headed by influential businessmen with names such as Davison, Dickie, Ellershausen, Clarke, Hart, McMullen, Benjamin, Lewis, Bragg, White, Stehelin, and Campbell. The the big three of the 1870s were E.D. Davison & Sons of Bridgewater, S.P. Benjamin, also of Bridgewater, and William Chisholm of Sheet Harbour. Between these three, more than eighteen million feet of wood were produced annually.

Steam was powering mills by the 1880s, and portable sawmills came in around 1890, allowing greater flexibility and moving the cutting further away from the rivers and streams. The first portable sawmills were used in Hants, Colchester, and Cumberland counties but they were widespread by the end of the first world war. Steam was the principal power source in mills from the early 1900s to the late 1940s when diesel took over.

Pulpmills have been operating in Nova Scotia since the 1880s. In 1885, William Chisholm had Canada's first sulphite mill built and operational at Sheet Harbour, and pulpwood was exported from the province as early as the 1890s. During the First World War, demand increased markedly for pulp for newsprint and explosives, making it a lucrative business. At the same time, lumber prices climbed as Great Britain was forced once more to look away from the Baltics to satisfy her needs. The postwar crash came in 1919, with lumber suffering more than pulp. Many logging companies went bankrupt, leaving vast tracts of woodland up for grabs at bargain prices. While lumbering continued at vastly reduced profits, pulp made large inroads, and a number of companies operated over the next few years. Some changed ownership and names frequently because of poor business skills and fluctuating markets, and many had one thing in common: American investors.

New England held the majority of U.S. paper mills. With such a concentration came depletion of fir and spruce stocks, so a roving eye was cast for new suppliers. Most Canadian provinces had banned the export of unmanufactured pulpwood from crown land by 1920, but Nova Scotia had no such law. Even if it had, the province still possessed an abundance of privately-held woodlands—more than ten million acres worth—much of which could be had cheaply. Nova Scotia was easily reached by water from the eastern seaboard, and so the Americans moved in. Some preferred merely to buy pulp, but

others were anxious also to own the land upon which it grew to ensure future supplies.

One of the biggest land grabbers was Boston-based Hollingsworth & Whitney, which purchased huge acreages in Annapolis, Kings, Queens, Lunenburg, and Cumberland counties totalling more than half a million acres. While selling a considerable amount of sawlog stumpage to local contractors, their primary concern was pulp for their mill in Winslow, Maine. This they shipped out of Bridgewater by boat, and from other points in the province by rail. By 1927, more than two million acres of timberland were held by American pulp and paper companies. That same year, however, exports of pulpwood from crown lands were prohibited and most companies went bankrupt when the Great Depression hit.

World War Two followed hard on the heels of the Depression, and seaborne exports of pulpwood were zero by 1941 as the Battle of the Atlantic raged and ships for other than the war effort were in short supply. What little pulp was shipped during the last three years of the war went to the United States by rail. It was not a business for the faint of heart:

"The pulp and paper industry in Nova Scotia…suffered directly from the effects of the economic and political extremes of the times. New technology helped profitability by increasing output and quality, but poor business acumen and the vagaries of war and the depression compounded the difficulties of this somewhat risky and

Camps were among the last of traditional ways to go. Improved roads phased them out during the 1960s and by the 1970s few workers spent a night in the woods. Those that did, in some cases, had the luxury of mobile trailers, one of the improvements over the days of old. (Harold Porter)

very competitive sector of the eastern North American economy." (Ralph S. Johnson, *Forests of Nova Scotia*, 1986).

Three companies each operate their own pulpmills in Nova Scotia today. Stora Forest Industries, a Swedish company, began producing pulp in 1961 from their mill at Point Tupper in Inverness County. In 1967, Scott Maritimes Pulp Limited, a subsidiary of American Scott Paper Company of Pennsylvania, opened its mill at Abercrombie Point in Pictou County. The third is Bowater Mersey Paper Company Limited, today part of the American Bowater conglomerate. The original Mersey Paper company began operations at Liverpool in 1929 but was bought out in 1956 upon the death of Izaak Walton Killam, the founder and principal stockholder of the company, by Bowater Corporation of North America.

It has been fifty years since chain saws first made the crosscut obsolete, mechanization began to replace hoof power, better roads and transportation made river drives impractical, and the last of the axemen were seen "passing upriver to their winter exile." Canadian folklorist Edith Fowke defines folktales as "all types of traditional narratives that circulate orally." Among these she includes personal experience narratives, "the kind of material often termed oral history." *Wood Chips & Beans* is such a book. It is not a history of forestry in Nova Scotia per se. Two excellent books have already been written on the subject: Barbara Robertson's *Sawpower* and Ralph Johnson's *Forests of Nova Scotia*. Rather, this book is meant to be entertaining and informative, historically representative of those times, but in no way definitive in scope. Hundreds of mills and woods camps employed thousands of woodsmen. Through a collection of memories from choppers, sawyers, mill hands, teamsters, yarders, cooks, and river drivers, we are able to look back at the end of an era, the last days of the axe and crosscut saw, horse and ox teams, wagons and sleighs, pickaroons and logjams. This is a story about a way of life that has disappeared.

James Moore

James Moore, 82, lives in East Uniacke, Hants County, and spent thirty-four years in the local lumber woods. When not logging, he and the "missus" also ran a small farm, harvested crops and hayed. A lifelong horse enthusiast, he left the woods in 1956 to train and race sulkies for the next thirty-five years. At one time, he had seventeen horses under his control.

I was thirteen when I went in the mill. I carried softwood and hardwood slabs the first job that I done. Slabs was off the side of the lumber where they sawed it. They were burnin' the slabs and they was whole length. You know what them'd be like. A big butt end and you'd pick it up in the centre and be draggin' it. I didn't hang at that too long. Then I went drivin' a team—I was fourteen—and I drove team for about three or four years and hauled logs out of the woods. And I went in choppin', yarded, canted, done anything that come up. You couldn't be independent. I worked for George and his son Georgie Cole right back of East Uniacke. They logged and sawed the year round. They weren't a big one [operation].

The Brooklyn Lumber Company logged in east of here. They were named after Brooklyn down here.[1] I didn't work for them, I was too young then. A big outfit, had about, I think, four or five sets [camps] in. They bought lumber from everybody that had some and logged it. They started in the fall and logged, got it out in the winter, and in the spring they river drove [on the Herbert River] down to Brooklyn. They had a big mill and they sawed it there. They was here seven years and they cut forty-seven million feet of lumber. They finished in 1920, they had all they wanted of it.

They had camps over to Mount Efram. It was an old farm way back in the woods. They had camps in Beaverbank; I don't remember just all how many they had there, two, I think. They logged in on this side of the Beaverbank Road and then they logged two cuts on the other side. Into the King Dam they had a camp. And they had a camp down

"Log camps, one log on top of the other, and notch them in and caulk them with moss…. They were warm, a log camp." (Bear River Historical Society)

on the Herbert River in Rawdon; they called it Happy Home.

Sometimes they'd have twenty-five or thirty men to a camp. Course the fellers that worked on the road and that, they stayed at one of the camps. And the cook and cookee. They always had a cookee, sometimes two. There'd be some of them stay there from the time they went in in the fall 'til they come out in the spring. [Local people], they'd stay at the camp and come home on a Saturday, Sunday. There was an old road went right through to Rawdon and down through to Brooklyn. They had what they called a tote team, they hauled in the grub supplies and that. They'd have to do all the camps and they'd keep makin' trips. Down in Rawdon, Charlie Moxin had a store and they dealt a lot there.

Log camps, one log on top of the other, and notch them in and caulk them with moss. They'd have tar paper and poles [for the roof]. They'd put a tier of tar paper and then they'd lap it and put a pole in between and that held them down. The wind never got a rake at them in the woods like they would outside. They were warm, a log camp. In my time, they were buildin' them out of boards.

Some of them was built double, like the cook had his end and the choppers and them had theirs. Sometimes the bunkhouse was separate, but not too often. Mostly, they had a partition in between; the cook slept out in his end where he cooked, and the other end was for the men. They'd be probably thirty feet long by fifteen feet wide, I suppose, wide enough for a table, and they had bunks run along the side where they slept. They'd be two bunks high. Everything was poles, there was no boards or anything. The stable was poles too. Maybe the last year they got some boards in. They made a bed out of boughs. Some of them fellers could make a bed just like a spring, stuck them all in, all the one length, and keep stickin' them in and goin'. Them old fellers, they'd work and make a nice bunk. The bough beds was all done away with when I went; had straw mattresses [then].

Dirt floors, but not the cook's end. They used to have a set of adzes.* You got the [pole] floor down and you adzed her all off so the cook could get around without breakin' his ankles. Sometimes the men would adze the bunkhouse off. They adzed the table off pretty good. There would be windows in the cook's end and they used to put a window in the other but not too many in the bunkhouse. They couldn't put them in the side, the bunks was there. If they shifted camps, they'd take that window and put it in the next one. They used to buy a stove, but sometimes they'd have a barrel stove. The cook had a wood range and plenty to work with.

It wasn't too many of 'em washed or bathed. They wasn't all that way now. There was some fellers that bathed, you know, get a tub or somethin'. One feller used to run down and jump in the lake. He'd strip right off, put somethin' over him and he'd run right down where she was open, where a run went out, jump into 'er and jump out and run for the camp agin. They washed themselves around, some of them more than others, but in my father's time, some never washed all winter. Some fellers would wash their clothes Sunday and dry them.

Brooklyn Lumber Company wouldn't cut nothin' under ten inches if they didn't have to, if it wasn't in the way. The walkin' boss was Willie John Chisholm. He went and marked out where they couldn't go. Say you had a piece of timber in there, why, he'd go and blaze up a line so they wouldn't get in over on you. You cut everything if it makes lumber. You didn't take no rotten stuff. Say there was one there six or eight inches on the butt and it was in the way, they'd cut it, but if they cut it down, they took it out, they never left it. There wasn't a great lot [of hardwood] cut, nothin' like the softwood. Spruce was the main wood and fir, but if it got too old it would start gettin' red [rotten]. They made "deal"; it was three inches thick and six, seven, eight, nine, or ten inches wide. You could cut them anywheres from seven feet to twenty, accordin' to how much the

* An adze was a hand cutting tool with its blade at right angles to its handle and usually curved inward, used for dressing timber.

"When the choppers was choppin', there'd be three men in a crowd. There'd be two men choppin' and one man makin' ready." (Bear River Historical Society)

tree tapered, to get the most out of it. It went overseas and they resawed it over there. I cut pit props too for three years. They went to England for the mines, to keep 'em from cavin' in.

They used the Blenkhorn axe 'til a nice little axe come out they called the Spiller in 1920 or '21. The Blenkhorn was the number one axe, the best one you could buy. We thought they had somethin' if they got a Blenkhorn. It wouldn't cost maybe a dollar and a half. There was always somebody in the village made handles and sold them. The Spiller was a nicer little axe. They was thin, and the Blenkhorn was a heavy axe and quite thick; it would be approximately two and a half, three pounds. You had to do a lot of grindin' on it, but the Spiller you didn't. And she stood up too, as good as the other one unless you missed and hit a rock or somethin', you'd have to do some grindin'. But you give 'em a good grindin' when you started, without you ground 'er too thin that she bent.

When the choppers was choppin', there'd be three men in a crowd. There'd be two men choppin' and one man makin' ready. You come up to the tree and you put a notch into it. And that notch is goin' to guide it wherever you want it to fall. Then you take your crosscut saw—they're pulp saws now, but they were crosscuts then—and you started on the back of the tree and you sawed in evenly, kept the same on each side. When she was sawed pretty well up, they had a wedge they'd put into it and that would tip 'er and she'd go down. They measured it and cut the logs out and go to another one. The choppin' was just left, but it never built up like it does now. More lumber's wasted now than there was them days; they didn't waste nothin'.

The "swamper" come along and cut the limbs all off it and snouted it so the yard horse wouldn't be hung up all the time. He'd cut a snig road about so wide so the horse could get to the log. The yard teamster has a set of dogs,* drives them into the logs and hooks the whiffle tree onto that—that's what the traces is hooked to the horse— and he'd drag it out to the brow, that's what the pile of logs is. They put down skids and things to keep them off of the ground. There'd be two men rollin' 'em up. They never yarded them too far because there was pretty good timber and they'd fill up a brow pretty quick.

* Dogs are made of iron, bent usually in the shape of a U with sharpened ends for gripping or holding logs.

Once it's browed, two horses come with a set of sleds. Oh God, I don't know how many teams they'd have. I'd say maybe an average anyway of three teams to a camp. They had a set of bob sleds, one trailed, and they loaded both sleds; the logs was long enough to go on both sleds. Once the sled team takes it—we're talkin' about loadin' in the winter now—he goes right to the landin'. Now the landin' is the mill yard, pond, or whatever. On the lake, they piled them all onto it. In the spring, between the time it broke up that they couldn't sled and that, they'd yard right to the river and put them in. They made sled roads, like from here to the river, and two men worked onto it all winter as they sledded if there was a little slue in the road or rock or anything. That was their job; they looked after the whole road.

Soon as the ice went out of the river and lakes, they started a river drive. The river drivin' was all done when I went into the woods to work. My father, Theodore Moore, was on the river drive every spring. Anybody could drive. There was some fellers wouldn't, but most of them from around here went on the drive. They'd get about a month of work or pretty handy to that.

There'd be places on the river the logs would all pile up, a jam they called it, and they'd have to dig them out and blow them out with dynamite, loosen them up so they'd float. They generally had a couple of Indians that done that. They'd come in from outside. It's only the Indians that was experienced at river drivin' that come, generally about two or three. They're good on logs and they're good with the boat. They had a boat there in case a man went in and couldn't make it on his own. Sometimes they wouldn't have them, but mostly they had a couple that looked after the boat. They

"They had a boat there in case a man went in and couldn't make it on his own.... They used to get in that boat and go down there; well, no car'd go as fast." (Bear River Historical Society)

followed the rear down, that's what they call bringin' down the last of the logs, rearin' them down. They used to get in that boat and go down there; well, no car'd go as fast.

If you'd good luck, you could move a lot of logs, and if you didn't ...that was one thing you couldn't judge. They had the river named all the way what problems they'd get into. They had a place down there they called the Devil's Jaws. It was bad for tyin' up logs because when she come over, she went down end first. They'd have two or three men there waitin' fer it and if they'd get the first log out, they was all right. Course, to me, it was fun to watch it, I was only a kid. My father would never allow me near the river. All right to stay back on the bank and watch, but we was never allowed around it too much.

There was a couple of 'em hurt, I guess, but not too serious. Drownin' would be the nearest thing, if you went down and got caught and the log took you down. I didn't see it or nothin', but I used to hear them talkin' about [a man], he got tangled up. I forget how now, but the water took the logs and he went with them. I think he got beat up a little but it didn't kill him. I don't ever remember of anybody being killed.

On the river drive the cook always had a cookee because maybe he'd have sixty men there and have to put lunch up for them. Another thing they'd have is a lunch carrier. The men would get up in the mornin', eat their breakfast, and they'd be gone. Then the lunch carrier, there'd be two of them, they'd go with a big basket on their back, all they could carry full of grub, out for about half past nine, ten o'clock, and give them somethin' to eat. One feller'd take and go that way [upriver] and the other feller'd go that way [downriver]. Then they'd go back to the camp, load up again, and give them their dinner and a lunch in the afternoon because they'd be out 'til dark workin' on the drive.

When they was up here, at the Billy Moore's Spring they called it, the river drivin' camp was there. Then down the road four miles there was another one. They used them for loggin' and then in the spring they used the same camps for river drivin'. They followed the water. When it was too far to go down the river, they'd move on down, cook and all.

It's only a guess for me, but it must've been fifteen miles anyway, or more, just countin' the miles on the river they took them from up here to Brooklyn. I think they said that about three miles up the river, there was just nothin' but logs. They peeled the hardwood so it would float. Generally, if it was a big one and you took a strip about that wide [twelve inches] off of it, it'd float it. Now in peelin' time, startin' in May, they used to peel the whole thing. The sap would start to run and you could peel what you cut last winter.

They started in here at Ned Lake. They had dams to back 'er up. Like Long Lake, I think there was five miles of water on it. When they dropped that old gate, the water rolled back from here to those trees out there and then she'd come. There was always two men tended the gate. My father and another feller tended it the last year they was here. They done it all hours; they timed it. However long it took them to walk to that place and heist 'er, that's the time they had to leave to be there. Say it took the water three hours to get there, well, they'd have to be three hours ahead of the water to heist the dam. They had one, they'd heist 'er, I guess, about two o'clock in the mornin' to get the water down to them for seven. It's like a big frame and there's three posts into it with holes right through the three of them. They'd have a pole and heist that up. It takes quite a little bit of strength of pullin' to open 'er up for the day's drivin'; the water keeps comin' and layin' agin 'er. That's when the rush of water comes and that's when the rush of logs went. They'd leave 'er open all day or they'd go back and shut 'er down. If they left 'er on, they'd be wastin' and lose their water.

The mill starts to saw when the logs come in. Take them all summer to saw. You take a drive that's still three miles up the river, why, that's quite a bit of lumber. They had a mill crew worked in the mill when she was runnin' and then they was home or somewhere's else when she wasn't. She cut eighty-five thousand [board feet] a day. They made nothin' but lumber at the mill down here, three-inch stuff. When it was shipped overseas, they made whatever they wanted out of it. They used to load it right there in Brooklyn onto flatcars; the railroad run right through the mill. As they sawed it, they had a couple of men and a team there and they just put it on the wagon, took it over and loaded a car. When the car was loaded, they shipped it out, to Windsor or Halifax I suppose, accordin' to where she's goin'. It was all overseas stuff.

Now Coles and them little fellers, they made the lumber for local [markets]. He had a little steam mill, she cut I don't think over twelve thousand a day. They was portable mills in the woods. You had to move the mill and set 'er up. She had to have a bottom to set on, skids and things. As they sawed, you had a pile of roughage that you couldn't sell, the old stuff that they had to take a shim or somethin' off. It was chucked aside and you boarded the mill in with that.

There was quite a few little mills that'd get a hundred thousand out, saw it, and ship it locally. You take Elmsdale mill there now, I remember when it cut in on the Beaverbank Road, you could buy the boards then for six dollars a thousand. If you went in the woods [now] to cut by the thousand, I think they'd want ninety dollars a thousand to cut it round. Then, you got a dollar a day. Say your timber was good and clean and fairly thick, you'd get a couple thousand a day, but if it was rough stuff, you'd do darn well if you got a thousand.

Say I owned some timber. I logged it, hauled it out to the mill, sawed it, hauled it down to the station, put it on the cars, and shipped it into Halifax for thirteen a thousand. But they made money at it. They sawed and shipped a lot of ruffage too, stuff that was red, startin' to rot. These little mills used to sell a lot of that and ship it for a smaller price.

You worked for a dollar a day. Not everybody, no. If you was wheelin' sawdust or somethin' you wouldn't get as much as the fellers runnin' the mill. In the mill, you got a dollar a day and boarded yourself, but in the woods you got a dollar and twenty-five cents and your board. But you was glad to get it; it was good money for the times. That was back in the hungry thirties, and they were hungry by times. We used to walk from East Uniacke out here and down by Bill

Lynch's, ten miles to go to work for seven a.m. on the highway. And we'd work all day and walk back, for two dollars and sixteen cents a day. Used to cut pulpwood for a dollar and a quarter a cord. We cut it five feet long and get a cord and a quarter a day, back before we got the power saw.

Back in 1935, '36, or '37, I had the first [power saw] that was around here. It was a Hornet, that's what they called it. God damn'd old thing was a hornet too! There was always somethin' wrong with it. A feller that sold it to me told me he had one and, God, he liked his great. I think he was just puttin' on to sell me. I didn't keep it too long. And Jesus, they was big buggers then. Holy God, it was a day's work to lug it around, now I tell ya! It weighed around thirty or forty pounds. You lugged that all day, and snow up to there, you didn't go dancin' that night.

I don't know how my father'd ever got us all as far as he did if it hadn't 'ave been for the Brooklyn Lumber Company. They paid better wages than the rest of 'em. Everything stopped down there loggin' [in 1920]. There was no big outfits loggin' then. Father was lucky, he got in with Coles and he was there every winter for I don't know how long. He couldn't stop because he had ten of us to feed and a dollar a day to feed us off of. He was pretty near sixty-two [when he died]. He was an awful man to work. He'd lift and drag to keep them sawin'. He never let up.

They're ruinin' our country [today]. There won't be nothin' to do after they're done. They're takin' everything and givin' us nothin' for it. I'm blamin' the government. They should've put a limit onto them that they can't clear cut. I can take you back there in the woods and you can look as far as the eye can see and there's not hardly a twig standin'. That was our main industry, this lumber.

Everybody sempt to be happy them days. You'd get in the woods, you was happy as hell. Everybody sempt to be good natured and do anything for you, always helped one another, talk to one another, and no argument or hard feelin's or nothin'. But today, it's not that way so much. You know, we went right out of the Depression to hard times. And now, times gettin' harder than they was two or three years ago, or I think they are.

When you look back there was a lot of good ol' days and a lot of bad ol' days. You can always see where you could've improved it a little. Like when we walked down here to work ten miles, worked ten hours, and walked back home ten miles. I don't think you'd be quite as happy if them days come back. But by the looks of things, they may have to.

Henry Young

Henry Young, 80, lives at Branch LaHave, Lunenburg County on the family homestead. A teamster in the lumber woods for more than half a century, he still enters ox teams in the Bridgewater Exhibition after sixty-six years. "My health's about as good as can be expected. I've got a good woman and a good family. And money, I don't plan to take any with me anyway, so it don't matter if I got it or not. So I don't think I could ask for any more really. I'd say I've had a pretty good life as far as I can see."

My father, Alvin Young, hauled a lot of vessel timber because at that time they built vessels all out of wood. That's seventy, seventy-five years ago, but I remember when they done it. We got a lot of timberland. He used to work home here some winters and log with oxen and horses. Used to take it down to Larry's Shipyard, down Dayspring below Bridgewater. They used to go down to the ship-yard in the fall of the year and get an order for so much of each kind, like the deck, futtocks, knees* and, oh, I don't know what they called it all. It was mostly spruce. Pine would make a futtock. They had to have a big crook into 'em and a pine would grow crooked. That's what you'd go for, a piece of crooked wood. Then you'd hew it off with the crook on both sides. We sold hundreds of 'em.

It was a broad axe at that time. There was an old feller, David Wagner, he was a good man with a broad axe and know'd how to hew it out by hand. They used big hardwood for vessel timber too. Saw them out in four-inch plank; they called them ceiling plank.* And we used to cut a lot of railway ties years ago. We had a lot of hemlock; that was all hewed by hand. My father got so he could do it, and I used to score it. I'd notch them in on the side and he'd hew 'em off. It was just in later years that they started sawin' 'em to the mills.

You take from 1925 up through the 1930s, the Depression years, she was pretty tough doin'. When the first war was on, that made times a little better for awhile. After that got over in 1918, she started

* Futtocks are one of the curved timbers that form the lower frame of wooden ships. Knees are curved timbers used as braces in building wooden ships. They can be naturally curved or sawn to shape.

* Ceiling plank was used as the inside planking of vessels.

to slump off some and kept goin' back there for quite awhile. 'Til we got up to the second war come on, you might say we was in a depression. There was more people than there was workin' and there was no wages. But still, people could live off of it. If you could get a dollar a day at that time you could live.

You had nothin' to pay money out for. You had no electricity, no telephone, you didn't have nothin'. You had just a little farm like we had here. Father would keep four or five cows and sell the cream. They used to churn butter and sell it. Keep a flock of hens and have some eggs and raise some young pigs. You'd take your butter and eggs or whatever you had to Bridgewater and trade it off for groceries. You'd take a load of wood of some kind in and sell it to get a little money to buy a bag of flour or sugar or whatever you wanted. That's how they made their livin' on these little places. They'd work them as much as they could, and then they'd go in the woods for a couple of months at a time. Usually three months was a pretty good run in the winter. That's the way they done it.

Things have changed so much over the years that it's hard to believe. They really ain't got any appreciation for what it was like at that time. We got things so much better. And people don't have to work as hard and they get a lot of money, some of 'em, for what they do. When I worked, I had to work ten-hour days. That was the shortest day you got. When they drove logs on the river, twelve or fourteen hours was your day.

My first attempt at the lumber woods I was fourteen years old. They were cuttin' pulpwood up Solomon Brook and I went up there with my brother-in-law. I think it was for Hollingsworth & Whitney. They drove their wood in here to Bridgewater and loaded it on boats or boxcars and shipped it away. There was no place around to sell pulpwood at that time.

They had hard dives for people to stay in. They'd build any kind of a damned hut to keep men in. Log 'em flat and stog 'em with moss or stand the logs upright, then put a roof on, tar paper it, and then stog that with moss. They'd put bunks in for the men. They called 'em bunks, but they just took boards and made a place for you to make your bed. If you wanted somethin' to lay on, well, maybe they'd have some hay in the shed for the horses. If there was no hay, you cut fir boughs, put them in the bottom, and then you put a long blanket over it. And the food wasn't too good. They didn't have much to make at that time. You know what they'd have back sixty-five years ago. They had the same most everywheres; that went on for quite a few years.

I worked down east some in the woods too, down Beaverbank for

John C. Horn. They had a mill. That was a rough outfit too. I worked for Isnor's down there some. They had a big box factory there to Grand Lake. There was a lot of lumber companies down below Halifax, Truro, around Shubenacadie, off in back of Oxford. I worked one winter with Creelman's in back of Oxford; they were quite the lumbermen. Down east they used to call it. If a man from here wanted a job any time of the year, you'd go down east somewheres; no trouble to get work down there. The men up here were good woodsmen; they'd know that and always hire ya. But they had some pretty poor outfits to keep their men. Oh terrible! My Lord, I'll tell ya, we stayed in camps that I don't believe some people today would keep a dog in, it wouldn't be good enough. You don't know how men had it that time really. You had to take it or leave it. There was no choice. There was so many men and no work.

That was before the Mersey Paper Company operations. Then somewheres around 1927, '28, '29, along there, the Mersey started their outfit. Well, then, that's where we went to work mostly after that time. They didn't have it too good at the start either, but they kept improvin' over the years, after the second war. At the last of it they had cots with a spring and mattress and good cover.* They had good cooks and they fed good. They had about the best accommodations for men that there was as far as I know around here in the woods.

When they started that outfit up, they didn't know where in the world the wood was all goin' to come from to build that mill up here to Brooklyn [Queens County]; that's the paper mill. That's a long time ago and she's still goin'. Oh boys, I'll tell ya, they know'd how to do it.[1] They got a sawmill down here at Oakhill but that's just for sawlogs.

They started in cuttin' four-foot [pulp]wood....Well, when the second war came on, there was a shortage of men, a lot of them went in the army. Then they went to cuttin' pulpwood in log lengths—eight, twelve, sixteen feet—because it didn't take as long to get a thousand cord of wood. They'd have a slasher, somethin' they put the wood through, and there was saws in it and chunked the wood up into four-foot lengths. That's the way they done it then and they're still doing it as far as I know.

Lake Rossignol was the first place they started loggin'. I drove oxen haulin' four-foot wood. I didn't always drive teams in the woods, but I drove a lot. My father worked there an awful lot teamin'. At that time a good ox teamster was just about the same as a truck driver is today. He's got to have the experience, got to know what to do. If he don't, well, he can't drive it. Everybody couldn't team a pair

* In the very early years, Mersey Paper Company used a type of bed called a 'muzzle loader.' These were one-man rectangular wooden boxes, open at one end, stacked side by side and in tiers. Muzzle loaders were space-savers and in theory at least, warmer than conventional bunks.

of oxen. He could try it, but he couldn't do it, not right. And they couldn't drive a pair of horses, or even one horse. They didn't have any idea. It was just somethin' that you were born with and you learned to do it.

Harold Verge was the superintendent when they started there. He had charge of everything. You had to do as he wanted done or you wasn't around him very long. That's the kind of man Harold Verge was. He was born around here and he know'd everybody all out around here and the French Shore. Everybody kept oxen and he know'd the ones, most of 'em, that was good ox teamsters. Sometimes maybe he'd hire somebody that wasn't so good, but not too often. He didn't keep him long. It was more to it than just drivin'. You had to know how much feed to give an ox or horse, hay and short feed, had to look after your team, tend it good. That was one thing they were pretty fussy with. If he couldn't drive a team and know how to use it, why, he wasn't there.

Harold Verge would go around the country [province] in the fall of the year to buy oxen for in the woods. At that time there was lots of 'em. Out around the French Shore they had a lot of well-broke oxen. He'd buy anywhere from ninety to a hundred pair every year. They used to beef a lot of 'em through the summer or anybody wanted a pair of oxen in the spring could buy 'em. It was quite a business. Sometimes maybe a pair they'd have quite awhile, but he bought a lot of new ones too. Around Christmastime they'd move in with their oxen. A hundred pair I guess they had up here at Caledonia at the barns.

We went to Caledonia to go to the Mersey woods. If you wanted to drive a team you took your whip with you and you took a pair of bells. They didn't have nothin' like that themselves but other gear they had—the yoke, chains, pads, and the straps. They had yoke makers there if you had a yoke that was no good. Yellow birch is easy to work and tough when they get dry. You had bells to make a noise. You put them around an oxen's neck and they rattled. They made a noise and sounded nice on a frosty morning. That's the only reason I know of. There's small ones and large ones, anywheres from one inch to five inches. We generally used big bells in the woods.[2]

There'd be a lot of men around that time…just double the men that he [Verge] wanted. Some of them would have their job [before going]. I generally had mine, my father had his. He know'd us fellers and that we'd be there. He'd pick out the ones that he wanted and take you in the barn and show you what team you was goin' to drive. Sometimes you got a good team and sometimes you got a poor team.

Harold Verge was Superintendant of Woodlands for Mersey Paper Company from 1929–1955 when he died suddenly from a heart attack. He was known as 'Bull of the Woods,' a universal logging term bestowed upon certain woods bosses for their toughness. There were none tougher than Harold Verge. (Dr. Wylie Verge)

He didn't know that. I never had no trouble drivin' oxen.

When you drove horses you didn't have to take no gear at all; they had everything. The Mersey Paper Company started in with oxen the first of it, then they got into the horse business. They used to go out West and bring them in here by the carload. I believe there were four big barns up in Caledonia and they'd take 'em there and break 'em. A horse was a good thing to yard and they done a lot of yardin'. I drove a lot of yard horses. They had as many horses on the last of it as what they had oxen.

There'd be a lot of men that didn't have a job. Say I was a teamster and you were a pretty able-looking man, you'd get a job for what they called a striker—help handle the wood and load it, cut it loose and keep the road fixed up you're haulin' on. If there was a hole, skid it up. Two men worked together. Every teamster had a striker.

He'd [Verge] tell you where you was to go, what camp to go to. That's where you headed for when you left [Caledonia]. Sometimes we'd go in to Camp One around Lake Rossignol. It was their base camp after awhile. When they first started there they had no road around the lake, just a trail cut they could drive cattle through. They took the oxen around and toted their supplies and the men across in a boat. You were in there all winter, three or four months. You left your family and your wife behind and you went. There was no gettin' out.

Well, sir, I'll tell you what we was paid when we first started teamin' for the Mersey Paper Company. If you worked by the day as a striker, the wages was a dollar and your board. If it come a rainy day, you didn't get paid for that. If you lost two days a week, you didn't have much left. But if you was a teamster they'd pay you twenty-five dollars a month I believe the startin' rate was. Then they got it up to thirty dollars, I remember. That you was sure of. If you didn't get out to work you got straight time, your time went on just the same regardless of how the weather was. If the road wasn't fit to haul or there was stormy weather you looked after your team. The man that was loadin' sleds didn't get paid for his lost time, but he still got his meals. That's the reason why I always liked to drive a team because if you got into a bunch of bad weather you didn't lose no money. Sometimes if you had a team of your own they'd hire you to haul by the cord. I never did, but there was different people had to work for what they got by the cord.

If you was drivin' a horse team some of 'em would get up at four-thirty. You had to get up a little earlier because there was more harness; the harness for a double team is quite a lot of work. You had

to feed and water and harness 'em. With the oxen you'd get up five o'clock and go out. You'd feed 'em, clean your stable out, give 'em water if they wanted a drink and then you'd give 'em their short feed. We generally fed the oxen bran and meal. You'd do all that before breakfast. Then you'd go in the camp and get your breakfast about six o'clock. Then you'd go to the barn and yoke your ox and you was always out before daylight in the wintertime. It didn't get daylight until seven o'clock and you was in the woods ready to load by daylight and you didn't get in until after dark, they kept you right there.

You'd give 'em their dinner. If you couldn't get to camp, you'd take a bag of hay. They didn't get short feed at dinnertime, just hay and water. In the evening you'd leave the woods just about dark, around five o'clock in the wintertime. You put your team in, give 'em a little hay, go to the camp and get your supper. Then after supper we used to sit around, smoke, and talk a little. Around seven o'clock, you'd go to the barn and tend your team. You had an oil lantern, everybody had one. You'd give 'em their water, short feed, and hay and fix 'em up for the night. They had rugs for the oxen—and the horses the same—when you put them in the barn so they wouldn't get a cold. You'd take the rugs off and comb 'em off, groom 'em up good for the night. About nine o'clock you'd go in and go to bed.

You worked six days. Sunday you had off, but you still had to be there. You might go to another camp [to visit], but I never did. Maybe you'd want to write a letter home to your wife. Maybe you'd have

"The Mersey Paper Company started in with oxen the first of it, then they got into the horse business. They used to go out West and bring them in here by the carload." (Harold Porter)

some clothes, socks, and underwear to wash. Some of 'em used to go in and they wouldn't shift clothes at all, but I never done that. I always tried to keep my clothes clean. There was no comin' out of the Mersey woods at that time. Later years when they got trucks goin' in there, then we come home every week. Every Saturday night you'd come home, go back Sunday evening. Then we had it good, then I liked it. This was quite awhile after the war. Yeah, things got a lot better.

Some places would get lice in the camp and then you was in trouble. Lice in the lumber camps down east was just a common thing one time. When you got home and they'd had lice in the camp that winter, you had to make sure that you took your underclothes and stuff off and threw them outdoors before you came in to have a bath. The Mersey Paper Company never was bad for lice; once in awhile, but not too often.

In the winter, lots of times the weather was cold and there was no snow. Well, they wanted to haul wood. They rigged up things they called a watering cart. It'd be a big puncheon or a barrel onto a wagon. At night when it was cold, they'd take that back and put the water over the road. It would freeze and in the mornin' they'd get a couple of inches of ice. They'd have good haulin' for three parts of the next day. They done a lot of that.

They had their own blacksmiths in there done the ox and horse shoeing and kept the sleds in repair. You had to have 'em sharp shod in the winter for the ice. They wouldn't stay sharp long on the frozen ground, about a week. You'd have to take 'em off, sharpen 'em, and put 'em on. When the snow came you didn't have to get 'em shod maybe for a couple of months. In the summer you just had a flat calk.

They drowned, I believe it was four teams that I know of up there in the lakes. There was two one winter up Lake Tobeatic went through the ice and right under, one team right behind the other. The teamster got clear. The sleds and load on shoved 'em right under the ice when they broke through. There was another place up there they lost a couple of teams. They never lost an oxen that I know of. That's the only times I know of anything happening. Oh, they may lose the odd animal, but if they did you never heard nothin' about it.

There's different breeds [of oxen]. They're bred up a little more now with the Hereford and Durham and like that than they were years ago. Years ago, you could take a Jersey cow and a Hereford bull we'll say and breed that. Well, that would give you a good ox to work. He wasn't very heavy built, but there was a lot of them kind of cattle around years ago. They ain't got nothin' like that today. They'd be a lighter made cattle, more of a dairy breed. Now, we generally try to get the Hereford and Durham crossed if we can. I find them about the best of any. Sometimes we'll get a brockle face with a red body and sometimes we'll get a red body and a white face with your Durham and Hereford cross. We don't work these oxen today. You try to get them mated up as good as you can because we take them around more to shows; they look better.

I'd say [the best then] was what we called a mongrel breed, a Durham or a Guernsey crossed with a Hereford. They were kind of mixed up at that time. They didn't have the purebred structure that they got today. At that time colouring didn't matter. My father had lots of them, a red one and a white one, as long as they worked good. That was the main thing. They had a lot of oxen seven feet around the girth [2,800–2,900 lbs. team weight]. The heavier team you had, the better. I drove oxen for the Mersey Paper Company that were smaller, about six foot, eight or nine [inches], but they were a little too light.

They ain't an oxen until they're four or five years old. When they're three years old they shouldn't be worked too much in the woods. They're just steers as far as I'm concerned. You could do a lot of work with 'em, but to work for the Mersey Paper Company haulin' the wood you wanted a good team. They had to be tough to stand it, because you had to work 'em all day. The bosses wanted you to load pretty heavy. They'd watch you for that. You daresn't go out with half a load on, not too many trips. If it wasn't good goin', you'd put a cord on. Then if you got out where the road was good, you'd put two cord on, maybe three. They had outfits that they could put four cord on. I know of one team up there that hauled eight cord in one load. They was a big pair of oxen; I remember the team quite well. The road was good and they had the day picked to do it. They wanted to beat the record. There was no team could haul it unless it was a real good place, because that would be out of reason.

You get a good one, you keep 'em as long as you can; I'd say ten or twelve years [average]. You can start a little when they're two years old; just a little, not too heavy. The first thing you should do is get them to lead good, put halters on and lead 'em around. I used to break a pair of calves in a bow yoke.* Then when you put the head yoke on they know what to do. Then you put on a little load with a wagon or a sled; get 'em to haul a little by degrees. That's the way it was done and that's the way you still got to do it if you want to make a team.

Some of 'em don't work good together. One that's slow and one that's smart, well, them won't work good. You get two slow ones or two smart ones, as near as you can. The side you break 'em on is

* The bow yoke was used by English settlers. The wooden beam rested on the neck with a wooden bow encircling the neck and extending below. With this yoke the animal pulled from the shoulder. It was a favourite training device for steers. The French head yoke strapped to the horns and the oxen pulled with their heads.

where you want to work 'em. The right hand is the "off" one and the left hand is the "nigh" ox. That's what we called 'em. [They were also given names, popular names being Bright and Lion, Spark and Diamond.] They'll understand you after a while. They understand your movement and they understand when you speak to them. Now, they're dumb animals, but you can learn and train 'em to do most anything. If you want to go this way [left], you go *haw*; if you want to go that way [right] you go *gee*.

Same way as a horse. You can learn a horse gee and haw. I drove a lot of 'em around the woods yardin' and they'd learn that just as easy as could be after awhile. They're a lot better for yardin' than oxen, they're quicker. A horse team haulin' on a road in the woods, well, you could make two trips in a half a day with a pair of oxen what you could make three with the horses easy. You may get four. They're quicker, smarter, they walk faster.

I worked at different jobs, it wasn't only teaming. In the spring of the year after we had our plantin' done, you'd go up in the woods until hayin' time. You had to cut [pulpwood] and spud it—take the bark off of it—and pile it. June was a good month, a lot of sap in it. My father and I and everybody around here done a lot of that. They [Mersey Paper Company] had what they call a bonus day. If you stayed until the thirteenth day of July you got I think it was a dollar a cord extra or fifty cents, I remember that. They wanted people to stay until peelin' was pretty well over.

Then we'd come home and make hay. That was quite a little job at that time. You make it with teams. You mowed it all with oxen and raked it. You weren't baling hay like you do today. My father generally had a small horse, what they called a driving horse, that would do the rakin'. Haul it in, fork it on the wagon by hand. You didn't even have what they called a hay pitcher at that time to take the hay up in the loft. Fork it all by hand, all loose hay. I forked a good many loads up in the loft.

After that was done and we had a couple loads of grain dumped, then we'd go in the woods again sometime the last of August, first of September. You'd work there a couple of months cuttin' what they called rough wood, pulpwood that you wouldn't have to peel, like spruce and fir. The hemlock you used to peel in the summer. We'd stay there until Christmas tree season, along the last of October, first of November. My father always cut Christmas trees. We bought the trees from somebody else, cut 'em and sold 'em to a man over in New York. He was the first to come around here and buy Christmas trees.

When that was done, then we'd have a little leisure time maybe in between that and Christmas. We'd go out in the woods home here a bit and get some firewood, a few logs or somethin'. After Christmas was generally haulin' time. We'd go in the woods again and haul wood for the Mersey Paper Company. If you had a good winter it didn't take so long, but if you had what they called an open winter, sometimes you'd be there 'til the last of March anyway. As long as the haulin' stayed, you was there. If there was ice enough you'd haul it right out on the lake and unload it. Some of those lakes would be full. If the ice wasn't solid to get on with a team you'd have to pile it off on the shore of the lake. Then in the spring they'd roll it out and drive it.

I worked around different places on mills here. Then I used to work for the Department of Highways a little in the summertime. Just when the right party was in. You know how that goes. They'd haul gravel with teams; I remember when this road up through here was all done with teams; that's the way they graded the roads. They got small graders and it took two teams to pull it. That was quite a thing when you got a job with the highway with your team. You wouldn't make much, maybe a couple of dollars a day.

I was a jack of all trades, to tell you the truth about it, all my life. That's the way it was done, how we made our livin'. I done that a long, long time.

Myrtle Whittemore

Myrtle Whittemore, 95, was born in East Uniacke, Hants County. She is a sister of James Moore. Following her husband Joseph to the lumber woods, she spent various years from 1925 to the mid-1960s cooking in camps and mills in Hants, Lunenburg, and Halifax counties. In addition, they ran a small farm in Rawdon, Hants County, before selling it to move to Halifax, where she finished her cooking days with Barrett Lumber Company. Her story deals primarily with the four years she spent during the mid-1940s in the lumber woods of Lunenburg County.

The first time that I was in a camp to cook was in back of Grand Lake in 1925. His name was Alan MacDonald from Enfield. Had fourteen men that winter. I was only there from after Christmas until March. When I first went in I'd never cooked in a camp you know, and I told them I never did. I was afraid I wouldn't judge for to have enough for their dinners or somethin', but I did. I was kind of scared to try it, but I come out all right.

I wouldn't 'ave been in the woods if my husband hadn't been

there. We was never allowed around the lumber camps before we was married. Oh, no! But there's an awful lot of women cooks in the lumber camps and they have for years. There was just him and I, so he had to be away to work, so when they wanted me as a cook, I thought I might as well work.

I was down in Lunenburg County four years. I went the fall of 1943. We worked for Harold Campbell from Halifax. It was on the Chester-Windsor highway. I cooked for the woods crowd in the winter, and in the summer for the mill crowd. He owned the mill. I'd move from one camp to the other. They supplied everything, I just cooked. They brought in enough stuff for a month or more at a time. He was a good provider, fed his men well. They had to feed the men good. I had forty-eight one winter, but for the mill crowd they didn't have so many. They only had about twenty, I think.

The men had their camp to their self; I was never in their camp. I had none of the lumber fare. I took my own bed with me and my own bedding. I had my washtub and washboard with me to wash our clothes. I washed my husband's clothes and my own and kept them clean, and ironed them. Oh, no indeed! I didn't go without no bath! I took the washtub. I don't know what the men done, but maybe they done the same thing, I don't know.

We were in the cookhouse; my husband and I had that to ourselves. Just a cookhouse and a dining room, but there was no separate dining room, one camp. I had a bedroom right in the cookhouse. It's just the same as if you're in your own house. You're not in where the men is or nothin'; just see them at mealtime. The stove and sink and your counter, things like that, was all at one end of the camp and the other end was the table.

We had to have breakfast at six o'clock, dinner at twelve o'clock, and supper at six o'clock in the woods. Only on Saturdays, it was five o'clock; Saturday night after supper, after the day's work, they'd go home, the ones that was handy. Back Sunday night, but no supper Sunday night; they had to have their supper before they come. That was in the bargain. The boss said to give no supper because they'll be comin' in all hours; I didn't have too many on a Sunday.

My work for the day was to get up at five o'clock and get the fires goin' to get their breakfast ready by six. Just the one stove…and big pots. They wasn't the iron pots, they were the enamel ones. I had lots of dishes and lots of everything to work with. It's not like years and years ago, like when my father and them worked in the woods, I guess that wasn't so very easy.

I'd give them beans, and if there was hash left at night they got that

and cold meat. Always had that. And cookies for their breakfast, and bread and butter. Molasses, that was always on the table. I always had a dish of prunes cooked and a dish of apple sauce on the table for them all, just for breakfast.

The homemade beans they liked. They stayed more with a person, I guess, to work on. They'd bring in the big bags of beans; sometimes they were yellow-eyed and sometimes just the plain white ones. You baked beans every day. What would be left in the mornin' I'd give them at night with hash and meat and stuff like that. It was all fresh meat. You changed every day to give them a different dinner. Some days you had roast pork, some days roast beef, and steak. Fish twice a week. Always had to have potatoes, that's somethin' they always looked for. I had a great big, long pan and I used to make that full of hash. And always pie. But now, I couldn't think of it; it'd make me tired to think of it.

Everything was on the table and they waited on themselves. Enamel dishes and long homemade tables for a camp. Long? I guess they were. They set forty-eight men to a table and they all had room. Never allowed no talkin' at the table. They could do their logging and everything out in the daytime and not wait 'til they get to the table, 'cause you couldn't hear if anything was gettin' low on the table. The boss didn't allow it anyway. They'd argue so. This feller would say he cut more logs, and another feller would say he hauled out more

A lumber camp cookhouse of unknown origin. Some cook-houses were separate from the bunkhouse while others had both under one roof (N.S. Museum)

logs. This feller, an ex-policeman, he was at the table, and he was talkin' and talkin'. "No talkin' at the table!" I said. He told me afterward, "You're the first woman that I ever shut up for." That was the only trouble I ever had; I did have to tell 'em to stop talkin'. If they got low on bread or somethin' like that, they would ask, but I'd keep an eye on the table. Always have plenty of bread on, but sometimes the bread plate would get a little lower.

Each man had their own place at the table. So this feller came there to work and there was just a place at the end of the table. He said "no." So when he come in, I didn't notice. I thought everyone would go to their place. He set into another man's place. And I saw this man goin' up and down beside the table. What was it he said? "I'm like a squirrel," he said. But I put this feller out of his place, and he had to come and set at the end of the table. He didn't like it, but he set there the rest of the time he was workin' there. I didn't let him get the best of me.

They all came at one time. The first man would be done and he'd bring his dishes over and I'd start washin' 'em. As I washed them, when the men was done, I cleaned my table off, white tablecloth, you know, the oil cloth, put the plates and my mugs back on and turned them upsides down. Had my table always set. Then I just had to put the food on when it come time. I had a little cookee, a young fellow, to help get the wood in for me and was supposed to help with the dishes. I always got the vegetables ready, cleaned off the food and stuff that was left, and everything like that. The boss used to tell me I was doin' his work and mine too.

There was no coffee then in the woods. Good job there wasn't. Tea was enough to make for a crowd of men, let alone make coffee. They used to make great big teapots. You put the tea in, all loose tea, and fill that up with boiling water and let it steep. There was a strainer in the spout for to pour. Put the milk in and pour it into pitchers, put it on the table, and then they helped themselves.

I had a day to cook my pies, a day for cookies and things like that, because I couldn't do it all on one day and get the meals ready. I had a schedule. Like today, I'd make pies for today and tomorrow. Then tomorrow, I'd make cookies and cake. I made bread every mornin'. I used to have the bread mixed some mornings before they come to breakfast. I never got it so they had to come onto it as you took the bread out of the oven or I'd 'ave never [had any left]. I always had lots of bread baked ahead. Oh, my land, yes, you'd use a half a dozen loaves, maybe eight [a day], but I made big loaves. The loaves you get now look like little kittens alongside them. You had bigger pans for

"Had my table always set. Then I just had to put the food on when it come time." (Fred Ellis)

the lumber woods; you could put two great big loaves in one pan. I gave them white bread, brown bread, and raisin bread. Saturdays, I used to bake two lots of bread so I wouldn't have to bake on Sunday. I didn't cook on Sunday. I was there and got their meals, but I didn't do no baking.

It just took eight pies for a dinner. I cut them in good pieces because the pie plates was big. And they always seemed to have enough. I told them, if there was any left, to clean it up. Every day I gave them a different kind—apple, mince, pie filling in cans—and puddings. I always gave them cookies: molasses cookies, sugar cookies; morning, noon, and night they was on the table. And cake: I used to make molasses cake, white cake, make them with raisins, and make them plain. I kept shiftin' around so they didn't get the same kind all the time. There was three things I used to like to make. That was bread, pies, and molasses cookies. Seems like that just come easy to me.

My camp was always clean for anyone to come into. I never kept it lumbered up nor messed. I kept my camps clean 'cause there's nothin' any worse than people comin' in to eat in a dirty place. Board floor. I'd sweep it up in the mornin' and at night. I didn't have to wash it because it was too hard; it wasn't one that was planed or anything. It was a double floor, so there was no draft comin' up. Now today, I guess, the camps is more up-to-date. But the camps was warm; they insulated them with birchbark or somethin' like that because they had to or things would freeze. I used to fill it [the stove] up at night when we went to bed and there'd be hot coals in the morning. It was cold, but they worked just the same in the woods.

I always had my evenings. They never had no lunch after they had their supper. When they come in and got their suppers, it wasn't back to my camp until the next mornin'. I was no hand to work at night. I couldn't sit down and do nothin'. I used to knit socks for my husband. In the summer in the mill camp, when I was down in Lunenburg County, I used to go to Chester every Saturday night with people who lived just a little piece from me, a man and his wife. My husband would go some. Chester's a pretty little spot, stores and everything. I went to a show out there one night. Oh, yes, I got out.

I would always go to bed at nine o'clock 'cause I had to, to get up early in the mornin'. You get your rules from the boss. Where I was, lights out was nine o'clock. Whether they all did or not, I don't know. Maybe some of them was in bed before that. Oil lamps: washed your lamp shades every morning. I don't know if they ever washed them in the men's camp, but I washed mine, rinsed them off, and polished them up 'cause I like a good light. There was two for each table and one for my sideboard.

I was paid by the month. It wasn't very much. The cook got no more money than the rest of the men got, but you'd think they should've. I must tell you the honest truth, I forget; it wasn't very big then. Only maybe a dollar a day. I earnt my money, I know that. There was a lot of work. The doctor told me my feet showed I walked a million miles. I felt like tellin' him, yes, I did. It was hard. I think that's what gives me the arthritis so bad now, standin' on the hard floor so much. My feet swell so bad. But I'm not sorry that I worked. I earned my money honest.

I could never say that I didn't have good providers when I cooked. Well, I wouldn't 'ave stayed, that was just it, because it's always the cook gets the name. If they don't get much food and stuff like that, it's the cook that gets it, it ain't the boss. As long as I cooked, the different places I cooked, I never had a complaint about a thing. No, I made that bargain when I went that I'd stay for a couple of weeks, and if I didn't suit them, to tell me, and if the boss didn't suit me, I'd tell him. That's the way I was hired and I stayed anyway. I often wonder myself now, how did I do it? But that's what I went to do. Them days is over with. I never think of it, you know. I guess pretty near all them's dead I cooked for, so the cookin' couldn't 'ave been so good.

Charlie Kelly

Charlie Kelly, 80, of Cookville, Lunenburg County, was a cook for thirty years. He spent many of these in various woods operations around the province. He learned his trade as a young boy when he was a cookee for the crews building the hydro project on the Mersey River in the 1920s. He eventually went to work for the Mersey as cook in their Rossignol camps during the 1930s. At one camp, he had four large woodstoves working at one time, with one stove reserved solely for boiling and baking beans. It was common for him to bake two hundred pounds of flour a day during the river driving season, cutting back to a mere one hundred pounds a day during the winter season. His wife Florence was a noted woods cook in her own right, as were her sister, father, and grandfather. When asked to reflect on his years in the lumber camps, Charlie simply says, "Oh, she was quite a life."

This feller was cookee'in' for me. The men come in after their day's work, hungry, and had a big supper. One fellow says to my cookee, "We ought to go back to the lake and see who can jump in first." Well, they all jumped in the lake and he [the cookee] was the only one that come up. Three had gone back. He was a good swimmer and he got two of 'em; one feller drowned. They brought him out and I'll never forget. They never called me by name, they called me "cook." They said, "Cook, would you mind if we bring that body in the cookhouse tonight?" I slept in there, you know. Well, I wasn't goin' to say no. I says, "That won't bother me." Between the tables, they pulled two benches out, and they had him layin' on there and had a blanket over him. I could've swore them blankets moved that night. I can remember that just as well.

This fellow and his partner was cutting by the cord and everybody was in a hurry. This tree leaned back the wrong way for 'em. They was wedgin' it to put it where they wanted it. There was a Jesus big rock behind it. This fellow went up beside the rock and was standin' while his partner wedged it. It split up the stump, come back and took one leg right off. That was the pitifulness looking sight I ever seen, the men carrying him out on a stretcher and another feller coming behind carryin' his leg. Now that was a pitiful sight. If the doctor, Dr. MacDonald, wouldn't 'ave been there to tend him, he'd have bled to death right there. I never thought much more about it. I was down to the exhibition [thirty years later] and we was tryin' to get over to the ox pull. It seemed like wherever I went this fellow [in a wheelchair] was in my way, right beside me lookin' up at me. He says, "Are you cook?" I says, "No, I'm afraid you've got the wrong fellow." "No, did you ever cook in the woods?" The moment he said that, it hit. He had both legs off; that one was buggered up too.

I went to Camp One up there, that was the main camp. It got so many bedbugs in there one time they had to move out. They fumigated it and after that you could go in the camp with a broom and sweep 'em up in wind rows. Oh, it was wicked.

I remember one time, one of the foremen, he says, "How full is your molasses barrel?" I says, "Pretty near empty." He says, "Do you mind if I go have a look at it?" I knew. "I think I'll bring you up a full one," he says. "That one there's not goin' to last long." So he had it down in the woods; he was about half drunk all the time after it got good. The men knew it, but they couldn't figure out where he was gettin' it. So they kept watchin' and they found it. A whole bunch of 'em got shined up there. Harold Verge come in and that was the end of that. Him and the beer was out. You wouldn't be there long if you got caught.

This chap had his leg cut real bad, may as well say it was off. To get a doctor up there took a long while. This was up across the lakes to Camp Five. He was layin' in the bunk and sufferin' somethin' awful. You could feel him take hold of a pole there for pain. I was goin' to have turnip kraut for dinner and you need vinegar for that. I told the cookee to go down and get some. He come tearin' back and said the vinegar's all froze. "Good," I said, "Bring it up anyway." Laurie Hann was a blacksmith. I told Laurie to heat an iron bar and bring it down. We drilled a hole in that barrel and he rammed that hot iron in. All that come out first was alcohol. After we got the alcohol out, the vinegar started comin'. After he was gone back to his blacksmith shop, I went in and said, "Basil, I got something here'll take the pain out of your leg." I told him what it was. "Get it quick!" he says. He couldn't walk at all before. I don't believe it was a half hour after that, he come out: "Cook, you got any more of that good stuff?"

Fred Ellis

Fred Ellis, 75, of South Brookfield, Queens County, worked as scaler for the Mersey Paper Company. When he returned from overseas following World War Two, he said, "No more of this foolishness. If I've got to go back in the woods again, we might as well starve home." Long periods of continuous separation from his family while scaling had taken its toll. He then moved to Halifax and worked as an electrician until he retired to South Brookfield thirteen years ago. He passed away from cancer a short time after granting me an interview. Of life in the Mersey woods, Fred said, "It was pretty rugged, but you got by."

It was no such thing as it is today. You had to get work. Today, people have got the world by the tail and a downhill start. Nobody in those days cared two hoorahs whether you lived or died. If you didn't work, you just didn't have any money and you didn't eat, so you got a job wherever you could get it. Most of the places, if you didn't take the job, there was a big line-up behind you and they were right ready to grab it.

My home was in Milton. You can imagine, in the middle of February, jumpin' on the back of an old pulp truck and drivin' out here [South Brookfield] twenty-five miles. It was the only way you could get out, to hitchhike a ride. We come out here and searched around all day long for some place to stay at night. Room and board was fifty cents a day. Next day we got a job over here; there used to be a big mill, Nova Scotia Wooden Ware, right across the river here. That burned down in 1944. It was a big operation. There was a three-storey building and approximately a hundred people working there.

Those times everything was shipped in wooden boxes. Do you remember old orange crates? They had a veneer mill there and they made thousands of them and shipped them out down south for Sunkist. That's where the majority of them went. Depending on the size of the box the customer wanted, you would make the sides, ends,

Nova Scotia Woodenware Limited, South Brookfield. Many factories such as this produced a myriad of wooden products ranging from barrels, boxes, shingles, sashes and doors, casks, buckets, and furniture. It was very much a wood dependent society until World War II. (Canadian Parks Service)

top, and bottom and they would all go strapped in a bundle we call shooks. The boxes would be assembled wherever they were going to use them. Most of the veneered products—strawberry boxes, fruit hampers—would all be made out of hardwood. The softwood would be used for those boxes companies would ship their goods in.

They made buckets too. At that time we used to get an awful lot of candy coming in regular-sized buckets. You'd make the wooden bucket and wax it inside, paint the outside and a big cover on it. They'd send them out by the thousands, one inside the other. I forget how many would go in a stack, but you'd have the train car filled right up to the doorway. There was a railway that went up the south shore from Halifax to Yarmouth; another one went up through the [Annapolis] Valley to Yarmouth. From Bridgewater there was a branch line that went right through to Middleton. Another branch line from it came across from New Germany right into the mill. Everything would be put on the boxcars right there by the mill.

You worked for ten hours from seven in the morning until six at night, one hour off at noon. One dollar and twenty-five cents for ten hours, twelve and a half cents an hour. Now, could you see anybody today working for that? And I don't mean you were just fiddling around; you worked for ten hours. If the mill shut down at five-thirty in the afternoon, you were docked half an hour.

The wood would come in from the [Medway] river, and of course it would be just saturated with water. You'd cut stuff and it would be piled on trolleys and run out through on a narrow-gauge railroad to the drag hill. It would be run off of that on another set of rails into an area where it would take maybe two days to dry. That's what most of the steam from the furnaces would be used for. The sawdust went down in chutes with endless chains, and all went out into a great big bin. There'd be fellers with big rakes hauling that to a hole [to feed the furnace].

Most of it was just manual labor. Of course, kids, which was all we were at the time, that's all you would get. Your old experienced hands would be running the machines. All you would be doing is dragging wood to them and taking wood away. Eventually you'd get a set job, but they could take you off that and give you something else; if that saw shut down you'd be given something else to do.

I heard they [Mersey Paper Company] needed scalers and I put in an application. They said, "Yes, you can have a job. Report to Camp One." When I went for the Mersey in 1938 I got sixty dollars a month and food. That was a big jump, but you were back in the woods all the time. If you wanted to come home it was two days out and two days in. If you wanted to stay home for a week, you didn't get paid. There was no such thing as holidays. The only time you would work in the woods on a Sunday was during the peak driving season. It was just straight time. Now, you get double time at least on a Sunday. No such thing then. When the boss wanted you to work, you worked.

I got a trip across [Lake Rossignol] on the boat from Lowe's Landing to Camp One. They said, "Now, you've got to go down to Porcupine Lake and see Billy Simpson," who was foreman. "The scaler will show you how to do it." That was way down towards Shelburne. It took me three or four days to walk from Camp One around to Camp Five. He took me out in the afternoon. "This is where the men are working." They were scattered all over creation. They planned to cross the ice in the winter from a camp to haul the wood, but to cut it you had to get around the lake, so we were tenting. He showed me the next morning [how to scale] and he said, "Well, I'm going." He went and left me and there I was. Billy Simpson helped me out a lot, but you have to learn a lot just by keeping your eyes open.

To scale a pile of wood you get the length and the height, and of course you have to check the length of each individual piece to make sure that it is forty-eight inches or, in the case of hemlock, fifty-two. That was just a quirk of the company. That's what they wanted and if you didn't get it, somebody else did. They were cutting their own wood, so they could tell you what they wanted.

If you put all the big ends out you get a bigger section in front than you got in the back, so you have to watch what's goin' on. Instead of them piling one section with the top out and the next one back, alternate, some of them said, "Oh, there's a new feller. We'll put it onto him. We'll get ahead of him this time." A couple of fellers were working together. There was this big flat rock that came out and right down, so they cut some little short logs and they put them along, butts out, in front of the rock. Then they piled the rest of the wood and they filled the whole back end with brush. Well, I thought to myself, "There's something wrong here. I better check this out." Sure enough, I found it. They laughed, "We thought for sure we had you that time." Oh, you got onto it after awhile. A full cord would be four by four by eight, which is 128 cubic feet. Well, now, you could never get 128 cubic feet for the simple reason that you had round pieces coming together and you had holes through. You would have to estimate.

Looking at a piece of woodland, you've got awful cutting maybe around the edge, and then you've got some good stands that are close together and maybe eight or ten inches, just right for cutting. If you got very good cutting, one man working by himself with spruce sometimes could average two cord a day. There were no such thing as chain saws those days—crosscuts and bucksaws or Swede saws some people call them. But if you averaged one cord a day you were doing fairly good because you'd have to take time from the good spot and pick up all the stragglers, a tree here and a tree there, but they'd have to be cut. Everything four inches on the top end they wanted. You didn't dare leave them in the woods or the walking boss would have ten fits.

There were fifteen camps there one time. They were so spread out and had so many men at each camp that you didn't have time to run from one to another; you'd be on the tote road all the time just walkin' back and forth. If you had sixty, seventy men cutting every day and they were cutting by the cord, they'd work through, Sunday didn't mean anything for them. They'd usually cut during the week and they would pile the wood Saturday and Sunday. It would have to be piled along the roadway so teams could get it in the wintertime. They'd usually have a camp and the scaler would stay at that camp. If you only had maybe twenty, twenty-five men to a camp, one scaler would do that today and tomorrow he'd go to the next camp and do it and come back and do the first one.

There was always some arguments [about the scale], but if they couldn't give you proof.... We used to have a lot of people from Poland and so on. You couldn't talk to them too well, but they were darned good workers, excellent. Sometimes they got a little bit difficult to get along with, but we always managed somehow.

The height of ground between two watersheds goes up between two lakes: Boot Lake and Little Tobeatic. When we logged in these areas back about 1940, the pulpwood would be landed at Boot Lake. From Boot Lake there was a sluiceway over the height of land to Little Tobeatic. From Little Tobeatic you eventually went down through Big Tobeatic, down through Tupper Lake and so on, out to Lake Rossignol, and down the river to Liverpool to the mill.

I suppose the engineers got up in there and found the shortest and easiest way to get their wood across was to build this flume [sluiceway].[1] It was almost a couple of miles long. They had to put a portable mill in at first to cut all this lumber. They had a big diesel engine which would be driving a pump to pump water up and out into this sluiceway. It would also be operating endless chains, four or five at least, which men would be hauling the wood in. It would go up, dump into a box, and the flow of water from the diesel would be sending it shooting out through this flume. It had to be high enough to get over the height of land. When you started, it was about thirty feet high, and when it crossed the height of land, it was down in the ground. It was quite an engineering feat at that time.

Spruce and fir were just cut, but if you didn't peel hemlock you might as well leave it in the woods because it'd go to the bottom just like a big rock. The biggest one that I scaled was four foot across on the butt and that had to come down through. Across the top [of the flume] it had to be in excess of four feet to be big enough to take a four foot stick. Deep, it would have to be at least two and a half feet because you had to have water enough in there to float these things so they wouldn't be draggin'.

You had four men along the full length of this sluice on a walkway. You'd have just a pickaroon* so you could drive that into the piece and walk along and assist it. If it started to catch, the water would back up behind it and spill out over the edges; then you'd never get the damned thing down. The four people working on here had to work together. If one of these big junks came—and they only came occasionally—the first fellow would have it with a pickaroon. He'd

* A pickaroon, or pike pole, is a long-handled pole with a sharp point on one end that was used by log drivers.

The sluice between Boot Lake and Little Tobeatic. Started in 1935, it took five summers to complete. Mersey Paper Company moved 50,000 cords of wood through its two-mile course. (Fred Ellis)

be going down and when he would see the fellow way ahead of him, he'd let out a hoot and that fellow would come up and take it. Eventually, you had to assist it the whole way down that flume. It was only when they got a big junk that they had anything to do. There'd be days that you wouldn't do a thing. They would go along just about the speed that you could walk. Then the river drivers would have to take over and get it down the brook from Little Tobeatic to Big Tobeatic and from there on it was somebody else's problem. You had to work with the water you had. In the springtime all the little lakes would be dammed and you'd be holding back water. When the water was gone, you couldn't go any further. Maybe it would take three or four years to get down to the mill because it was a long ways to go.

I wasn't involved in building it. The only reason that I was around it too much, there would be times, especially in the spring of the year when this thing would be in use, they weren't cutting and there's no need of scalers if you're not cutting any wood. If there's nothing to do, well, this [walking the flume] is a good, easy job standing around. You more or less put in the time because it was two day's walk out to Caledonia. At that time, it was about twelve miles from Caledonia to Lowe's Landing. If you could get across on a boat to Trout Brook which was their base, Camp One, well, that's fine, but if you couldn't it was twelve miles around. It was a long ways up in there from Camp One to Caledonia, so the result was you didn't come home for overnight.

You went in the fall and stayed until Christmas. Then after Christmas you come in and stayed until after the hauling was done when the ice was breaking up. In the wintertime you'd have to check off all of the wood when it was hauled out of the woods to make sure that you were getting it all. You knew what the cut was in the summertime, and in the winter it had to match. There'd be a two-sled road go into the edge of the swamp and around to the lake. Maybe you'd only get what you call a two-turn road: a trip in the morning and a trip in the afternoon with a pair of horses. You'd have a number of teams of oxen hauling out from the stump to the two-sled road with just one sled with a rack secured to it. Called them a dray. They would haul the wood out to where they were using two sleds.

After that, there'd be the drive work. Then all summer they'd be cutting pulp. In the summertime was when we'd be busiest. In that period of time they had to get all their hemlock cut because when the sap finished running you couldn't peel. You might get home once in between times. Some of the farmers used to figure that once they got their garden in, then they were going in the woods to peel hemlock until it was time for haying. So you had a bunch coming and going most of the time. As long as they had a certain number of bodies cutting, [Mersey didn't object] because they realized most of the people were farmers and woodsmen.

They'd be cutting spruce in the fall too. A lot depended on how much wood they got cut during the summer months. In the fall when they finished their cut, everybody would go home. In between times I've left here in the morning on a bicycle, peddled through to Annapolis down as far as Kingston and was there three o'clock in the afternoon and had a job with the Spur Fruit Company pickin' apples. It was a hard pull I'm tellin' ya up over Mickey Hill here on gravel roads. It was a dollar and seventy-five cents a day we got; that was pretty good goin'.

They used to put up pretty good camps. They were all built on the same style, separated halfway back, half for sleeping quarters and the other for the cookhouse. Camp Five was made of upright logs and would be twenty by maybe forty-five feet long and able to sleep sixty men. Along the roof the [stove]pipe would come down and then along horizontal, and then down to the big stove that would carry a four-foot stick. On that stove you'd have a great big washtub that the cookee would have to keep filled with water for washing when the men would come in. On each side of this horizontal pipe you'd have a rack, just a couple of poles down and along. Everybody would have a great long handle with a cross on it. He'd come in with his wet clothes, hang them on that and hook them up over. Well, you can imagine! You talk about getting gamey and ripe, but you got used to it. You only had what you could bring in on your back, your own personal belongings, 'cause you had to carry everything in. Now you got men that won't go in the woods unless you can get them home every night and all this tomfoolery. I just wonder what some of them would do if they really had to get down and scratch.

In the corner of the sleeping quarters there was a little cubicle for the boss and scaler, and in there you'd have a great big box. We always called it the wong'n box but spelled it *van*. Don't ask me why.[2] When I'd report anything, I'd report it as the van. They'd have mackinaws, pants, tobacco, most anything you wanted. If you didn't have your own saws and axes to take, the company would supply them, but you'd have to buy them. One of my jobs as scaler was to look after that, to see that it was all charged out properly to certain men. A report would go in with my report of the wood they cut and that would automatically come off before they got their money.

"Camp Five was made of upright logs and would be twenty by maybe forty-five feet long and able to sleep sixty men." (Fred Ellis)

The supplies would be brought in and put in a storehouse, just a rough shed, at the foot of a lake. From there it had to go by wagon in summer and by tote team of some description in the wintertime. To start off, a tote team would take you a barrel of flour, a hundred pound bag of sugar, a bag of beans, a case of dried apples, a case of dried prunes and all the salt, pepper, and spices that you wanted. There'd be meat come in every week, maybe a little oftener than that depending upon the number of men that you had. It was up to the cook then and we had pretty good cooks. Course, when you're working hard, a feller said you could eat most anything when you're hungry enough. They had beans twenty-one times a week if you wanted them. There'd be possibly four long tables and every so far there'd be a pan of beans, a pan of apple sauce, and a pan of prunes. Now that was there all the time, but you didn't have to have it. Over and above that you'd have stews, sliced meat, and all that.

I used to marvel at these fellas making pies. They'd make fifteen or twenty a day. I told Harry Wile one time, "I'm going to see how long it takes you to make a pie." He rolled the bottom crust, filled it, rolled the top crust, put it on, ringed it around and stamped it. In less than two minutes he'd have a pie ready for the oven.

There was no alcohol allowed. You could smoke and chew. Especially this time of year [summer months] it would be mostly chewing tobacco. They used to have rules and regulations. If you wanted to smoke you'd go to a certain designated area where there's a pool of water. All you had to do was pull the moss back and haul out a few granite rocks where these hemlock used to grow and you'd have the most beautiful water that you ever wanted to drink. We really never had any fires. Oh, there's been a few little instances that could possibly have developed into fires, but there was always enough people right there to confine them.

Some fellas would bring in a little violin or somethin' with them. I remember this little coloured fella from down Shelburne. Instead of walking way out around, they'd come up through the woods and get a job. He'd come in after a day's work and there was a big flat rock near Camp Five. He'd get up on that thing and he would dance. You'd see the sparks just a flyin' from the spurs on his shoes from this old rock. He'd dance there for about five minutes before he'd go in the camp. Sunday nights there'd usually be a singsong. They could play cards if they wanted, but there wasn't too much. They were usually tired enough after supper if they worked hard all day that they weren't too anxious to have any entertainment. They had to get up early in the morning.

What they're doing today is something out of this world. It's all over; they've rimracked the country. They take these great big machines in, and what they don't cut down they destroy anyway. What it don't smash down, it cripples to such a point that it can't grow up straight if it wants to. I've got no use for them at all. Why, I see some of the wood that goes along here; I wouldn't have accepted any of it when I was scaling. But now it don't make any difference, I guess, as long as it's not a limb, they'll take it.

John Taul

John Taul, 84, lives at Pleasant River, Queens County. He was thirteen years old when he first went to the woods with his father, George, as a cookee at camps in Enfield for John C. Horn. Over the years he has worked in the lumber woods at various places, mined gold, hunted, trapped, guided American sportsmen, and been a river warden. "I done a little of everything, I guess." While gold mining is a story in itself, his brief anecdotes about it give an insightful comparison between work above and below ground, a life many men endured to survive during that era.

In the old days that was a different thing altogether. You had a crosscut saw, a peavey, an axe, a measuring pole, a sledgehammer, and a wedge. You'd go out in the morning with the stars in the sky and you'd come in when they was out—for ten cents an hour. Nowadays, you got a power saw and a tree farmer and there's nothing to it. Don't have to cut a road. Just fall your timber and the tree farmer comes in, hooks onto it, and takes it out.

I can remember when the only way you could get in the woods when I was a young feller running around was by a pair of snow-shoes. It'd be up to your belt in the woods. Oh, yes, the winters was harder. Me and Angus Lowe, we used to have to take our provisions on hand sleds, enough to last us all week, and go back there on the old Annapolis Road, cook for ourselves, and cut pulpwood. Work all day, come home, and start cookin'. And cold! That old camp, you could look right through it. I remember one night there before Christmas, it come a real cold night. The only way we could keep warm, I'm tellin' you straight, one fella had to stay up to keep a fire while the other slept; we'd take turns. Saturday nights, we'd walk out, well, I'd say twelve miles one way and go back again Sunday night. Them were the days. That was tough old times.

It was all hard work in the woods, but the toughest job I ever had was loadin' logs with a peavey. They put skids on a truck and two men roll these big sawlogs up on them with peaveys. Hard work? None harder. You'd be so tired that you didn't think you'd ever make it out. No wonder a feller's legs is gone.

I worked in the lumber woods and sawmill for George Lewis from New Brunswick for ten years. Bill Mullen, he come from New Brunswick; he was manager for the Eddie Company. He got it cut and George sawed it by contract, so much a thousand. George Lewis got killed in his mill. He had his mill all set up and runnin'. He went down below to see how the gears was goin'. The main shaft had a piece stickin' out on it. He had a sweater on and that got caught. His son was with him and time he seen what was goin' on and got it shut off, he was beat all to pulp.

I worked mining gold off and on for must've been ten or twelve years. Too long. Both my lungs are eggshelled from rock dust. Them days, you see, in the old days in the mines they had no water on the machines. You take a stoper, that's a machine bores the holes, you're drillin' overhead, you couldn't see your partner for dust. You were takin' that all in, you had no protection. Now they have hollow steel that the water goes through and that kills the dust. Now they got everything. I worked in Molega for Colonel Olands for seven years and up in King Mine in North Brookfield. When Olands come there first he paid us a dollar and seventy-five cents a day. That was before the war.[3]

My grandfather, John, and Uncle Bill were both killed in the mines, four of 'em in one night, in here to Middlefield. That was before I was born, but I understand they were takin' the roof out; it was pretty rich up there, I guess, and they went up too far. The whole damn thing come down; took four days to muck them out.

The old fellas, at the first of it, had no machines. They used to hand drill with a hammer and steel. Hand steeling they called it. Two fellas, one twist it and the other fella come onto it. They had long steel, different lengths. You'd have a short one to start with, take it out and put the other one in, and pound on that awhile. As you got down, you put another one in and another one, until you put the finisher in.

I seen a fella blowed up in a mine: Bobby Sutherland, a good old friend of mine; me and him used to trap and hunt together. He drilled in a miss hole, a hole that had dynamite and a cap in it. They had drilled that off the night before and shot, blow'd 'er. But sometimes one hole will cut the other one off, cut the fuse off, and that won't go. You got to be very careful. He had his hand on his partner's shoulder, learning the young feller how to crank the machine. The drift, a tunnel are the same thing, was about a hundred feet long and only about four feet wide. Boy, she went right in that miss hole. *Bang!* The young fella never got hurt at all. Bobby, there wasn't a bone into him wasn't broke. Took him right out the drift. In one of them machine holes, they'd have six or eight plugs of dynamite. That'd be somethin'.

I seen Archie Belong get killed. He was puttin' in a turn sheet where you pull your [ore] car in and turn it around. They heist the cars up on the skip. They run the car on, the skip comes up, and you pull the car off. The skip drops just like that when the bell rings. Nobody touches that bell except the fella that tends the skip. That's to signal down below [three rings, then two]. Archie said to the young fella, "You want to watch that skip, they rung 'er down." Archie had that piece of rail just out over the shaft far enough that when she come down she hit it. It come up and hit him. A steel rail and it bent that rail just like that [nearly double]. His head was like an eggshell; he never knew what hit him.

I done everything. I helped the feller up on his back stope, taking the dynamite up to him to load his holes and carrying his steel. I tended deck a lot up top and used to make all the loads. The fuse and the cap that went in the dynamite, that's what they called a load. They'd give me the order for the loads, so much powder, so many loads. All them fellas knew just how much dynamite to put in a hole, what would break it. If you were timbering, you'd come up and get timber and take it down. Some would be muckin', shovelin' the stuff up. I'd sooner work in the mines [than the woods]. It tain't a healthier work, but its nicer down there, just right; all the same temperature, winter and summer.

Alan Hunt

Alan Hunt, 78, is a lifelong resident of Greenfield, Queens County. His family, one of the original settlers of the community, long noted for its salmon fishing and lumbering, ran a small sawmill for a number of years at Molega Lake. Alan is a veteran river driver on the Medway, which runs through Greenfield. "That's all we ever did in the wintertime was cut some logs…and bring 'em five or six miles down the river."

My father, Linkard Hunt, was born in 1885. His father was Boardman, and there were two more brothers, Porter and Lemuel. As far as the logging goes, it was Porter, my grandfather's brother, who started this logging operation in the late 1880s. Porter was the contractor and Lem acted as second-in-command. The operation, the way I understand my father, was mostly around Jordan Bay, Seventh and Eighth Lakes, in that district. Whoever had the sawmills in Milton…he contracted to cut and deliver logs; he had nothin' to do with the actual timber itself. I think he probably wound up we'll say about 1912.

They had to use boats to bring all their freight in over the water in the spring. It was all rowin'. Those carries were not very long and they'd probably pull them through or maybe pole them. Some of those men would go up in there in the cutting time, from June on, stay right through 'til freeze-up and come out on the drive and not get home 'til the last of May. One time in particular, my grandfather and Uncle Lem stayed there all winter and their job was supplyin' the camp with moose meat. Thirty or forty men, I suppose; it took quite a bit of meat.

They'd have to make their camps. They were quite primitive, I guess, made of logs and just poles and bark for the roof. Spruce bark makes damn good waterproof roofing. It's very pliable when it's green. Turn 'er upside down and put the bark side down; the other side's slick, just like it's varnished. You put that up and shingle it; it flattens out while it's green and pliable. You don't even have to use poles…. I think ol' Uncle Port had stoves[4] in his day, but before that they just had a fireplace in the middle with a smoke hole in the roof. Those days a man had to walk twenty miles in the woods and he had to carry what little personal belongings he had and his quilt. Usually it was just one quilt, regular homemade wool; they were warm. If he bunked up with a guy, they had two quilts.

They'd move their supplies in and then summer cut in peeling time, spudding time; that would be June and July up until August. June and July were the best. They'd maybe get a little the last of May, but it don't start gettin' very good and loose until June. You could peel a little in the full moon in August, but it'll tighten up in between then. Just fell the stuff and knock the bark off of it. It was mostly spruce and hemlock, I guess. It was all done with axes. Probably ol' Uncle Port, on the last of his career, was using the crosscut saw.[5]

The cutting crew, there was one man felling and two spudding. You probably stood on top of the tree, take your axe, and start the bark. You just ring it about four feet apart around and cut down as far as you could reach on both sides, then take your spuddin' iron and roll it off down each side. You could roll off a junk about four feet long. I used to make 'em [spudding irons] with just a piece of car spring; it has the right curve in it. Not real thick, about an inch and a half; make a point on one end to go in a wooden handle and sharpen the other end. After they were barked, they floated better, and they had this greasy, light piece of wood to haul out to the ice through the frost and snow.

After peelin' was over, then they had to start movin' in their winter supplies. Soon as it got enough winter to go on the ice, they started hauling stuff [logs] out and puttin' it on the ice using horses, but oxen primarily. They'd move their oxen in on the ice and leave them all summer; just turn 'em loose to roam around and graze on the old meadows. There was lots of meadows around the lake shores.

My father was twelve years old and he went up there one winter. The ice was bad. My grandfather had a small horse and took this up to work on the lakes to bring the supplies and stuff. He took a man along, and my father, and if the horse fell through the ice, they had a man big enough to pull the horse out. The ice was bad all that winter and they couldn't put a regular-size horse on it.

One problem they had, they smashed those great big trees down, took the bark all off the top of 'em and then they was layin' there with the limbs drove down into the earth. When they came to 'em, everything was froze solid as hell and they had a helluva job breakin' 'em loose and rollin' 'em over so they could pull 'em out. I remember seein' things in Uncle Port's ol' woodshed he made, like a peavey hook, only a big one, with a ring in the end of it. They must've hooked

Headworks and crew winching in a boom of logs. This style varied slightly from that described by Alan Hunt in the type of crank handle being used. (Lillian Scott Perry)

that on the log, put a pole through it and tied a chain to the end of the pole and tied their ox on that to roll the log over.

They'd get it all on the ice and make their booms all around it. When the ice went out, they started boomin' it across a series of lakes from Eighth Lake down to First Lake. This was on the Mersey, on what's now the Rossignol. They came down to Indian Gardens, spilled the stuff there and drove it to the mill. I don't think that particular outfit would ever have as much as a million feet. That's an awful lot of logs in one boom. Maybe four hundred thousand, somethin' like that. I just remember Uncle Lem, he was an awful ol' windbag, braggin' about him bringin' the biggest boom down the Rossignol that anybody ever brought. That was the time he had four sets of headworks. Usually they had just one. He had two headworks pullin' the thing and he had two more, one on each side, so they could steer the tail of it; they'd have trouble on the lakes when they hit a point.

They make a raft of logs, I'd say about fourteen, sixteen feet long, twelve feet wide. You lay crosspieces across each end and you pin them with wooden pegs. You bore through the crosspiece with a two-inch auger down into the centre of the log under it. You make a pin that will fit a two-inch hole, but it wants to be swelled a little on the first end so when you drive it in it goes in tight, the swelling on the end holds it. Then you mount your crank, a wooden spindle, with a crank on each end. You put pork rind in, greasy part out, for a bearing, and that'll last forever. It's mounted on poles that are all pinned with wooden pins. The crank itself, the handle, is made of about inch-round iron. It goes across the spindle between this rack. You take a piece of spruce about six inches through and split it, make an inch hole through the middle of it and that fits over that crank. There's a couple of bolts through it on each end. Part of the crank is flattened so a bolt would go through and the crank is fastened to the wooden spindle. That's your headworks.* All the people that boomed across the lakes used it. they had a system like that around the mines. It was the old well curb, only this was two cranks, a crank on each end.

The headworks is tied right on the boom. I'd say the crank has two hundred to three hundred feet of rope on it. It's quite a long rope, just about what the spindle on the crank would handle and not pile up too big. If it got too big, it'd turn too hard. It's pulled out and there's an anchor on the end of it and an anchor rope on it with a float. Two men tend that. They row out to the end of the warp [rope], drop the anchor, and stay there where the float is 'til they wind the boom into the anchor. Six or eight men on the headworks wind it up, hopin' to God that the anchor will get a good grab. Sometimes in the mud, they'd wind 'er all the way into the boom without goin' an inch.

Oh, my God, it took half the length of your warp to just gather in all your slack. They always talked about takin' your slack boom. Everything settled back, logs all spread off, and it gets loose as hell. Your boom might be way the hell and gone too far away from your source of power, whether it's a headworks or what [motorboats were used in later years to tow booms]. You want to wrap 'er in a little tighter and put it together, and it takes half the length of that warp to get goin'. And when it does move, I don't imagine it does a quarter a mile an hour. If there was wind, they always tried to get in a lee shore somewheres and wait 'til the wind goes down. Lots of times they'd have to wait a week 'til the wind changed.

There was a young fella, Roy Swicker, well, he was an old man in my day, his father drowned himself throwin' out anchors. When he threw the anchor out, the buoy line tangled up around his foot and he went out with the anchor and drowned. He left Roy an orphan, twelve years old, and he went up in the woods for Uncle Port and the first job he did was felling. Twelve years old! Link talked about it. The trees was big and they come down and went off like that [sloped away at the base]. He had an old pair of leather shoes and they were all wore off on the sides from hangin' on the side of that stump.

Somethin' else that's interesting, they didn't have the facilities to

* Another type of headworks, a capstan, used a vertical spindle with poles inserted through holes which men pushed against while walking 360° turns on the raft.

make the iron boom chains that was used later. The booms that they made during the period I'm talkin' about, when old Uncle Port was doin' his stuff at the very, very first of the 1900s, they bored a hole in the butt and top of long spruce or hemlock. They'd probably be fifty feet long, maybe a little more. Spruce were better 'cause they were straighter. They made the pins like I was tellin' ya about, long enough to go in that wood so far and left the head up. Then they took a great big ol' horse's rope, splice an eye in each end of it and they'd end up, it'd be about [two feet] long. They called them horse cocks. So they had the hole in the top and butt of this boom log and they drive that [pin] through the eye of the horse cock so it drove in tight. It was made small enough and bored deep enough that it just come down level and in fairly snug against the eye of that rope. If they wanted to break their boom, they had to knock it off with an axe, then bore another hole, and have another pin to put it back together.

If you had to get across the lake, you didn't leave it in the middle of the lake. They stayed there all night and all day, and all night, the next night…they stayed right with it. They had a camp or some kind of cookin' facilities somewheres and somebody tended it and brought food out. You started daylight 'til dark, rain or shine. You was workin' against time. Water was very important; as the water went down, you was losin' money.

When they came to the first carry between two lakes, they had to get off enough of their spare boom to take down through and set a snare on the other end. Course, it didn't take as much boom to catch it as it did to eventually go around the whole thing so they'd have enough slack boom for a catch boom. Probably they'd sluice enough through so they could take another bunch of slack boom through and keep addin' to the catch boom below. The waterways between the lakes must've been quite good channels 'cause I never heard of 'em havin' any trouble with drivin' the logs through those passages. Spill it through, boom it up, winch it across to the next lake, and go through the same thing again. First Lake was about eight miles long before it was flooded when the power development come along. The other ones were, in comparison, four to six to eight miles. It could be eight times 'til they got to the Indian Gardens, then they had about, I suppose, twelve or fourteen miles to drive it down the Mersey to Milton.

When they got to Indian Gardens, there was a dam, kind of like a reservoir, and when they brought their booms in, then they had to sluice through this dam. There was other operations, other log drives, comin' down the river at the same time. As they kept gatherin' together, they kept workin' together. When they got to Milton, I don't know how many mills was there, but there was more than one. They had what they called pickin' gaps, separate booms, a boom goin' into one mill, another boom into another mill. They had sturdy platforms out to the end of these and fellers tended that, a bunch of 'em with pike poles. Each lumberman had his own man on the pickin' gap takin' care of his interests. Each log was stamped on the butt or there could be a blaze on the side; they put letters or somethin' with an axe. They had to look at every log and put it in the right boom.

The camping life, there was somethin'. On those river drives they had four meals a day: one 'fore daylight, one in the middle of the mornin', one in the middle of the afternoon, and one after dark. The cook and his outfit followed the drive. They'd move ahead of the drive and set up. When the drive got too far past them, then they had to move agin. They set up two great big lean-tos facin' each other. There were at least two cookees and their job was to keep a damn good big fire goin' there all night. When those fellers come in, they were all soakin' wet. They come back that night and slept in those open lean-tos, that was their livin' quarters.

It was all open fires. The cook baked his bread with reflector ovens and they set up a bean hole. They probably lived ninety percent on beans and bread. That cookee's job was to follow the drive, build a fire and give 'em a hot meal twice durin' the day, first and second lunch they called it. Old Uncle Port, on the last end, he got himself a portable cookhouse on wheels, like a camper trailer today. Along the Mersey here, there was a road downriver. It must've been a rough son of a bitch.

The Medway wasn't as big a chainwork as the Mersey, but it was a long one. It's a bad, rough river and shallow; a lot of places for logs to hole up. It's a hard river to drive. The first people who brought logs down that was the Mitchells. They had a mill in Mill Village and brought a drive of logs down the Medway every spring. They were goin' through the same rigamaroles that I've been describing. Then later on, ol' Henry Davison had a big steam mill just about at tidewater at Mill Village and he brought drives down the Medway River for years.[6]

The people in the village of Greenfield built a gang mill somewheres along 1836. That's a series of [vertical] saws, each one is set for a specific thickness; they were water-driven. The log was rolled onto two little carriage things on a track, then they'd start the saws goin' up and down. Quite a lot of it would stick out over the carriage. Some of them had a ratchet feed; that one in Greenfield, I don't know if that

had a ratchet or they just pinched it ahead with a peavey. Those particular ones were pretty slow. They use the same system now, only it's more modern.

It was kind of a co-operative thing. There were seven or eight in the group and they had access to land all around Ponhook Lake and the Medway. They brought their own logs in. There was other outfits that had logs around the waterway and they brought them down to that gang mill. It was right in front of where I live. That operated for quite a little while, then I guess they didn't get along too well—for some reason or other they got tired of the co-operative system—and they sold it to ol' Henry Davison and then they used to rent it from him to saw the logs.

Along about 1912 they had a shingle mill and grist mill, water power, on the other side of the river. An old Catholic priest moved into Little Ponhook...and he moved a mill in there and brought a crew. When they finished, the Freemans, four or five of 'em, bought that mill from the Catholic priest and set it up beside their shingle mill. The operation then was what you called custom sawing—everybody in the village cut a little bunch of logs to sell for their use, put their mark on it, bring it down, and pile it on the bank and it went

"The camping life, there was somethin'.... They'd move ahead of the drive and set up. When the drive got too far past them, then they had to move agin." (Bear River Historical Society)

through the mill. The feller on the other end, the tallyman, had to keep track of each log. Maybe he'd have eight or ten different tally sheets.

Those ol' fellers were awful stupid. This gang mill I was talkin' about. It [log] went through and they had eight, ten, or twelve boards with the bark on 'em. Then they had to take edgin' off the side. They didn't have the edgers they have today; they had one saw and they ran that board through one side and took one edgin' off. They had pins so far apart...put the square edge of the board against those and push the board through the saw agin. There was at least four or five in the village—ol' Parker Crowell, John Crowell, Ed Joudrey—all had half their fingers sawn off like that. I don't know what the hell it was about it. They'd be holdin' the board, kind of pushin' it along, and it come to the saw, they just didn't bother to take [their hand away], they'd just push it right straight through that saw.

And today, somebody fall out of a boat like that [Roy Swicker's father] with a rope around 'im, the other guy sittin' there, all he had to do was take hold of that rope and pull 'im back to the boat. He probably just set there with his mouth open; course, the buoy thing probably went with him—it was wound around his leg—there was nothin' probably for him to get hold of. The fellers on the headworks were too far away to do anything and they would've had no boat. The ol' boys was scared of the water to begin with, but they went river drivin'. Ninety percent of them couldn't swim. Swicker, whether he could swim or not, the anchor had taken him down.

On the river drives, there was always bad accidents. A log would go down and stick. The first thing, half the logs in the drive would be all piled up. That water, there'd be tremendous pressure. Oh, God, you got workin' on the face of that jam, and if you were able to loosen the key log, that's one place you don't want to be. You want to get out of there just as fast as God will let you. There's been a lot of river drivers [killed], particularly out through New Hampshire, Vermont, and northern Maine. There was an awful lot of logging off those mountains. The ol' boys, a river driver get drowned [in those states], they put him in a pork barrel, bury him, and hang his calk boots on a tree. There's a picture of one, way back in the 1800s, in a book *Tough Men & Tall Trees*. When they put in a power plant on that particular river [in the United States] they dug out one of 'em. It was a long ways from anywheres. That was, I suppose, as handy a way to bury them as any.

Hilton Scott

Hilton Scott, 87, cannot recall when anyone but a Scott brought log drives down the Barrington River in Shelburne County. The annual event was cause for celebration. School and business closed as the community gathered at the river for picnics while lumberjacks rode the first of the logs through spring freshets to the Scott sawmill at River Head. River driving on the Barrington ended in 1957, but the lumbering continued, and today Stanley Scott and his twin sons, René and Raymond, operate the family sawmill, a business spanning five generations. The Scotts have also been long known as athletes, winning many sportsmen titles in log rolling and related events. The most noted of the family is Stanley's brother Phil, a nine-time world log-rolling champion, who still travels the globe demonstrating his skills. In recent years a number of the Scotts have showcased their talents in the Great Canadian Lumberjack Show.

As part of the Loyalist Bicentennial Celebrations in 1983, the Scott family staged a fifteen-mile log drive on the Barrington, complete with community suppers and lumberjack contests. The Canadian Broadcasting Corporation filmed a vignette of the re-enactment, titled "The Last River Drive." Hilton Scott, as elder statesman, was given the honour of rolling the first logs into the river, it being sixty-five years since his first river drive.

I'm the oldest member of the Scott clan in Barrington. I had four brothers—Andrew, Harold, Ken, Tom—and a sister, Alice. Andrew and I are the only two left. When Barrington was first settled there were sixteen families and they called them the proprietors. My grandmother was a Watt and her father was one of the proprietors. The old guy that came here first and started the work, Thomas Uriah Scott, had a cookhouse up the Jordan River, just up from Jordan Falls bridge. They got together somehow and he came here after they were married and took over the family house when the old people died.

There was a big piece of land set out for the proprietors and their heirs forever. It goes up to Woods Harbour and nearly to Clyde River and anywhere on that you could go. They did quite a lot of loggin' on that. The crown land, the lease for a hundred acres was so much for ten years, didn't cost very much, so they'd move there and log it for maybe two or three years, then lease another piece.

When grandfather first came here, one of the first things he did was he went up to the head of the lake and found where the township line ran. That was the edge of crown land. Then he came back a little bit to the first brook he saw, and took up that piece of land. It was part of the proprietor's land. He gave it to me, his cabin and the whole thing, when I was fifteen years old, probably because I was the oldest grandson and because I carried his name [Hilton Uriah] too.

As far as I can figure it was the early 1870s when he took up that land.[1] He had a good little camp. I'd say it was fourteen feet square, logged up about four feet, and then it was boards from that up to the top. The roof went on a slope and at the top was a two-foot square opening where the smoke went out through, but most of it stayed in the camp. Just a fireplace in the middle and a Dutch oven in the front. Then they had a hole dug out to cook beans in. They just had iron kettles with iron covers. He'd rake out the coals from that hole, then put the kettle in, shove the coals over it, and build a fire again. That's how he cooked the beans. Had no floor [it was dirt] and no door [an opening covered with a blanket], a hole in the roof, that's all [no windows]. It had fires inside and that give a lot of light. Probably they went to bed when it got dark. They slept on ticks filled with meadow hay.

Grandfather and my father, Uriah Pitman, built a water mill on the branch of the Barrington River; that was the first one. They had a push carriage that you could saw short stuff on, but no long carriage like they have now. The first one of these went in the little steam mill which was built in 1906, just about a half mile difference down toward the main river. I started working there when I was thirteen. Grandfather was gettin' along in years then and I helped him fire the boiler. They shut it down after about twenty years. It was kind of shaky, only a wooden building, so they quit it. Tom [Hilton's brother] took over then and they had a diesel engine, and at the last I think they used electric power.[2]

My father had a small mill above his house for quite a while where he sawed laths and shingles. He kept that more or less until Tom started in at Black Jim's about fifty years ago. An old Indian, they called him Black Jim, that's where Andrew and Tom built the mill. From where the mill is now, it was just across on the other side.

There was a big store down at Port La Tour, Consolidated Trading

Scotts' steam mill built in 1906 on the Barrington River. (Lillian Scott Perry)

Company, and they took care of a lot of the lumber and laths for the fishermen. About every week or two, a pair of oxen would start at five o'clock in the morning and haul a load down to Port La Tour and come back the same day. It's about twenty-five miles return. Sold a lot on Cape Sable for boatbuilding. They never trimmed boat boards; they were big at one end and narrow at the other. Saw them live, just put the damn log on there and saw.

On one side of Great Pubnico Lake was a settlement, probably a dozen families. My grandfather and my father bought the places as people moved out, so [eventually] they owned the whole of Great Lake Hill [headwaters of Barrington River]. The first winter I spent there I was eight months old. They had a cookhouse and an addition where grandfather and grandmother stayed. Our family had a camp of our own alongside the cookhouse. We was out to Great Lake four or five years. Usually after Christmas, we left school and spent the winters in the lumber woods; we went back in the spring to school. We liked it. All we had to do was set rabbit snares and eat. My father was the boss and grandfather was the cook. He owned part of the business, but he did the cookin' part. The basic thing was beans, salt herring and moose meat...rabbits, ducks, anything. My grandfather was the best cook in the world. He gave me a recipe for bread when I was eleven years old.

We usually took supplies in when we went. Horses were no good. The ground, a lot of it, was soft, and a horse, their hoof is in one piece and when they stick their foot down it's like a suction cup, they couldn't get it up. We used oxen all the time. They crawl right along as long as it's halfway up the broad side. The old man would go up in the fall around Tusket, go back in the country there, and hunt somebody that had a pair of oxen. He'd walk them home from Tusket. If he wanted to keep them [rather than beef them after the winter's work], they'd drive them back in the woods and just keep run of them every three or four weeks. He'd know just about where they were. They'd feed on the meadows. Then he'd haul them out again when he wanted them to make hay at home. They were the only critter before tractors came around.

They had nothin' but axes then. If they were running two camps, they'd have eight or nine choppers with double-bitted axes. When they first started, they had the old pole axe.[3] Then one of the times we was at Great Lake, the old man came out, as he did every week or two; when he came back he had a double-bitted axe. They didn't like that, said they'd cut their head off. The old man said try it. At the end of the day, one fella that chopped with the old man, an old fella from Villagedale, he says, "If you're goin' out, get me one of those axes." From that, it went all double bits. They never cut them down with a crosscut saw, only when they wanted to cut the logs in two.

They drove down the Branch probably three or four years, but it was small and a helluva job to get logs down. It would come up and down so fast that the logs were high and dry. Most of the time it came from Great Lake and Wabei [on the main river]. Starting from Great Lake, there was Whistler Point, Wabei, Mushquash, Big Falls, Little Lake and there was about four rapids from there down and they all had names. There was Polly's Place first; that was up to Great Lake. She was an old Indian woman. I don't know what she did, but she was a medicine woman, I think, more than anything else. The next one was a small rapid at Wabei. It was all smooth going from there down to Big Falls just above Barrington Lake. There was Weir Falls, then Sorrow Falls, Island Falls, Chrissie's Falls, and then Phil's Falls by Tom's place.

The Indians were the best of river drivers; they were catty. The chief one was John Glode. Joe Pictou was one of the other principals. They travelled from at the head of Great Lake, an Indian reservation we called the Gravel Pit. They were good people, all of 'em, the

Joe Pictou, right, and son-in-law Philip Paul. "The Indians were the best of river drivers; they were catty." (Col. Sullivan)

Glodes and Pictous. You could trust them with anything. Grandfather had a little shack down by the steam mill at River Head and they'd come around. They played with us, and the kids played around until they got big enough to go to work. The old women would make baskets. The old Glode, Victoria, that was Johnnie's mother, she was older than Methuselah's goat. She was the chief basket maker and you should have seen her with a drawknife. John Glode and Joe Pictou were the last of the original Micmacs; they were full Indians. The others were just half Indian and half French. An old Indian that used to live here said, "They're just white enough to make 'em a damn fool."

My father was never a good river driver, but Tom was excellent. From the time Tom and I was two years old, we were on the logs so we didn't scare worth a damn and a blow. I was a bit fussy [choosing a log to ride], but Tom, he only weighed about a hundred and thirty pounds and he could ride a whiplash. Sometimes in the millpond, maybe two hundred feet by half as wide, we'd run back and forth on the logs just for fun. He could go anywhere, but I had to watch what I stepped on. If I stepped on a log that was small, first thing I was down to my ass. He was about like a cat.

The only accident they had was Uncle Walter. He got his leg almost cut off, and he pretty near went for it from where they could get him home. Otherwise, there wasn't. The ones that were good on the logs went on the logs and the ones that were no good on the logs, they stayed where it was firm on the bank, which was me most of the time. Mostly I drove oxen.

My father was postmaster for River Head for thirty years. He was also game warden for thirty years, so he kept pretty busy. One time the old man had a little store and he used to get molasses by the tierce, that's like two barrels—halfway between a barrel and a puncheon. He also bought and sold hay and feed and all kinds of stuff like that. One day we loaded up with hay. "Well," he said, "you might as well take the molasses since you're goin'." We only had sleds and there was no snow within fifty yards of the platform where the molasses was. He said, "Do you suppose we can carry that?" It weighed about thirteen hundred and fifty pounds. I said, "I'll tell you one thing. If we can't, and your brothers Walter and Charlie don't come along, you're goin' to go one hell of a long walk before you find somebody that can." So we did it, grabbed a hold of the damn thing and lugged it. We took hold of the bottom of it on the edges and then he took hold of my wrists and up we came. He never worried about me after that.

We used to smoke kyaks: string them up on sticks, put them in the roof of a [smoke]house, and build a fire under 'em. Oak sawdust makes the best smoke. That old fella [father], he'd go in there and there'd be smoke comin' out of the cracks everywhere. Bye and bye, when he got the fire goin' just where he wanted it, he'd come out and *"Phew!"* Another thing I seen him do, every once in a while he'd run into a hornet's nest. He'd just pull it off and pull it apart. The hornets would fly around and light on his hands. He'd just leave them there awhile and he'd snap them off. Never stung him. He wasn't quite as big, but he was his father's son.

Grandfather was a good man. Powerful. About six feet two tall, two hundred and ten pounds. When I was a quite small kid, all along the Barrington River there was about five miles of meadows on both sides. They were all owned by different people. Sometimes there'd be twelve or thirteen pairs of oxen with loads of hay, one right behind the other. They made the road themselves. We was comin' down there one time and there was a place corduroyed and it was broken up in places. The first one in the lineup was Matthew Watt and he had a son that was drivin' these oxen. Uncle Charlie, that's grandpa's son, he was drivin' my grandfather's oxen. Grandfather said, "Charlie, unhook your oxen and go around in front of Matt's load, get hold and pull him out." Old Matt came storming around and he said, "Not by a damn sight, you won't!" The old man just grabbed him by the neck and the ass of the pants and fired him in the alders. Just the same as you'd throw a bag full of clothes, with no more effort. He says, "Now

Thomas Scott, Sr.,
Hilton's grandfather,
left; Uriah Pitman
Scott, Hilton's father,
right. (Lillian Scott
Perry)

damn ya, stay there!" So that was him. It was a word and a blow, and the blow came first. But he was a good ol' fella.

He was workin' on the Pubnico Road one time. I think he had a pair of oxen there. The boss of the place had a wooden shack that he stayed in. The rest of 'em stayed in tents. Somebody said, "Who the hell does he think he is?" The old man said, "I'll fix him." He rolled the feller's caboose full of rocks and nobody could roll them out, so he had to stay in the tent. Oh, he was a hard ol'…. He came in my father's little store one day. He said something, I don't know what it was, and he just took his fist and slapped the casing around the door and split it from end to end. He was getting old then too. Even as an old man, whatever he said was it.

They were the best woodsmen that I've ever seen. The old man, if anybody wanted any kind of a log—a spar for a boat, a log for a mackerel trap—he would tell them exactly where to go to get them. A lot of times when we were sawing logs for laths and stuff, he would start out in the morning and I would start out with the oxen at the same time. I knew exactly where he was going and by the time I'd get in there, he'd have a load chopped. That was a long time ago. It was good fun and a lot of work, but I wouldn't have missed it for anything in the world.

Irene Jones

Irene Jones, 81, lives in Upper Ohio, Shelburne County. Her husband, Cecil, ran a small woods operation on the Roseway River. The family also raised dairy cows and sold the milk to the Yarmouth Creamery. Irene's father, Fred W. Bower, was founder of Shelburne Woodworkers, an economic mainstay of Shelburne County for more than seventy years.

To go way back, it was called the Shelburne Fruit and Pickle Company.[4] I remember when we were kids we used to pick blueberries and take them down there and get four cents a quart, after about a three mile walk to get there. We thought we were rich. In 1919, they enlarged onto it and formed the Shelburne Woodworkers. They used to buy logs and saw them into lumber and they had a shingle mill. My father was the manager at that time. There was always a small store in connection with it. My father owned that and when they amalgamated into the Shelburne Woodworkers that store went with it, and they added on and had a big grocery store. I worked in the grocery store after I finished school as a clerk. Gradually there was no sale for [fish] boxes, so they just sold lumber. In later years it got so hard and expensive to get new mill men that could saw or plane lumber they found it just as cheap to do away with their mill and they now buy their lumber, but the Woodworkers still have the hardware part.

Cecil always had two pair of oxen. He owned a lot of timberland, at one time about eight hundred acres, and he cut for himself. When they went into camp they would be five or six miles from here up in the Indian Fields direction. He also had timberland across this lake [Jones Lake] and when he cut those, he brought them out to the edge of the water, put them in a boom, and took them across with the headworks. His mill was right down the cove of this lake. At one time his mill was down the road about a mile, his first mill. That belonged to my husband's father, Lorenzo Jones. It was a water mill and had been there for years. When his father died, he took over the mill, but during the high water one time, it took it out.

Up in the Indian Fields he worked there maybe ten different

seasons. Those days they had oxen into the camp to be fed, so he would stay every other weekend and let the men come out. We're talkin' between 1939 and 1950. The rest of his time he spent across the lake here.

I used to cook for my husband, but I never went to the camp to cook. I always done my cooking here and they took it back themselves. When he was in the woods, he'd have five or six [men], and river driving time he'd have ten. Then when they started to saw in the spring of the year there was a little camp right down below where the mill was. We only had two or three that stayed in the camp, but they come up here and got their meals. We didn't have room for them in the house because we had seven children of our own. The other men that he needed were just from this section and they went home nights.

It wasn't easy, I'll tell you that. I used to cook for a week at a time. One team would be out and they'd take the food in Monday morning. Then I'd have the whole week to do the cooking again. I'd start about Wednesday. I would make a great big pot of stew and a great big pot of baked beans, and a pot of corned beef and cabbage. They used to have salt herring and they would cook that themselves. I'd make a basket of molasses cookees and one of sugar cookees and one of doughnuts and probably twenty loaves of bread ready to go in each week. Probably ten or twelve pies. As I look back, I wonder how I ever did it. But you know, you got along. It's there in front of you, so you do it. Those days you didn't think anything about it. You did what you had to do.

For a while those days we had a delivery truck from Shelburne Woodworkers come up once a week with your groceries. If I didn't go down or couldn't get down, you could always phone your order in and that was delivered on a Thursday. You could get your flour in hundred-pound bags, and a bag would do me about three weeks. Everything else was bought in large quantities.

When the Woodworkers had their mill going, Cecil sold a lot of his lumber to the mill and we used to charge our groceries. For several years we didn't know where we stood with the Woodworkers because you don't sell lumber every week. When we sold lumber, that was credited up to us and I charged my groceries. Before we'd get that settled up, I'd have another grocery bill. But in the end we always got settled up with them. Regular customers charged their groceries and paid each month, but there was quite a lot that paid cash, people they didn't really know and if they could trust or not. If we wanted a hundred dollars in cash we could always go there and get it on our lumber. In those days that's the way they worked.

I used to keep account of everything we bought. This particular month, it was in 1945, there was five men, and at that time we had four kids, and our grocery bill for the month of March was forty-five dollars. You can't get enough now for a day, can you?

Melvin Bower

Melvin Bower, 75, lives in Upper Ohio, Shelburne County, on the Roseway waters. His father, James M. Bower, worked the woods and was a widely known guide. Melvin retired six or seven years ago after a lifetime in the lumber and pulpwood business, but his son and grandson carry on the tradition today.

Do you know my power bill here now costs me a year as much as an ordinary family on this river earned in one year? Now that's quite a thing you come to think about, isn't it? One thing I can say, I was never hungry, always had plenty to eat, and we was comfortable, but I mean you never had nothin'.

I don't think in my life we ever had a welfare person on this river outside of maybe one. Everybody made their livin' but had little money. They looked after themselves. You had to get everything in, apples and potatoes, and you preserved; and up home here we had moose meat. All had a few acres of land and that's what they worked on, that was their livin'. Now, you couldn't live off that today. See, they didn't hire nobody. If they had a son come up, he worked with them a little while and most everything they had they cut themselves. I imagine if they cut fifty thousand, that would be a big year. We used to sell for ten dollars a thousand alongside the road. Now you never got no money out of that; that's how you got your groceries years ago. You cut a few logs and Shelburne Woodworkers would take 'em. And your taxes, I believe in Upper Ohio, the most of it went to pay your schoolteacher. We'll say a teacher got one hundred and fifty to two hundred dollars a year, that's what they had to get out of the community here. And they talk about things today.

It was a good life. You take them poor people—everybody was poor—but a lot of them people just loved to go in the woods in the wintertime. You went in and had regular meals. Your meals must've been good, because in the spring of the year you were just as healthy as you could be. I hear on the television, "Oh, what a miserable life." It was a good life! Sure, it was a God damn sight different than city

life. You was back in the woods, but you had really good, heavy clothes on and you had your camp. People them days, most everybody, were well dressed. You had long underwear and heavy pants, sweaters, and heavy shirts. You were dressed for it, you didn't mind it. One thing, the old people always built a log cabin. You could build them out of boards and tar paper. Well, that was cold, but you put your logs up and you had a fire goin' all day or half the night; those logs got warm and that would keep your building warm. You had good big logs in there. A log camp was ten times as good as a damn old tar paper one.

You had plenty to eat, you were warm, and the rest of it come. You had a crosscut saw and if you had a good filer, that wasn't hard work. Once you got used to that, two good men on a crosscut saw would saw all day and you never minded it hardly. You knew how to work back and forth onto it, and if you didn't have a fool on there that held her in too hard, why, you had nothin' to it.

My neighbour up here and another feller, if I'm not mistaken—now all they was doin' was sawin' 'em down—they put 125 of them big hemlock down in one day. Now I'm tellin' you, that would make some of these boys talk with a tree saw. And they was big, them wasn't little hemlock. You never had a hemlock there under two feet through. That stuff's all changing isn't it? Hard to see some big old

"Two good men on a crosscut saw would saw all day and you never minded it hardly." Pictured are Raymond and René Scott giving a demonstration. (Lillian Scott Perry)

hemlock now. I don't imagine they'll ever be back again. I suppose some of them was five hundred years old. Yeah, never be back.

I started when I was fourteen, right across the lake there. We contracted for Isaac Bower. My father and I had contracts for twenty-one years with him. I drove teams for years. I used to come out maybe every two weeks to get provisions: groceries for the camp, and hay and feed for your teams. Then I was a contractor for Jack Cox, who was one of the biggest landowners up here. I done all his contracting. I must've logged forty years for Jack Cox. I imagine I cut a million, a million and a half feet a year.

I remember ol' George Davis, he was a big logger for Jack Cox. They owned a lot of land together. They used to [river] drive down to Sutherland's mill in Clyde. They [Sutherland's] were big loggers. The two in my time was J.J. Cox and Shelburne Woodworkers. Them days, that was all virgin timber. You'd get more off an acre than you would now off fifty acres. Across the lake over here we logged there for years and only a small piece of land too—less than a thousand acres. Oh, my heavens, he had some timber on it.

We used to pay a dollar a day and found. I had one of the greatest men workin' for me in the woods down here and that man had a wife and three if not four kids home, and if you got four days a week in you was doin' good because you didn't get paid for a rainy day. I often wonder, now how could a person live on four dollars a week? I don't know what we got, but I imagine we only got five dollars a thousand for puttin' those damn logs out—for cuttin' 'em, haulin' 'em out, and puttin' 'em in the lake. Some difference. Now, my grandson here, he's got a big tree farmer and he could go here and put out two or three hundred thousand in a month with three men. My, my, my.

All my young life everything was river drove. Them days I used to go cookee with my father. The first river drive I went on to actually work must have been right around the war. That would have been for Sutherland Lumber Company. They put big drives over here on the Clyde River. The first year we went, you talk about life, that was a hard life in a way, but you made it. I think we were thirty days the first time before we ever seen anybody but ourselves. We got down here what we call Roy McKays and the water give up and we had to leave 'em there. That wasn't halfway down; we were miles from the mill. Come a rain in June or July, we took 'em again. I think we got 'em in that time.

We had just a miserable drive. Ol' Glen [Sutherland] put 'em in whole length and you couldn't get nowheres with 'em; shorter logs, you'd been all right. You take a spruce fifty feet long, you generally

Shear logs would be placed at strategic locations along the river, usually on corners, to keep logs flowing smoothly. (Lillian Scott Perry)

junked them off in the crooks because you had to saw him off anyway. They put the things in whole length and you want to get them in the river whole length! A little top comin' down river. You'd have shear logs on the [river]sides, so when they come in, it'd keep 'em goin' straight. Now that son of a bitch would come in—it'd be underwater about six inches—and he'd go right underneath the thing and catch behind a rock. You took your peavey and kept pickin' it until it broke and went downriver. Oh, your hands! The only way you'd save a peavey, it had a nub onto the top and when you broke it [jam], that's how you caught it with your hand. Man, that would get so sore and when it got good and sore, you'd lose your peavey.

We had two big dams up here on the Clyde—big dam to Russia Lake and a big one in Long Lake. We started in Russia Lake, then we went out into Auger Lake, then Sand Lake, and into Long Lake. Then you had to go from there into Barclay Lake. Then you were all through with your headworks. I suppose we'd have two or three hundred thousand in a boom. There was no more lakes then; you drive 'em from there on. The upper end [of the Clyde] is hard, but once you get down below what they call Cub Scootch it's a good river. You only got one bad falls down there—Trout Hole—that's bad, but the rest of it is good, you can go fast. But above is a bugger. Tree Falls is kind of bad, but Martin Falls is the worst: big ledges and big drops, she'd jam up there. We got caught in Trout Hole, must have had half the drive in one plug. We worked there for days and days to get that out of there.

The worst place I minded was the darned lakes. On the river you didn't get that wind and you could work to keep yourself warm. But out on the damned lake all you were doin' was crankin' [headworks] and, boy, that could be cold I'll tell ya. We went down across Long Lake in a northeast snowstorm, rain and snow. Holy ol' cow, that was cold!

As far as gettin' wet, if I ever fell overboard I'd go right to the camp and change my clothes. I couldn't work with wet clothes on. Now, my brother-in-law down here, Herb Harris, he was wet every day and he could work all day with them wet clothes on. I couldn't. After I got wet above my knee, I was gone. No damn way was I stayin' and workin' with my back wet, no siree.

You always had troubles. I remember one time down here at the end of the lake, we must have had two hundred thousand out there. One of those freak things happened. We had that boom tied ashore with our grab chains and it come with a big southeaster. The next thing our logs were goin' up the lake, the boom and the works. It come a big rain and started the ice above the lake, and when that ice come the boom couldn't hold it. It straightened them heavy chains, the links, right out. Once it broke clear of shore, the boom wasn't tied together. What a mess we had. We worked there for a month getting them damn logs again.

After [river driving] was done, you didn't have a damn thing to do. No way to make a nickel. The government used to spend, I suppose, four or five hundred dollars a year on the roads. If you were lucky, you got on there. I believe you only got a dollar a day for ten hours. My father used to do very good. He used to trap quite heavy and that would give you cash. Fur was fairly good them days. I remember one time he come home with a wildcat and gave it to mom to buy herself a winter coat for eighteen dollars. That was a big thing them days, 1935, somewheres along there. And he guided. He'd have four parties in a month for moose huntin'. He always had that. And we used to guide Americans in the summer time fishin'. We'd pick up a little bit of money there. You had to scratch at everything.

This Isaac Bower I was tellin' you about, his father, Winthrop Bower, was a big lumberman. And Parker [Bower], they was brothers. Winthrop was the businessman and Parker was the worker. They built tram roads through the woods and hauled their logs. Your rails was logs and two oxen walked one ahead of the other in between these two rails. His wagon had big cast-iron wheels [with] a big hollow out of it and these phalanges went down both sides. Your axle went in through your wheels and that would work back and forth for

the width of your rails and keep it on. If it happened to hit a rock that old cast would break out and you had to get another [wheel]. My God, he hauled a lot of stuff out. He had a big mill down here to Shelburne, right where that Irving Station is as you go across the Roseway River, right there somewhere. I never saw it. I guess he had everything there. That sheathing in the porch, he made that, and he had a dory shop.

I often think now that ol' Wint must have been a pretty damn good engineer. He built that thing through the woods, I'll say three or four miles up on the Indian Fields, about four miles above here. He had another one first out here to Harpers Lake and he had mills out there. I suppose they were steam mills them days, had to be. Just think, building that back through there and all them bogs. He had to bridge them all. A bog was the best place to go, it's level. If you go through rough country, look at the digging you'd have to do to get that level. You couldn't go down too steep a hill 'cause you had no brakes and your oxen couldn't hold it back.

You lay stringers in the bog, good logs, and you cover them over with poles for your oxen to walk on and then you lay your track on top of them again. You corduroyed the damn thing. Just think of how many thousands of poles it would take to cover that. You can still see some places yet where the old thing was.

They come across the Indian Field Road. He had two poles that he put across the road and he bolted them to his other ties and that's how he come across the road. I seen them unbolted and laying around in

"They built tram roads through the woods and hauled their logs. Your rails was logs and two oxen [or horses in this case] walked one ahead of the other in between these two rails." (N.S. Museum)

the summertime for fellers to go up and back with teams. He had two wagons and they were hauled off in the alders there. In the fall of the year, he started logging and I suppose he'd log there all winter. They used to double sleigh in the wintertime too with oxen, but I imagine they would shovel the thing off. Them days, manpower was nothin'.

When I was a kid, we used to do a lot of cat-hunting with dogs. I used to go up around here and walk out that old tram road; it was good walking them days. When you start through this country buildin' a road and you had no dozers, all you had was a pick axe and a shovel, and you had to keep that road pretty level. He was quite an engineer, I'm tellin' ya.

We worked up here about five miles to the Pine Island. That was about two miles back across the bogs. Boy, I'm goin' to tell you, that one bog there, I know that wind come right from the North Pole. That was the coldest damn winter I ever seen in my life. Talk about cold! Up in that ol' camp in the morning and out with your oxen seven o'clock, you jumped around to get warm. The biggest trouble I used to have was my feet. Herb Harris used to work a lot with me. He said, "You're wearing too many socks. Put on one pair of socks and your feet won't get cold." The next morning, it was cold and frosty, but the sun was out. We went across to get some stave wood for the barrel factory down here. I put on one pair of socks and my feet got so cold I tried to make a fire and I couldn't keep still long enough to get it goin'. I said to that boy, "Look, if I ever get to that camp, it won't be no one pair, it'll be three pair." That was the last time I ever put on one pair of socks. Ah, I'm tellin' you, we used to have some fun.

I would say somewheres around 1945, 1946, was the last drive that went down there [Clyde]. I imagine I brought the last out of Horseshoe Lake down through [the Roseway] we'll say 1950. On Long Lake from 1955 to 1965 I boomed logs fifty to sixty thousand at a time, but they [river drives] were long gone; we had an outboard motor then. I was the first one up here ever got trucks to haul logs; that was in the war. The only time you'd river drive then would be somewheres to get 'em out. We cut across the lake, bring 'em over here and boom 'em, then I'd have a haul out down here. I had quite a few of them around the country. You had a ramp and a haul out with the winch. You'd haul your logs up with a winch, load 'em on your truck, and go with 'em.

The lumber business today is the worst I ever saw in my life. The mills today, they're so big and produce so fast that your local market we'll say is none. They'll come in from Quebec or New Brunswick or somewheres and they'll just dump it—I suppose they try to turn it over—and the mills here can't compete with it.

You know, there's more young trees growin' today in Shelburne County than there ever was. My answer to that is, years ago my father and all these fellers were deer and moose hunters. Land, barren land, was worth nothin' and they burnt it every two or three years to make feed for the moose and deer. And they didn't just burn an acre, they burnt hundreds of acres. Now, for the last thirty-five or forty years that hasn't been burnt and that is all comin' up in young timber now. I don't know what it'll make, but the old way was you went in and if there was a big log there you cut him down and that let the sun in and that's where your little fellers would grow right up. I seen my father spend five or ten minutes looking where to fall a log that it wouldn't kill a little tree. Today that's all the difference because you haven't got a feller that knows how to cut a tree. When I started loggin' in the woods, I sawed down with an old feller and I learnt from him. But now, you can go out, get a tree saw, and go in the woods. Now what the hell do you know about knockin' a tree down? That's the kind of things ya got. If you got a bunch of little trees, that's a good place to fall your log isn't it? And it'll smash 'em down when it comes down. The old fellers wouldn't have done that. The old fellers would have felled it somewhere else and saved them little trees.

Then you come in with a damn tree farmer today with all kinds of power. Well, that log is laying that way [crossways] and when you had your team, you couldn't haul it out that way. You had to haul it out straight somewhere 'cause you didn't have the power did ya? Now you hook on that and bring it up and you kill everything that's there. Now for clear cutting, I'd have to say yes, that's the only way to go with the machinery today; otherwise, you'll kill everything anyway. I think it's goin' to be a long, long while before you ever see [the forests] come back again.

Herbert Harris

Herb Harris, 68, is Melvin Bower's brother-in-law. He lives in Lower Ohio, Shelburne County. Never one much for chopping or sawing, his love of the lumber woods centred around river driving. When other children were playing ball at recess, Herb could be found re-enacting log drives with small sticks on a brook that ran through the school property. Habitually wet from playing around the water, his grandmother offered to buy him a ball if he could stay dry for one week. Herb won the bet but caught the worst cold of his life. A strong horse-lover, he believes money could still be made using horses today in the woods. However, he fears the skills required to be a teamster will soon be lost as the old-timers die off, because young people show little interest in learning the trade.

I guess that's been my occupation, doin' woods work, all my life. I pretty well made a living off woods work until I started into Christmas trees twenty-four years ago. It was mostly contracting. I sometimes had three pairs of horses and three drivers, and I'd go haul logs for somebody, so much a thousand. In between times, I'd be on my own land for the local market.

I quit school when I was thirteen and went to work in the woods. In the winters [teaming] was most always my job with Jim Bower and the Sutherland Lumber Company. When I started with Sutherland Lumber Company, that's when they first started to log into Long Lake and Clyde River. My job was to take in all the lumber and stuff they needed to build a dam. I was fourteen years old and my guide was eleven years old. There was no road in there, just barren country. Chester Bower, Melvin Bower's brother, was my guide. He had been in there with his grandfather and knew where to go. We had a pretty young crew. It'd be fifty-four years ago. That's when we first started to be able to sell a few logs again. For a long while there, the Depression, there was no market at all.

I remember we used to have a wooden fence over by the ox barn door. I used to have to get the end of the yoke up on this fence when I was yokin' one ox; I couldn't reach to hold the end of the yoke up. At that time, now and again, somebody had a horse, but, see, there wasn't much money anywhere and oxen are pretty cheap. They don't work very hard and you can't do much with 'em, but you grow them up yourself and when you're done with 'em, you sell 'em for meat and get your money back. They haven't really cost you a cent except for the shoes and yoke.

Oxen don't sweat and they get so hot; first thing you know, he's got his tongue out, and if you don't stop then, he dies. You couldn't do anything hardly with them [in the summer], they were just useless. Oh, they'd make hay or somethin'. I know a couple of them died that way, just from the heat. And they're slow anyway, even in the winter. And then they've got two claws and, in the summer, sticks and stuff go up between those when you work them and that gets all sore. It's too cruel, you just can't drive them anymore.

They're slower [than horses], but you can't haul any bigger load and they are steady, no doubt about that, slow and steady. If you wanted to go to town now, what would you take? I've got a van out there or I got a little tractor. Would you take that old tractor? It's slow and it's steady and you can depend on it. Taken dollar for dollar in the winter, I guess probably financially, your oxen would be better. But what are you goin' to do if you want some logs out in the summer? They were just useless in the summer.

I was an ox lover 'til I used horses and there was so much difference. Every horse has a disposition. Well, oxen do too but there is very little difference in oxen, but in horses there's a great difference.... I seen two choppers come in with a horse. One guy stayed down in the woods and cut the logs. The other guy stayed out on the brow, unhooked the horse and sent it back, rolled his logs out, looked after the landing, and helped load the truck. The horse went back and forth all day long that way. Wherever he heard the fella down in the woods, he went for that. Well, you'd never get an ox to do that.

It's something like your Fords and Chevs and one thing and another. One guy will say there's nothing like a Ford, and another guy will say the Chevs are better. Same way with horses. I guess I liked Belgians the best. I've had all kinds and some of 'em I liked and some of 'em I didn't.

Harness is quite more costly than an ox yoke. It's a lot more for to learn where it goes and to adjust everything than there is to an ox yoke. I never worked for Mersey Paper Company, but I used to hear them say when I was a boy, you went there for a job teaming a pair of horses, they took your harness all apart and threw it in a barrel of ol' used oil. "There's your harness; put it together." Every buckle was undone. If you couldn't put it together, you didn't get the job. They do it to save the harness purposely, but also to find out what you knew about horses.

I think a horse is more economical than the skidders. One of those tires cost as much as a horse. The parts on these skidders, any little breakdown, is a thousand dollars. Another thing, you go logging today with your power saws and skidder, a good day would probably be thirty thousand feet. Well, that's almost a winter's work for your ol' oxen, and that whole winter that man would be makin' a day's pay. So now they cut that down to one day with a skidder. Same thing's happened in the fishing industry. They used to go out and have a big boat and then they'd go out from that with a little dory, and there was always plenty of fish and they was makin' a living off those fish. But now they go out with a big dragger—I don't know much about fishing—but they bring in tons of it. You can't meet the demand; fish don't spawn that fast. Like when they started to build these big mills and the government was assisting them, they said because they employed so many more men, but what happens to your logs? Where they goin' to come from? You can only go so big. I always claim that you'd be a lot better off if they'd assisted the little man and had ten of them in one county instead of one big one.

My first river drivin' experience I was thirteen years old; went down the Clyde River, from Middle Clyde down. It was only a small drive. I was more or less getting experience. There was only, I think, six of us. When we first started, my father was rowin' the boat and he took some guys out. "You jump out on these [logs] and take these out." The logs were all in a big stillwater. He kept going around. "You jump out here." When it come to me, "Jump out." "No. I don't know how to do this." "Jump out!" So I got out. I'd never been on a log with calk boots on. It was a great big log; you couldn't hardly fall off it. I kept tellin' him my calks were stuck in the log. Afterwards, I realized it was just fright; you couldn't lift one foot. I really thought they were stuck in that log. "Don't pull the boat away. You'll upset me." Anyhow, he kept tellin' me he was goin' to go. Finally, he pulled the boat away and I stood there shiverin'. After a while, I got used to it.

I was always a little scared of bugs, big flies and stuff. So I looked down and here was a great big old long-legged—I don't know what he was—some kind of a fly crawlin' up on my log. So I said, "I'll turn the log over and drown him." So I rolled it over and nothin' happened; I didn't fall off. This big bug kept crawlin' around so I kept doin' that. I was on a place where it was only two or three feet of water, a meadow that was overflowed. Suddenly, I looked down and I couldn't see bottom. Then I was scared to death. After a while, I got a pole and positioned so I got on the bottom and got shoved back in where I could see shore. I never forgot that old bug that first learnt me to roll a log.

There were a few accidents. I know a fella got his ankle smashed. He was standin' on shore watching the logs go around a corner. He was tending a wing and one log came out over the wing, went in, and hit his ankle. His ankle was right up against a big tree and smashed it pretty bad. Had to bring him out with a pair of oxen. Another guy I know got his leg broke, but nothin' more than would have happened on land. About drowning, you always fell off of something and what you fell off was there. It isn't like you was out in a boat and the boat sank. The big danger, what we had to watch for, was in shallow water where there was a plug or jam and the logs got pounding and going and your foot went down and hit bottom. You'd

Herb Harris, right, and his cousin Milton Harris on the Clyde River. "There's always cold water under you and nobody wants to get into that, and you just had to keep doing things that sooner or later you was goin' to go in it." (Lillian Scott Perry)

be caught there. But if it was deep water, there was never anything to worry about really except getting wet and cold. I've had a doctor tell me since, you don't get cold from gettin' wet, you get a cold from gettin' dried out too quick. I've gone river drivin' with a cold and come home without it and wet every day and sleepin' in your wet clothes at night.

You only minded it [cold temperatures] in the early mornings. Once you got goin', river drivin' is usually hard work. You sweat more than you shivered. I remember one time we was river drivin' when every once in a while we had to take our peaveys and beat 'em on a log or somethin'; the hook would freeze up so they wouldn't work—gettin' kind of cold.

There's always cold water under you and nobody wants to get into that and you just had to keep doing things that sooner or later you was goin' to go in it. It was kind of laughable when somebody went in. I remember one incidence that we had a great laugh over. We were goin' from one falls down to another on the Clyde which was about a mile. When the water's high, if you go down the shores, you're wadin' in water all the time. So three of us was goin' down after lunch to tend this next place and we found a log that we could reach out and get a hold of, a great big old log, so we jumped onto that and paddled out into the current. We was goin' down this river and after a while it got kind of tiresome just standin' on this one big log so we paddled over and got peaveys into another smaller log, one about a quarter as big. That was nice. We were still on this big one, but the three of us had our peaveys drove in this other one; that made it comfortable, somethin' to lean on. We went quite a little ways and we went around a corner and came to a little run that wasn't a falls, just black, swift runnin' water. Right at the end of the swift runnin' water, before it went out into the eddy, you could see the water boiling up over something. I knew it was a rock.

Our big log was going sideways and we had no poles, just peaveys that we were goin' to work with. I saw what was goin' to happen. Our little log was on the downstream side. That was goin' to go over this rock and our big log was goin' to hang up there. So I said, "I'll play a trick on these fellas. When that little log goes over that rock, I'm goin' to jump it and go." Sure enough. Our little one went over that and we all three had the same thing in mind. When we hit this little log, it sunk, and we had to swim ashore, all three of us. Our big one stayed up on the rock there. We'd been safe as could be if we'd just stayed where we was.

There were small drives on this [Roseway] river, short drives, but the Clyde was the one that used to have the long drives. They went from Long Lake—that's four or five miles above Ohio—right down to the pavement, down to the 103. More than thirty miles by river, I imagine. It's a real good river, only it's wide and gravelly. Whenever you get a gravel bottom, the river gets wider over the years and more shallow, so when you had lots of rain and the water was high it was a good river, but when the water got down it was awful. It was so wide, your water was goin' everywhere. This river here, the Roseway, it's completely different. It's a long river and if you had a big rain the water would rise for five days before it gets to its peak. The Clyde River, it's up the next day, and the next day it's startin' down again. It [Roseway] was better in that way, but it has a lot more bad rocks and bad places in it for river drivin'.

You had to do whatever was there to be done. On the big drives, a million feet that they had on the Clyde, it was broken down into two crews. You had what we call the head channelers. They put on all the wings and got the logs goin'. Then they had what they called the rear crew come behind. You were either a head channeler or a rear crew on the big drives. But ordinary drives, whatever was to be done you done it to get that drive in, you had no place.

Sometimes you set on shore. I know one time in particular we were three days setting on shore with a fire goin', nothin' to do. They had a big jam on the side of a falls, and down below the falls about a mile there was five big rocks, sort of looked like they were put there on purpose to hinder the river driver. Between the two places was all good clear water. Another guy and I were sent down to these big rocks they called the Sisters to make sure that when this jam broke, we kept it all thinned out goin' through there.

The problem with that certain falls, there was a back channel and a meadow that went around the falls. When the logs would get plugged in that falls, then water would back up and go around and down over this meadow and in front of your jam you had no water to amount to anything. They worked at this jam up there for three days and it never broke. They just gradually picked the whole thing apart and the logs went by us three and four at a time. Every night we'd coax 'em. "Let us go back." "No, it's goin' to break today." So we sat there with a fire to keep warm and the other fellas comin' at night with the whole palms of their hands blistered. Just picked it apart.

One of the last drives I was on was for a fella from up in Weymouth. He bought a piece of land on the Clyde River and came down here and logged it. It was quite a big drive, about eight hundred thousand. He'd never seen a log in the water except in a millpond. He didn't know anything about it himself, and his woods boss had never seen a log in the water. They come down from up there with a bunch of guys that didn't know a thing about river driving and they hired about five fellas from around here that had been river drivin' all their life. We had to do all the work, and I mean all. They were scared to death of the water.

When they brought the first wagonload of stuff into the camp where we were goin' to start, they had two cases of dynamite. I guess they'd been watching movies. We used to set it off to call the men to lunch. Any amount of logs, dynamite was no good. We used to rig it up if you got just one cross log. If you had a wing of logs here and another here, a long one come down and got crossways, and usually it would be under water. On top of the water you'd do something with it and get it out of there. But under water, before you could do anything, other logs would pile on top of that. We used to have dynamite on a crotch stick and we'd light it and put that down over the log. When that went off, even one stick would cut the biggest log right in two—almost the same as if it was sawed—and let the whole thing go. Dynamite was good for that.

I remember one time we was on a long straight falls and we got this cross log in. We had this little trouble so we was puttin' dynamite onto the log. This guy was downriver, I suppose, a hundred yards and he was standin' there leanin' on his peavey watchin' what we was doin'. We stepped back, you know, 'cause water would fly when you cut the log off. Nothin' happened, nothin' happened. First thing, our dynamite went off right under this other feller's peavey. Soaked him. The stick we had it tied to got adrift and went down river. He always blamed us for doin' it on purpose. That's what happened to our dynamite; calling fellas to lunch and cutting off a log under water. It was no good in still water; you had to have the water pressure along with that sudden crack.

There was a lot more drives a hundred thousand than there was a million feet. These little short drives you went home, but on the Clyde River they had great big tents probably thirty or forty feet long with two little heaters in 'em. Usually pitched them on a bunch of stumps you had to lay on. The Sutherland Lumber Company had oxen and wagons then on the drives. About every third day they'd have to pick everything up and move down farther. You usually had to walk downriver a ways at night one day, the next day you was right at the tent, and the next day you had to walk back. That's usually the way it happened. Those big drives, if you got a mile a day, you'd be doin' great.

The big problem with river drivin' like on the Clyde, you had to depend on water and if you only got your drive half way to the mill for a year, nobody could finance that. In them days when you went in the woods, like for the Sutherland Lumber Company, you went in the fall, worked all winter, come out on the drive, and then you got paid for the whole season. If that drive didn't get in, you didn't get paid. It just wasn't workin' out. We always got paid, but sometimes we had to do a lot of arguin'. The last drive I was on we were supposed to get three dollars a day. The first ones, I imagine, two dollars a day. Boy, that sounds small now. Used to get almost double drivin' what you did for woods work. The last drive'd be about forty-six, forty-seven years ago; trucks were taking over.

With the trucks it wasn't so cheap per thousand, but they knew what they could do. Like the drive I was telling you about the fella from Weymouth done. They only came down as far as Upper Clyde where they could reach them with trucks on account of that same reason. They sawed in there—quite a big portable mill—and took the lumber back to Weymouth.

The only time anything ever scared me I went through underneath a wing where we had built out to a rock. That was almost in sight of home down here on the Roseway River. Those wings are usually all tangled up down underneath with logs. They come down, hit your wing, and sink under. I went to go out on this wing, just one log leadin' out to it and it was quite small, so I had to go fast. I stepped on a piece of bark, and almost like I done it on purpose, I dove head first right down in front of the wing. With the swift current, in no time I was under it. I had to go through and out the other side. No goin' back up stream. We was all schooled when you first started river drivin' to go downriver. If it's only two feet back up don't try to get back, go with the current. You don't have much choice. You can't swim in fast water.

Just to give you an idea of how much I liked it, when I was on little drives for Shelburne Woodworkers over on the Jordan River, about four o'clock one afternoon we decided we couldn't go any further; we ran out of water. The Sutherlands were still driving over on the Clyde River, so I left there four o'clock and had about two miles of muddy road in the spring of the year to walk to Jordan. I got home and the next morning I got my brother to take me over to Welshtown. An old road went through to Middle Clyde, just an old road about seven or eight miles that had been forgotten. It once was the road from Middle Clyde to Shelburne but hadn't been used for a long while. I was in Middle Clyde when they were eating breakfast to go on that one.

Oh, we had a lot of fun; I enjoyed it. I always said, if the Americans over there knew what sport river drivin' was, they wouldn't come here deer huntin', they'd come river drivin'. When you got with a good bunch of guys, you had a lot of fun.

Harry Lewis

Harry Lewis, 80, lives in Weymouth, Digby County. His father was a logger, and Harry began working the woods at twelve years of age. "There were nine of us in the family and I had to get out to work to eat." He opened his own sawmill in Weymouth in 1950 and formed Lewis Lumber Co. in 1954. He sold his interests to his son and son-in-law around 1972 but still remains an honorary member of sorts today. The mill was destroyed by fire in July 1991, but at the time of this interview was in the final stages of being rebuilt.

Weymouth was a real big town one time with shipbuilding, all kinds of export of lumber and several mills. One of the biggest mills—I don't remember it much—was G.D. Campbell & Company. They had a mill just about where the Esso garage is across the bridge. It must have been as early as 1890 when the Campbells were pretty active, and I would say they were the big people in the teens. The Stehelins[1] come along in 1896 and they started to ship lumber out of Weymouth too, but it had been shipped before that on schooners.

The Campbells used to drive their timber from Fourth Lake, Fifth Lake, Tom Wallace, right down [the Sissiboo River] to the mill and saw it. I seen a bit of it, but I never had anything to do with it. They run a store, and people would sell them their logs and work for them and take their pay in groceries. When the First World War started, practically all of Campbell's boys went to war—I think there was five went at one time—so that made a little hole in the thing and they faded out of the lumber business.

After the Campbells went, George Hankinson was the next man that came along. He was in the business, I would think, along in the 1920s up to 1935, in that period. They run a big lumber business. They done a little river driving. They cut the wood up along the river and had a portable mill at Gaudett Bridge; we call it Sissiboo Falls now. They also had one back at the branch where the Tom Wallace comes down and crosses the road goin' into Fourth Lake. They'd log all

winter and cut two, three, or four million feet and drive 'em down and saw it in the spring. They were a fair size operation.

In between, there came a pulpmill up here at Weymouth Falls. I can remember that but not too much. That must have been about the 1920s, maybe before, and that operated here for quite a few years. That didn't make paper, it made ground pulp. They put a railroad in three or four miles to connect their plant with this railroad. They shipped most of it from the wharf in Weymouth North, down to the States I would think.

Eighty percent of everything then was going into sawlogs. I've seen pictures with five or six schooners here loaded at one time. It would be going to West Indies and Bermuda. A lot of the exporters got into building their own ships, and I would say in that day almost one hundred percent were local sea captains.

After George Hankinson & Son, then along come Weymouth Shipping Company with a man by the name of Mr. Taylor who was married into the Campbell family. He did a lot of sawing and exporting. But by then, George McKeen from Saint John had come into the picture and they were exporting lumber across to England, Ireland, and Scotland. I would think it would be along about 1935, just before the Second World War. They [McKeen] would be really the exporter and Weymouth Shipping Company was just supplying the lumber. They had portable mills out around the country and they had a mill setting right down back of where Weymouth Motors garage is now, on that flat. They were doing quite a big business—six, seven, eight million a year. There were a lot of smaller mills, but

Stehelin Saw Mill, New France, Digby County, c. 1895. (N.S. Museum)

Weymouth Shipping Company was one of the bigger mills.

The Mullens and Sabines had mills in the back country. They're New Tusket and Riverdale people, but they would be shipping their stuff through Weymouth or Belliveaus Cove. Belliveau Cove was quite a big shipping port then. People by the name of Ben Belliveau & Company bought lumber from all over the country and shipped it to the West Indies and them countries. It would be the same era.

About 1930, I went to Bear River and bought pulpwood for about three years for H.T. Warren & Company from Digby. Tupper Warren was just amazing. You'd call him one of the R.A. Jodreys today. R.A. had more education than him, but not much; he had no education at all. He couldn't write his own name, but he had a big lumber and wood business, machine shop, and box factory in Digby for twenty-five or thirty years. He had a daughter and a son. The daughter was very smart and she run the bookkeeping end of it.

He bought pulpwood for Mersey Paper Company and shipped it out of Bear River on the old *Tilly*, one of the Mersey boats. It come right into the wharf there and carried four or five hundred cords of wood. I think more than anything this was just one of the things that Warrens went after, to get a contract to help the economy of the county. People couldn't sell wood anywheres.

I don't know how I got to Bear River. I went to work for Warrens and I'd never seen a grocery store, or a grocery, or never scaled a stick of pulpwood in my life. I woke up tomorrow morning and I was in Bear River buying pulpwood and paying for it with groceries. Course, I wasn't too long catching onto it. The store was mainly for people that brought in pulpwood. I opened it when I went there. We had the store where Frenchy's is now and piled the wood on the wharf. The Clarkes had a big lumber business before I ever went to Bear River, but right then it was, I think, one hundred percent pulpwood for a few years. The first six months I was there, I bought thirty-six hundred cords of wood and paid for it all with groceries except eighty dollars; that's the only money we spent in that time.

A lot of people cut wood; there just wasn't anything else in the 1930s when the Depression was on. They'd be practically all local farmers. In the group there might be one or two that would be a little bigger cutters, like Bern Alcorn and Roy, his brother, they'd cut a little more, but the ordinary people, ninety-eight percent, would only bring in what they needed to get to live on. They'd be there every day; that was their only job they had. Some people I can remember well. Hueys from way back in Victory, would take two days to get in there with their oxen time they left home, and have three dollars worth of wood. I remember him well, had a big family. How did they live and bring up a family?

Practically everything come from Saint John those days by boat. Of course the boats used to come in Bear River then too, but none of our groceries ever come in Bear River. They come to Digby first and were reallotted up there. Molasses was twenty-five cents a gallon. Eggs were ten cents a dozen. Surprisingly enough, sugar is cheaper now than it was then; a bag of sugar was about three dollars. Flour was cheap. Soda, tea, salt, ginger—no canned goods. There'd be axes and like that, but not so much hardware, mostly groceries. Their main store was in Digby, and perhaps if somebody wanted a coat, they'd bring it up. They'd be trucked up there in the summertime and in the winter they'd be hauled up with horses and sleds. They had trucks by the name of Defiance. Warren's made them right there in Digby for a long while. They might have brought a motor in, but they made everything else.

I hate to tell you what they were paying for wood then. The highest price we ever paid was three dollars and fifty cents a cord, rough, four-foot wood. There was skullduggery as far as that's concerned— you will hear people take nine feet for a cord of wood—but it wasn't so with the Warren's or me because a hundred and twenty-eight cubic feet was a hundred and twenty-eight cubic feet. That's how we dealt. If they had a cord of wood, they had a cord of wood. Lots of times you'd buy it out roadside and only pay two dollars and fifty cents a cord. We'd go scale it there, then pick it up. Harry Harris was quite a big trucker in Bear River then and he'd truck it in for those people. When you got more than he could handle Warren's would truck with their own trucks.

Warren's would have eight or ten of their own trucks, which was quite a lot for that time. The ordinary fellow would only have one and it would only be a small truck. A lot of them wouldn't even have a cab, it'd just be an open chassis and a hood on it. People would build their own cab on it to keep them out of the weather. And there was no such thing as a heater those days. Chevs and Fords were just comin' into being then. Jerry Lombard would say, "They were only seldom, very seldom." In the thirties there were very few, and you hardly ever see one in the winter. I would say around 1945 there commenced to be a little more.

When you had a lot of wood there, I would say it [the *Tilly*] would make a trip about every two weeks. You wouldn't do anything in the winter at all and if you had four or five thousand cords of wood, it would make six or seven trips to take it all up. I can't tell you exactly, but I imagine they might have got seven or eight dollars a cord for it. They'd send their own boat, but Warren had to do the loadin'. I loaded a good many there. Some of the boys tell me yet today, they got a pretty good day's pay, a dollar a day then, loadin' the boat, while the ordinary wage was about fifty cents a day.

When they come in to load a boat, I can see them now, sometimes two hundred men would come all at once. You'd only need a hundred and it pretty near broke your heart to turn them away. I guess you'd just take the first hundred that got there. After a bit, I suppose, the boys that had got a little used to it, you might prefer taking them, but most anybody could get a job because when you're handling wood, there ain't much to it. We never loaded any from the water; ours was always on the dock. We've had accidents. Some of the biggest trouble would be you'd get a little bump on the head once in a while. There were no hard hats in those days. Walkin' over the wood, people would roll their ankles over, but we never had a serious accident while we were loadin'.

I think it stopped altogether for a few years. Mersey perhaps got as much wood as they wanted closer to the mill. After Tupper had stopped buyin' there, the Lincoln [a pulp company from Maine] come on quite strong. Their local man was a boy from back here in Tusket, Stan Sabean. Lincoln owned a lot of land around Bear River and Lake Jolly.

Most of Warren's lumber was used in their box factory. There wasn't a lot of export. Long before, there was export to the West Indies and in the latter years, ten or twenty years down the road, they got in the export business in lumber, but the bulk of their stuff first was goin' mostly into fish boxes. They did make some others. They made sugar boxes for Atlantic Sugar in Saint John, but I would say ninety percent of their business was fish boxes. Maritime Fish Company was goin' strong then in Digby. They were big people and some that operated it were relatives of Warren's and they dovetailed the whole thing in so it made a pretty good [business]. They had big boilers for cookin' the fish and heating the plant. A lot of their waste wood, slabs and stuff, would go down to run the boilers in the fish plant, so it paid pretty good.

Warren had quite a few portable mills. They would have just been sawin' ninety percent live-edged lumber for their box factory. They didn't take any edgings or anything off of it. It all went in as it come, and for the box factory you got a lot more wood out of a thousand feet than if you were squaring it up. Most of this was spruce and fir. Hemlock was going into wharves. They're a wood it's almost impos-

sible to make rot, they'll last almost forever without creosote; creosote wasn't thought about then. They were using it as it came out of the woods or sawed it for timbers.

They failed out between 1945 and '50. The old gentleman died and it was left to the son and the daughter. I think times started to change and they couldn't quite keep up and they had to ingest a little more money in it and one thing and another. They sold out to Vanderwaulde in Montreal; they were perhaps quite well to do. The son and daughter stayed on a while with them and then they both passed away.

Pit props was a big thing here during the war. A man come in from overseas by the name of Naftel. He finally settled in Middleton. He had a pit prop and pulpwood yard in Digby, Yarmouth, Shelburne, Bridgewater, and Port Williams. During the war years, he bought thousands and thousands of cords of pit props for going to England to put in their mines. They had to be all hand shaved and they were anywheres from five foot and a half up to sixteen or seventeen feet long. Some of them were really logs. They were taking everything in that, in the softwood area—spruce, fir, pine, hemlock—it didn't make any difference. Hardwood was a thing that sold either for pulpwood or pit props.

I got into the stevedoring business and some years, we'd load as

Tupper Warren of Digby operated several portable sawmills in different counties. Pictured is a Warren mill at Five Mile River, Hants County, c. 1914–1923. (N.S. Museum)

high as a hundred thousand cords of pit props, which was a lot of stuff. I got in with some other people and we finally set up a company and done that for quite a few years, stevedoring pulpwood, lumber, and pit props. We done Yarmouth, Digby, and Port Williams.

During the war it was just about impossible to hire anybody. We had a pretty good nucleus of men within a twenty-mile radius here that were used to stevedoring, running winches, and all that kind of stuff, so we would take them with us. We'd set up a bunk house right in Port Williams. We'd hire a building and then board the men different places. We used to have our own beds and blankets and stuff for eighty, ninety men. I don't think we ever set one up in Hantsport, but we loaded several ships there with ground pulp for the Minas Basin Pulp and Power. As far as Yarmouth is concerned, we had trucks for travelling [back and forth] from Weymouth. When the war stopped, they might have used pit props, but they wasn't buyin' them from this country.

During the war too, we took ballast out of the ships as part of our stevedoring business. We must have done that for three or four years. The ships would come in from overseas loaded with all kinds of junk and trash for ballast. As a rule they were used to takin' a cargo over and bringing a cargo back; had to pay them both ways. But when they started to need a ship every two weeks it was another story. When they had to have the stuff quicker, there was nothin' to bring back from England.

I would say seventy-five percent of it would be bombed-out buildings in London. If it was brick and that kind of stuff, you shovel it in a big bucket, took it up using winches and dumped it over the side. We'd take it out in the Digby harbour and dump it overboard. There's one spot out there where they put it deep, terrible deep. Now, some of 'em had the most beautiful gravel in them you ever seen and if you got one, you'd bring it into the wharf sometime and use the gravel for fixing up your pit prop yards or roads. There was a few then that was using the water ballast, [but] they use water now more than they ever did.

My dad told me when he was alive that about seventy years ago when the first steam mill came in the country that they said there wouldn't be another log in the country the next year; they'd all be gone. Well, in my lifetime, I suppose we have sawed, to be safe, three hundred million in this area. Thank goodness that around here, what Bowater doesn't own, eighty percent is owned by private individuals and they do a very good job of selective cutting. This French Shore, they've been one of the best silviculture[2] people that I know of. Now the young fellas comin' along, some of them gets it and sells it to buy a car and the next week it's gone, but the old men done a good job and there's still a lot of big timber in this county yet.

Now a lot of the big stuff is not like it was. But a lot of it, if it hadn't been cut—and a lot wasn't—it would all have died anyway. Wood is like a man. You can say what you like, but if you run wood much over seventy years old, you're runnin' into real problems. The old heart commences to rot, just like a man. Another thing too: time has changed. Back in those days a lot of the timber was one by twelve, or two by twelve, or twelve by twelve for timbers and stuff. Today, you can't sell a piece of timber that's over six by six. Now, that's how it's gone the other way. They've changed their system of building. They were using twelve by twelve; man has got weaker, he can't lift a twelve by twelve anymore. Back seventy-five years ago when this house was built the studding was two by six. Now, a lot of the studding is only two by three, a lot of it two by four. They're doing some two by six again now because of insulation. There was a time when floor joists were two by twelve; now they're two by eight.

It has changed so much and I think the trucking business has changed a lot of it. The roads and trucks have got better and we're trucking logs today for a hundred and fifty miles. When you think of Mersey truckin' logs a hundred and thirty or forty miles back here over to Bridgewater and we had logs last year from Shubenacadie; we even had people call us from Sheet Harbour. Well, there wasn't any such a thing in 1912 or 1913 when the first automobile come around as hauling more than two or three miles. The first truck I seen would haul about five hundred board feet. Now, they haul seven thousand and then you get one of the big tandems in with thirteen and fourteen thousand on it.

Back in the olden days they figured if a mill sawed a thousand to a man he was doin' very good. If he had ten men in the mill and sawed ten thousand a day, you done pretty well. It's changed completely around today. If you got ten men in the mill, you got to saw seventy thousand a day to make a go of it. You ain't making no more money because you're payin' interest and you're payin' wages and so on. There's money in the sawmill business if you can get a certain price for lumber because of the fact today you sell the chips, which has got to be quite a big item for pulp and paper. You burned them up in them olden days as a rule. If you could have your chip business left you'd be real lucky 'cause you get sixty dollars a cord for your chips. If you saw ten million lumber you're sawin' about nine thousand cords of chips. At sixty dollars a cord, you got $540,000, which is big business, isn't it?

There are still a few mills, but a small mill just can't exist. The demand is different. The West Indies is stopped. It used to be a big market for hardwood staves for molasses barrels for Barbados. They were all building up in those days. Lumber and barrel staves, that's about the only thing that went down. Then they'd bring back rum and molasses so they had a better payin' trip back than they did down. This George Hankinson, I can't tell you the year it was, he told me the most money he ever made in his life, he sold the lumber for ten dollars a thousand. Can you imagine? Today we're paying forty dollars tax on it alone. Unless you can get three hundred and ten dollars a thousand for it today you can't make a cent.

Now, right in this new mill that they're building over here, they're going to be able to saw a five-inch tree that was going into pulpwood. By April this year [1992], everything going overseas has got to be dry kilned. A lot of the little mills are goin' to be forced right out of business because they can't afford to put in a dryer, 'cause a dryer is almost a million dollars, between eight and nine hundred thousand dollars. And a lot of the little mills have trouble selling their stuff locally and a lot don't get paid. That's one of the big problems with small mills. They run accounts with people and it don't take long for that to run up when it's three hundred dollars a thousand. You lose one customer a year, he might be the best customer in the world and somethin' happens to him, and you lost six or seven thousand dollars. You lost your profit just about on a small mill. A lot of them don't have barkers or chippers and, like I said, that's a big item.... We hope to make use of the whole thing, and if those small hydro-electric plants could come that they're talkin' about building, it would be the most wonderful thing that ever happened to the country. They'd take all this waste, there wouldn't be a bit of waste left because when you get into bark you're gettin' into environmental problems. There's a certain amount of acid in that bark that will kill the fish and plant life. So if you could dispose of every bit of this, which I hope you can some day, it would take all this. They'll take about thirty or forty trailerloads a day to run a plant. It would take all the waste of every little mill and you wouldn't be bothered with it. It's a big job to get rid of it.

This drier business...for export, the moisture has to come down to around sixteen or seventeen percent, which ordinary wood is up to twenty-seven or thirty percent. It is better for building because it'll last longer when it goes in your house. The main reason that it's got to be kiln dried for going overseas is to kill the bugs in it. There's two or three different names. You can see what they do. They'll bore in a log just like boring in with an auger. There's some great big white grubs will get in the pine and make a hole as big as your finger. There's worms gettin' in the wood that you have to watch out for all the time. You can take and build a house out of them wormholes and it don't hurt a thing as long as they ain't in there [alive], but if they are they keep on chewing and eat the house right down.

It's always been the case, but I think, like everything else in our environment, people have come to realize it more. Other countries are doin' it, so you got to do it. It's been talked about in Europe for four or five years—mostly Sweden—and all those people have come into the dryer business and they're forcing everybody else into it.

Our spruce wood is one of the better woods in the world as far as lasting for years. A lot of kiln dried is coming in from northern New Brunswick, Quebec, Ontario, and British Columbia. Their wood is not as good, [but] it's coming in practically the same price as it is the local for green. Who's going to buy green lumber if they can buy kiln dried lumber for the same price? It works better, it doesn't warp. The biggest trouble, they're gettin' stumpage very cheap and they have big mills and big production. There's a freight subsidy comin' in from B.C. that works comin' this way but just the opposite goin' that way. Where some of the boys are payin' forty cents a hundred goin' out, it's comin' in for five or six cents. It's a freight that's been on there for a good many years and it won't be changed I don't think.

I think the worst thing to do is kill your hardwood. You're not only killing the hardwood trees, you're killing the birds, the rabbits, everything else. You need the hardwood to go along with the softwood from my experience in it. I don't go along with this clear cutting at all. That is wrong. We've never done that. I agree that some of the worst things that happened is when they mowed this stuff flat. I'll go up where a piece has been cut between two pieces that we got and there isn't a thing anymore than on that floor. You look at that and then look at ours on both sides of it, but thank goodness that in ten years it'll be grow'd up again. It won't grow up quite so good because they take everything off now, limbs and all, and put it in a heap. It's a shame to see it that way.

It's our own fault. We got to the place where nobody wanted to work anymore. To get anything, they had to bring them big machines in to get this stuff out of the woods. Back in my day, there was hundreds and hundreds of men that knew nothin' but cuttin' pulpwood. Now in your day that ain't so and it's a good thing that it ain't.

I don't want to go back to the bucksaw days again. But we're takin' practically all of our stumpage to pay for big machines and we're devastating the country by doing it.

We need the pulp companies. There's a certain amount of wood that won't go into lumber, that's for sure, and that wood has got to go somewhere. You have to work the forests. And right now, with the market like it is, we see how bad it is without it, and it's real bad. I think we have seen right here in the Weymouth area results of not being able to cut. They've had to tighten the belt. Recycling, in one way, is a bad thing. It's affecting people right now awful hard, but eventually it'll be the best thing that ever happened. If you can recycle thirty or forty percent, it's going to help the forests—goin' to need that much less pulp—and in a few years your forests are going to see the benefit of it.

They are doing a lot of good things in the forests. They're doin' a lot of plantin' that they never done years ago. Right in our own local country you don't need much plantin', but there are places that you need to plant it after you cut because it'll take a few years to grow again. There's some land that won't reproduce anything and there's other land that reproduces too much. I could show you land that we got where, instead of being a tree every seven feet, which is the best it can be for real growing, there could be fifty in there, which in turn you got to cut some of them down or you ain't goin' to have nothin'. But every part of this country isn't like that. From Bear River this way, it's exceptionally good until you get to Yarmouth. Then you run into more barren country and they're doin' a lot of planting down that part of the county now. Some of the big companies I think are wising up a little too. They realize that some of the thousands of acres that they've clear cut, like Tom Wallace and Fourth Lake—it's late for those now—that they should have cut a little different.

Charlie Paul

Charlie Paul, 86, a Micmac from Ohio near Weymouth, Digby County, spent his entire life in the woods, hunting, fishing, trapping, guiding, and logging. He guided American sports with his brother, Philip, and Joe Pictou on trips from Bear River through to Kejimkujik, Liverpool, and Yarmouth nearly seventy years ago. He worked in both the Nova Scotia and New Brunswick lumber woods, where his specialty was river driving and breaking up logjams.

The woods have been my life. I worked when I was thirteen in a loggin' camp. I had to. There was just me and my mother; my father died on us. I had to help my mother so I went in the woods loggin' back up in Weymouth—Fifth Lake, Fourth Lake, Third Lake. G.D. Campbell, the biggest company in Weymouth, owned all that timber in there. I seen two million feet of logs cut back on the Weymouth [Sissiboo] River.

Them days when I first went, we had to chop the logs down; we had no saw. The choppin' axe, double-bitted, you had to have it right down sharp. Two years I done just choppin'. Then the next year I went back they had a great big ol' crosscut saw, but that was better than choppin'.

We'd go up there and cut logs in the wintertime and drive 'em down in the spring. I was one of the champion river drivers. When I was a young man, that's all I did. When I first started, I had a stepfather—he was a crackerjack river driver—and I used to work with him. The boss used to say, "Take Charlie with you, John," and we'd go to the river and I used to watch what he was doin'. That's how I got to be a crackerjack. If there's any kind of jam anywheres, I was always there to break it up. You had to look for where the first log come. There's always a rock down there or somethin' where this big log would come and stay. The rest of 'em used to pile onto it so you had to clean these logs up. Quite a job. By Jesus, I guess it was dangerous. I guess it was!

I had some close calls and I seen some fellers have some close calls. I had a fella, Henry Charles, I thought he was a goner. The foreman said, "Charlie, there's a big jam down the road and you're goin' down there and break it up. You better take Henry with you." We were the best fellers on the river. So we went down and, boy, it was jammed right across the river. It was the Weymouth River; that was the hardest river in Nova Scotia, big falls. You take Slow Gundy, there's a big falls down over there and down at Granite Rip, it's all rocks right straight down to Weymouth. In the springtime when the freshets are on, boy, you got some rough water in there.

We went workin' onto it. We seen the key log was down underneath there. We got down and tried to pry the damn thing over. All of a sudden, this bloody ol' jam took off! Jesus, talk about goin'! Had to run the logs, and logs goin' up and down every which way. You had to be just like a cat. My buddy fell in. I didn't see 'im; I was gettin' the hell out of there. When I was on top, I looked, and here was my buddy. There was a big log stickin' out of the water about twenty feet and he was holdin' onto it by his hands and feet. Good thing he held on there. If he didn't, they would come down and squash him, kill him.

Had some close calls, I guess I have. I'm goin' to tell you about one. It wasn't here in the Weymouth River, but up in Goose Crick in New Brunswick. The boss said, "Paul, there's a jam down the river and it's been there three or four days. It's causin' a lot of trouble. Will you go down and see what you can do with it? I'll send a couple of men with you." So two or three of us went down and we found where this river jammed up. It was a ledge and where the log come, he come across this side and went down. There was a big round hole and this log had jammed himself in there and was on the angle. We tried to lift it up, but we couldn't; it was stuck in there tighter than hell.

The fellers said, "Charlie, how the hell are we goin' to get that thing out?"

I said, "The only way we can get him out is somebody go across there and pry the thing out. Four or five pries might pry him out."

So they wouldn't go. They knew how to work on logs, but they didn't know as much as I did. "I'll go across and pry that thing out," I told them.

On the end of it, the water had to go down about forty feet, right straight down, just like that. I went across. There was a couple of shelves there. I stood on one and I put my foot on a log. I was stickin' my peavey in there tryin' to pry it out and it was movin'. I said, "Now, I'm goin' to come across." I had to run across, oh, it must've been half as long as this buildin'. But I jumped the damn log. I shouldn't 'ave jumped, you know; I should've walked across. When I took my foot off, I jumped on the log, and no more I jumped, the damn thing went. I got about half way and that was it. Thing went just like that and took me down. I went straight over these falls, logs and everything. Jesus!

When I got down below, all I could hear was just the water boilin', that's all. I didn't get hurt. I went way the hell down there underwater, way the hell out there about fifty feet time I come out. But I was all right, no logs struck me. When I got back up where my buddies was, they said, "Charlie, all we could see was just the legs and hands goin' down over that falls."

It's funny I'm here today, all that hard time we went through. A hard ol' life, but we didn't mind it. My brother told me, "Charlie, you're goin' to be crippled some of these days. You just watch. You've been river drivin', you've been in the water all day long. You're goin' to feel that some of these days." I didn't listen. Sure enough, I feel it now.

Clinton Miller

Clinton Miller, 87, lives in the village of Bear River, which straddles the county lines of Digby and Annapolis. His family was one of its founders in the late 1700s and by the late 1800s the community of two thousand was one of the most prosperous in Nova Scotia. Its economy centred around ship-building and lumbering. From 1831 to 1901, no less than 115 sailing vessels were built in Bear River and a thriving trade was carried on with New York, Ontario, the West Indies, Cuba, and South America at the turn of the century. By 1905, annual lumber exports were five million feet, along with three hundred thousand feet of wharf pilings and two thousand cords of wood.

The catalyst behind Bear River's commercial success was Clarke Brothers, the firm of Wallace W. and Willard G. Clarke, who formed a partnership in 1880. Merchants, manufacturers, and exporters/importers, they owned warehouses, ships, sawmills, a dry dock, a dry goods and grocery store, a furniture and hardware store, and thousands of acres of timberland. In 1891 they were considered one of the most enterprising business houses in the province and by 1897 had a business volume of two hundred thousand dollars a year.

In 1899 the Clarkes and William Miller, Clinton's uncle, built a stationary sawmill nine miles in the woods at Lake Jolly. It produced thirty-five thousand feet of softwood lumber a day, in addition to shingles and box shooks, and employed seventy-five workers. By 1903, a substantial community of two hundred was living at Lake Jolly. In 1915 the mill was converted to hardwood and manufactured clothespins, dowels, door frames, window sashes, and toy furniture.

Around 1920, Clarke Brothers began an ill-advised project to build a sulphate pulpmill at the mouth of Bear River. This grandiose venture failed in short order, and in 1923 the Lake Jolly sawmill burned. With the Clarkes' fortunes went the livelihoods of many village residents. Today only a handful remain who can recall those times of sail and lumber barons.

Lumber was king in those days, latter part of the 1800s and ran right up to the First World War. After the First World War, things kind of lulled off. Bear River did more business than Digby at that time. Digby was only the county seat and Bear River was the business centre, the main port. The old fellas told me, at one time you couldn't name a thing they used in those days that you couldn't get made in Bear River.[3] Old Mr. Tupper made all the blocks and sheaves for ships. The sheave is what the rope run over, and they made them out of lignum vitae, the hardest wood there is. Their own ships hauled it in here from South America. Grandmother told me when she first came here there were six ships being built on the stocks in Bear River. My grandfather and Uncle George Miller had their shipyard on the school grounds. Bear River was a real thriving place.

My grandfather, Obed Miller, and Mr. Edward Clarke, with a yoke of oxen and a two-wheel cart, were the first people to Lake Jolly with a team. Roughly speaking, it must've been in the late 1860s. They had a water mill at Lake Le Marchant [on the road to Lake Jolly]; there were six of them in it. They took a regular size lot, split it up and made mill lots out of it. They were something like two chains and ten links in width.* Grandfather got two mill lots, which made his a little wider. They split it up in the different names and operated the mill. The mill was built the same as they built all the ships around here. Each person took a portion of it. This is the way those old fellas did it.

*A chain was 66 feet; a link, 7.92 inches.

The last cut they made [at Lake Le Marchant], grandfather took a contract for a million feet of pine to Boston for ten dollars a thousand, delivered now in Boston. No wain, no knots, no bark showing on a board, and no board could be under eight inches. Now can you imagine what kind of timber they had? And they didn't saw it down back in the 1800s, they chopped it down.

The start of the Clarke Brothers, Mr. Ed Rice got a little money ahead and loaned them the money to pay off the Welches who went bankrupt. In the mid-1800s, there was a big water-powered sawmill at the Head of the Tide where the powerhouse sets now and that was Welches'. Then they owned the Bear River Trading Company and had a shipyard back of the store. They used to side launch them right there. So Clarke's bought up the assets, Will Clarke moved into the top floor of the trading company and lived there and that was the start. From there on, they grew and grew and grew. They owned three ships and had a mill out at Big Lake and Lake Jolly.

Lake Jolly was a going community. They had a school, store, post office, blacksmiths, two or three large horse barns, houses built—must've been fifteen families living out there. Mill hands, like single people, stayed at the cookhouse. They worked for thirty dollars a month and their board. The only time Clarke's would go out there was summer time. They had a big cottage built and they'd go there and stay. Later, they made it into the girls' dormitory for the girls that worked down in the clothespin factory. They had about twenty-five girls sorting pins and packing them up in wooden boxes. The dowels were all packed and tied by men.

From the time I was eight years old, I was going back to Lake Jolly

when there wasn't school. Uncle Will was the superintendent of the place 'cause Clarke's was out here with their business. Warren Wright was the millwright and the sawyer was another Wright. A millwright is a machinist who sets up the mill for operation. Wilfred Kennedy used to run the dowel machine. They'd take a board and start it in the machine and a dozen dowels come out of the other end. It was a big steam-powered mill—four big Scotch boilers and a big coiless engine.

What amused me more than anything, they had an old up and down mill, a series of saws hung on this yoke like and fastened in the bottom and the top. If you wanted inch boards you put the saws an inch apart and set them that way. They'd square up a big log from the rotary, run it down through the mill, roll it over on live rollers, and set it up in front of this up and down saw. Then they'd go to lunch. It was an hour for lunch and there'd be about twelve boards fall off it when they'd come back at one o'clock. They did away with that and put in a big band saw; it was much faster and cut less wood. That up and down saw was cuttin' a quarter inch and every four boards, that was an inch where the band saw was cuttin' an eighth.

They manufactured dowels, clothespins, sawed lumber, and had a sash and door factory. Hardwood had to be sawed and air dried. The stock was sawed around five-eights of an inch. They cut the stuff

Clarke Brothers, Bear River, were highly successful merchants, manufacturers and exporters/importers. Pictured in the background are their three ships and lumber wharves. (Bear River Historical Society)

five foot long and sawed it on the band saw. The boards come off and were shipped out in the yard and stuck there so the air would pass through. When they'd go to use it they'd load that on tramways and shove it in the kiln. Then it would go to the mill, stripped up, and they'd make clothespins out of it.

They were haulin' the stuff out of there with horses and oxen, wagons and bobsleds. Coming from Lake Jolly where they call Buckler Field—it was Charlie Harris's place in my day—right across the way was what they called the Halfway Place. In the evening the teamsters would load their oxen with lumber and come out there when it was cool. They had a big, long barn logged up with a roof on it. Fellas would bunk in there, get up early in the morning, and come to town. They were doing this in the cool of the day. See, time didn't mean anything to these people. They worked for a month, they were gettin' paid by the month, time wasn't anything to them at all. They'd get up at two o'clock in the morning, feed their cattle, have a little snack, then yoke up and come onto Bear River. It would take two or three hours to make the trip—and it was mostly all downhill—then unload and they'd get back before the heat of the day really hit. It took over four hours from Bear River to Lake Jolly with a yoke of oxen empty, not pullin' anything. That's how the transportation was. Then around 1917, '18, they started with Ford trucks, the old Model

T's, and they were hauling then, but the roads were pretty bad. They couldn't go in the wintertime and the mud would stop them.

Back Lake Franklin, they'd put men in the woods at a camp in October and they wouldn't come out until spring. Those days, there was no way to get home so they put their time back in the bush. Their wives would be running a bill at Clarke Brothers to live on, and in the spring they'd come out and settle up against the wages they earned and usually they wound up in debt.

Clarke's bought Uncle Will out around 1915, '16. Right at the end of the war, he went to Carleton by Carleton Lake [Yarmouth County] and built a mill and a clothespin and dowel factory. He didn't have enough money to build the mill, so he borrowed it off of his wife's sister, Mrs. Pru Gordon, from Worchester, Mass. Gordon had died but she had the money. He was the inventor of the automatic shackle on railroad cars. You've seen them shunt cars and they come together, he invented that. Corning Woodworth was his millwright. Most of the old fellas that had worked for Uncle Will wouldn't stay with Clarke's; they went down there to work. I was sixteen years old and went to work for him.

Right after the First World War, that's when they started the pulpmill down here. We laid everything, the prosperity of this community, right at the door of W.G. Clarke and his son-in-laws

Lake Jolly community. Nothing remains today to show where this once prosperous village was except for the occasional overgrown stone foundation.

An artist's conception of the Clarke Brothers' Pulp Mill, used to sell stocks. The finished project was quite similar, minus the elaborate docking facilities. The skeletal remains of one main building still stands. (Creighton Balcomb)

Cunningham and MacIntyre. MacIntyre was an honest to God con man. He went to New York and sold more stocks in this stuff. They bought an old run-down mill that was over in New Brunswick and tore her down brick by brick, brought her over on scows and put it back up here. The only new thing they put up was the stack. Then when they got the mill operating, they hadn't any water, and a pulpmill takes an awful lot of water to operate.[*]

* The mill operated only briefly, perhaps six months. Further details concerning its demise and the Clarkes are to be found in Wilbur Parker's account which follows.

In the thirties, that depression wasn't any worse for the people here in Bear River than the depression right after the First World War. All over Canada the fellows returned and they didn't have guarantees for their jobs like they did in the States. If you went in the army in the States, if you inducted, your job was safe when you come back. But here, you were just turned loose, that was it. There were thousands and thousands of men out of work. It was rough, really rough.

The last sawed lumber that I knew was during the First World War. There wasn't anything here in the early twenties; the thing had died right out. There was no market for their goods and then the mill burnt at Lake Jolly completely. When that burnt, it flattened right out. They still had what we called woodpecker mills—set up and saw a little winter cut here and there. Pulp took over and they've cut pulpwood since. There's been two or three companies—Brown Lumber Company, Lincoln Pulp Company, Mersey Pulp Company. They interchanged, you know, one would buy the other one out. Whoever had the most money, I guess. I moved away in November 1922 until May 1959. I worked in Boston, New York, and Philadelphia and wound up as a construction superintendent.

Wilbur Parker

Wilbur Parker, 83, lives in Bear River. He has been a scaler, timekeeper, truck driver, and cook for woods operations years past. His story is two-fold: it completes the Clarke saga and gives insightful glimpses into the last days of the tall ships that were so much a part of the Bear River timber trade.

Pulpwood put Clarke's on the rocks financially. MacIntyre was the big shot and instigator. He married one of W.G.'s daughters and he talked his father-in-law and all the rest of the Clarke family into it. They got a lot of American money in that. Oh, he was sharp. I knew him quite well. When I was a kid working in the bank, a young junior clerk, my job was to take bills and present them to different people. After he was broke and didn't have two cents, I had to go in his office and present this bill. He just says, "That's a nice looking document" and passed it back to me. He refused to pay it and we sent it back. That was the last of him; he moved out of here shortly after that and I never seen him since. That would be probably 1925.

The whole operation from the start was something anybody that knew about pulpmills would say it wouldn't work. I don't know how much they made, but I guess that mill only operated six months. The wharf they were supposed to build never got built and this pipeline wasn't figured in it and that cost them a lot of money. They didn't have enough water down there when the thing was built, so they had to build a six-mile pipeline. I would say the pipe was about two feet in diameter, Douglas fir. It made good work for the people of Bear River. I knew one of the kids only thirteen years old, Freddy Kempton, they took him out of school because somebody had to lay in the pipe to hold the staves in shape while they put bands around them. He got top wages, as much as the highest paid man.

Clarke's lost all they had gained over the years; that all went in the pulpmill. They lost everything. The trading company went into

The six-mile pipeline that helped drive the Clarke Brothers and a number of Bear River investors into bankruptcy. (N.S. Museum)

Pipe Line from East Branch to Bear River Pulp Co's mill at mouth of Bear River, Nova Scotia made of Douglas Fir 2 ft. in Diameter, 5½ miles long.

receivership; that was a big business. They were paupers. People around here lost their whole life savings.

All this pulpmill business here, some trust company down in the States had it and Lincoln got hold of it. Lincoln Pulp came down here from Bangor; they were a subsidiary of Eastern Corporation. Their mill was in South Brewer, Maine. We had lots of pulpwood here that could be shipped by water right into their yards. About all they were interested in was softwood, mostly spruce.

Their first operation, I understand, was in Moose River and Parrsboro. When they came down here, the first thing they did was survey everything. Clarke Brothers had owned thousands of acres. A fella by the name of Ern Wade was the surveyor and he had a crew for a whole year surveying all the lines out Victory, Milford, Tom Wallace, and back as far as Weymouth, I guess. Now the Mersey owns all that property. The Lincoln didn't fail up here. They wanted to convert their mill over to hardwood, they mixed it, and they had an abundance of hardwood on their own property in Maine. They sold all their property here [around 1960] to raise money for what they were doing down there in Brewer.

Those old shipyards is where all us kids played. There'd be two or three feet of chips all over. They were really active back in the late 1800s, around the first part of 1900, 1905, '10, around there. They went everywhere. I used to hear old Captain Goodyear tell about goin' around the Cape Horn. They'd be gone for months. There's been quite a few ships lost out of Bear River. I've seen wharves, both sides of the river; there was no place to park another one—eight or ten ships.

At high tide they could all turn around there. Alfie Chute made a business of towing with these small gasoline boats. They had good gasoline engines back those days. They'd get towed until they got through the two bridges.[1] They'd put the sails up after they got out in deep water off Bear Island. He had a lovely big motorboat and that was the transportation from Bear River to Digby before automobiles if you didn't want to go by ox cart or horse team. Down behind the schoolhouse there used to be two or three slips that went out over the mud flats to take them out to low water.

I remember seeing the last vessel that was built here. She was launched one rainy day at noon in 1913. My grandmother took me there to watch. That was Reg Benson's shipyard. I can just barely remember one of W.G.'s daughters being on that ship and breaking the bottle of champagne on the bow. Then they took the ship down and rigged her, masts and all that stuff, at Clarke Brothers' wharf.

The last end of it, the only thing I can remember them building from scratch were these big scows they used for taking stuff out to deep water where they had to top these ships out. They couldn't give a ship full of cargo in Bear River because the river wasn't deep enough. So they give her part of a load, then take her out below the bridges, took the scows out there, and they'd top them. I can remember when they built two great big ones, and when they launched one, Dube Rice was on the deck caulking and she went right across the river and hit the bank and he never even stopped working. He caulked warships in New York for the First World War. They were made out of steel, but he caulked the decks.

Oakum was tarred hemp. It come in a great big crate in hanks, rolled up and tied. You had to make it like big yarn. You kept pullin' it apart, puttin' it on your knees and rollin' it up, and pullin' it out like that so it'd hold together. You'd make up little skeins so when he [the caulker] wanted it, he'd start in with his iron, then when he got to the end, pick up another piece, lap it, and keep packin' it in. See, the plank would be tight on the inside of the ship, but they were made on a little bevel so there'd be room to get this oakum in there. After he got it in there, he'd hold this great big iron—I've still got one—and go along and drive it in with a great big mallet. After the seam was full, he had like a grease gun full of hot pitch and they'd squirt that in the seam to seal it. They did that all over the ship, on the deck too. The top wages when they built [vessels] was a dollar and a quarter a day. Most got a dollar and they worked ten hours a day.

Somethin' else I should tell you. They used a lot of knees. The cross timbers and the deck had to be fastened to the side of the ship. They cut these knees about like an angle bracket you buy now in the store. They had to dig out roots of spruce trees after they'd been logged—red spruce mostly, near as I can remember—and they shaped them. They were stronger than tryin' to fasten two pieces of wood together to make the angle. I've got a paper I can show you, a fella sold for the schooner *Josephine* in 1905, thirty-two knees for nineteen dollars and ninety cents. That's about sixty-one cents each.

How do you suppose they fastened them? They had a machine they call a trunnel [treenail] machine. As a kid I played around it. The pieces, I think, were hard pine about an inch and a half square and about two feet long. They'd stick them in a socket in this machine that turned. You cranked it by hand like an upright lathe. It'd make 'em round and sharpen them off just like a lead pencil. After they got that knee in place, the guys with these augers drilled holes through by hand and drove those things in. They had hot pots to make glue and tar and stuff. I would imagine they put glue on them when they drove them in those holes, then they'd saw them off and that's what'd hold them up there.

When we were kids, they were repairing vessels. They'd put new planks in and deck them. They'd bring vessels up when the tide was highest so they could get them on the blocks. They set on great big blocks so that when the tide was out the men could work in under them. When they put new planks in a ship, they had to be bent. They had this long steam box and they had fire pits—two of them as I remember—underneath it and great huge iron pots. They had covers on the pots and wooden chutes that went up into the steam box. After it was all cut for size, they'd put timber in there and steam it so they could bend it and keep springing it in with clamps and one thing and another 'til they got her in place on the ship. They did use some galvanized iron spikes because I've seen them, but I never seen them use them. They'd have to work fast, especially if it was underneath where the water was goin' to come up and float the boat. I would say that stopped in the late 1920s.

The old packet was quite the boat. The first was a sailing vessel, the *Citizen*, before they had the steamboat [the *Bear River*]. I'm the last guy livin' that worked on her. A one-lunger steam engine, the packet made her weekly trip to Saint John and she'd take whatever produce was here the farmers had to ship. Cunningham used to ship nail keg staves all bundled up. That would be a full load for the packet, and it filled a boxcar when you got over to Saint John. Seventy-five tons was her capacity. I don't remember she ever had that much on her. She'd be pretty low in the water with seventy-five tons.

Bear River shipyard, late 1800s. "When we were kids, they were repairing vessels. They'd put new planks in and deck them.... They set on great big blocks so that when the tide was out the men could work in under them." (Bear River Historical Society)

There was no wholesalers in the [Annapolis] Valley and none around Digby. Some came by train, but very little. Most times we'd have thirty or forty bags of flour and feed. Most groceries those days came in wooden boxes, not cardboard. We hauled several barrels of molasses. I remember one time we took a car over that belonged to the Methodist minister. Usually they'd go out Monday, very seldom later than Tuesday.

Coming from Saint John, the first freight they put off might be Victoria Beach. Then they'd go over to Digby to what they called the Iron Duke behind the courier office. That's tore down now; all you can see are remnants of the old wharf. They couldn't stay there long. They could only go in when the tide was right. Then they came up

and went through the bridges and at the old Victoria Bridge there was a wharf where we used to put off freight for Elmer Weir, a retailer/wholesaler in Smiths Cove. Then on the way out we'd stop at that wharf. Local people might have something to ship to Saint John to sell, even people that killed beef would send the hides over for Captain Woodworth to sell.

She did a lot of towing of vessels. I remember one was called the *Frederick P. Elkin*, a three-master steel ship. We towed her in, and when she was loaded we towed her out. We were on our way to Saint John. She got stuck in the mud flats and we couldn't pull her off because the tide was lowering. The two captains got chewin' the fat at one another, and when the captain of the *Frederick P. Elkin* started cursin', Captain Woodworth wouldn't take it. He said, "Cut the lines boys. We'll pick her up when we come back." So we let her stay there on the mud for three days.

I remember a pile of logs rolled down on Carry Henshaw and he was crippled up for a long while. Those days there wasn't any compensation, welfare, and all that stuff. He was an Oddfellow and I remember how the Oddfellows helped pay his expenses and things like that. That's the way they did it years ago. Like when Burton Frude got typhoid fever. The townspeople got together and made sure they had firewood and groceries and stuff. They were hard days, yet nobody knew anything different.

Orrin Pulley

Orrin Pulley, 89, lives in Bear River on the Annapolis County side of the river. He worked for Clarke Brothers at their Lake Jolly mill in 1918. Over the years he worked in ten different lumber camps in Nova Scotia and New Brunswick and river drove pulpwood in New Brunswick. "They don't work in the woods anymore. Them times we worked in the woods. Yes sir we worked."

How much do you suppose wages was the Clarke Brothers paid me the first I worked with 'em? They paid two different wages, just accordin' to your age. It didn't matter what you could do. You could take a man's place and yet you couldn't get a man's wages because you wasn't old enough. It ain't that way now. Man's wages was twenty-one dollars a month and board; I got seventeen. Six days a week and ten hours a day. Oh boy, times 'ave changed, eh?

Would you think I done a day's work in my lifetime you couldn't find a man today could do it? I ain't talkin' about power saws. I cut a cord and a half of cord wood with only the axe in four hours. And when I done that, my father, at the same time, cut a cord and five feet; that's a foot more than I did. Yeah, there was three cord and a foot of wood we cut in four hours. Split it too and piled it, yes, sir. There's no man and his son livin' today to be found could do it. No way, not just with axes.

I'll tell ya somethin' else I done. Course this wasn't choppin', this was walkin'. Into Chub Lake camp, we'd only been there a week or so. They just had the camp built. One morning we was eatin' breakfast and Decker McCormack, the boss, said to me, "Would you go to Bear River today and do an errand for your day's pay?" The day before we swamped a main road and there was some snow on the bushes. It was wet and dirty and we was goin' to do the same thing that day. Boy yes, I took him right up on it. They claim Chub Lake camp was fourteen miles from Bear River. I looked at my watch when I went out the camp door — seven o'clock. At ten o'clock I was in Bear River and I walked most of the way. Some, at the foot of the hills, I jogged a little bit. I stayed in Bear River from ten to three o'clock in the afternoon and struck 'er for Chub Lake camp and I walked in the camp right on six o'clock. Why, that five hours I was in Bear River, I could've made a second trip because I wasn't tired.

I'll tell you some other things that I've done that it took a good man to do. I put a kit bag on my back in the store in Clementsport and I carried it on my back seven miles. Weighed forty-seven pounds. Now, forty-seven pounds, when you come to think of it, when you carry forty-seven pounds seven miles it's quite a load. It taint nothin' for one mile but when you carry seven miles, that's a different thing. I never took 'er off 'til I got home. And a bag of feed or flour [100 lbs.], I could carry that a long way on top of my head. When they built the Joggin Bridge, I put two bags of cement on top of my head and carried 'em. They was eighty-seven and a half pounds apiece.

Oscar Berry was a strong man. I see Oscar Berry, in one of Clarke's camps out in Morganville field, lay a barrel of flour flat on the floor, reach down, put his arms around it, pick 'er up, then shift one hand down on the bottom of it and, a kick or two, it was on his shoulders. I couldn't even pick the barrel up off the floor that way because my arms was too short and they wouldn't go around it. Oscar had long arms. That was an able man.

Boy oh boy, I've seen some things done in lumber camps. A feller had an accordine [sic] and could play pretty good. He was quite an actor. He took a piece of haywire and put it across from one bunk to the other and he took his accordine and went out on that tight wire and played. He passed the accordine to someone and they passed him his sweater, and he stood on that tight wire and put his sweater on and took it off. Yes, sir.

I was quite a wrestler. I counted them up here a while ago and I think it was thirty-eight different men I've hooked up for to rassle with. I'll tell you somethin' you might not believe. I told a feller once I'd put my hands in my pockets and he couldn't put me down. You can believe it or you cannot believe it, but I put him down with both hands in my pockets. I pulled my elbow out, not my hands, and I throw'd my elbow up right quick in front of him and at the same time that foot went behind his leg. Just a quick step backwards and down he went, right flat on his back. Rasslin' is mostly with feet and, boy, I was quick. I rassled once with Charlie Baltzer and I stood Charlie on his head. Picked him up and turned him upside down. He was about two hundred and forty pounds.

I got to tell ya another one; this is a pretty good one. We was loadin' a pulp boat down here in Bear River and had her just about loaded. I believe that was 1932, I'd be thirty years old. Father was up on deck. Clayton Huey was there. There was him and two or three more. They had just tussled with a big block of pulpwood to get it in the place where they wanted it. One of them said, "Boy, it would take some able man to pick that block of wood up alone." It was four feet long and two feet or more in diameter; it was a big block of wood. And

Clayton said, "Well, there ain't no man in Bear River can pick it up."
I looked over and said, "Oh, I wouldn't say that." I don't know what
made me say that.

I went over to that block of wood and hooked onto 'er and pulled
it up out of where they had it placed. Stood it up on end, leaned it back
against my right knee, reached down with a pulp hook, and that
hand down there at the bottom of 'er, and I picked 'er up about a foot
clear and dropped it. Well, sir, it made Clayton mad. They was all
younger than me that was there and not one of 'em would try it.

Right about that time, it was gettin' crowded up there. We was in
each other's way, so Harold said one or two should go down on the
dock. I said, "I'll go." Bye and bye, another big block went up. Harold
was up on top. He come over to the edge and hollered down to me,
"Orrie, I believe you'll have to come up here agin. They got one here
they can't roll over." He done that because he seen it made Clayton
mad, you know, yes sir.

My father [Arthur Pulley] was as good an axeman as could be
found. Nothin' like him today. You talk about smooth choppin'.
When he cut a notch into a tree there was no ridges there. Why, so
smooth it almost looked like it was cut with an axe with a bit onto it
a foot wide. He always used a pole axe. I've known him to chop with
a four-pound axe and iron wedges to keep the handle on.

I'll tell you about how good he was with an axe. We was cuttin'
cord wood up in Mink Brook Lake. One evening in the camp we was
talkin' about how much better it was then than it was when they used
to only have the axe. There was a time when they didn't have crosscut
saws yet. Well, father said, "Boy, taint much better; taint any different than my time. I could chop a log in two as quick as you can with
a crosscut saw." We knew how to use a crosscut saw and had a good
one, just about brand new and it was cuttin' good. So the next day we
went to the woods and I kept that in mind. We was going to cut a tree
about two feet in diameter, a hardwood, for cord wood. I forget if it
was yellow birch or white birch. We cut a tree a little less than a foot
on the stump for a skid, felled that across to keep it up out of the snow.
We sawed 'er down. I measured two quarter lengths off and notched
'er. I said, "Now, we want to try you right on this tree here. We'll take
the butt one and you take the next one." Well, I suppose there'd be
no difference to amount to anything on them first two junks. He said
okay. He got up on it, axe up over his head. He said, "Whenever
you're ready, start."

I forget whether I pulled it my way or Chester pulled it his to begin
the cut. Anyway, when that saw moved, the axe come down. Well sir,

well sir, well sir. I wish that I had some of them chips that he cut out. He cut big chips out of that there tree, oh, I would say, between two and three inches thick and more than a foot long. To put in the stove, it'd make four or five junks of wood. When he cut halfway through, he jumped up—he didn't step around—he jumped right up clear, swung around and I don't know if he missed a blow with that axe or not. I figure we were just about halfway down through too. We tried to go faster, but we was doin' all we could. Well, we was almost cut off when she dropped and split, the end was a hangin' where our cut was comin' out. He hit three more blows with his axe and his block was off. If ours had been up so we cut our's completely off, we'd have made two or three strokes to cut 'er off clean. Man oh man, pretty well even. For neatness I'll tell ya, him and Reg Potter was smooth axemen. Oh dear alive, there's no good axemen now. Heaven sake, no smoothness to their choppin', only hagglin'.

Creighton Balcomb

Creighton Balcomb, 79, lives near Clementsport, Annapolis County. Creighton, like his father, Owen, before him, has spent his entire life around the woods. Besides working for a number of logging operations for the better part of twenty years from the late 1920s until 1942, he spent twenty-eight years on the railroad, retiring in 1973. When not working on the homestead, he cut winter wood for himself, hunted, fished, trapped bears, guided American sportsmen, and dug over a thousand barrels of clams in the Annapolis River for shipment to the States. "There was always somethin' to do, but not too much money handled."

I worked in the lumber woods a lot. I worked on the Chester road, halfway from Windsor through to Chester the year of '34 when we had the deep snow. Worked one winter at Tupper Warren's in Digby and another winter with Culp over the North Mountain. Another one with Burnaby up Youngs Cove; that's where I got my leg broke. Two different winters with Tom Fortière; one was to Lake La Rose and the other was in back of Tupperville. He had his permanent mill here in Annapolis, but back there [Tupperville] he had a diesel mill. Boys, I'll tell ya, they chewed up the logs. It kept the choppers some busy. There was times they couldn't keep the mill a goin'. They sawed around seventeen, eighteen thousand [board feet] a day. Another one in back of Tupperville in 1927 was for Cunningham who had the mill in Bear River. That was the first time. I was only fifteen years old.

I was home here goin' to school. Pop was back there markin' lumber and he wrote home and said if I wanted a job to the mill, come up. So I got on the train and went to Tupperville, the first time that I was ever on a train. The mill was back in the woods three miles on what they called Tupperville Meadows, a big bog and meadows. Cunningham had three portable mills. The man that owned this timberland didn't have any mill and he would pay Cunningham to bring his mill and crew there and cut it. There'd be a boss, cook, cookee, two men at the haul-up, a canter, sawyer, edger, a man to carry the edgin's and slabs away, a trimmer, a man to mark the lumber, and a man to wheel the sawdust.

The old feller that wheeled the sawdust from the big saw got the flu and had to go home. That was my job. Well, what a job! It was a big body [wheelbarrow] and I had to wheel it uphill in the hardwoods. I couldn't wheel it down over the slope of the bank on account of a brook runnin' through there where they had a pipe out to get water for the boiler. You couldn't put no sawdust in that. I was only young, and mister, work from daylight 'til dark. Pop got a dollar twenty-five a day and I got ninety cents a day, I think it was. But that was in the 1920s when dollars was dollars. I was supposed to wheel it from the edger too. The sawdust from the edger was nothing like it was from the big saw, not near as much. My gosh, the scoop that you had to scoop that up and put in the wheelbarrow was about [three feet] wide. You'd never see a snow scoop so big.

Ten o'clock they'd shut down to file the big rotary saw and oil the boxes and I'd get a little rest. They shut down twice in the afternoon too. The boxes are what the mill shafts run with, the belts. I was only there a day or two and the cook said, "How do you like your job?"

"Well," I said, "all right, only I get hungry." I was young, you know.

He said, "Whenever they shut down to file, that big pan of cookies over the cookhouse door inside are for the lumber crew." Well, he didn't have to tell me a second time.

I got a leg broke in the woods in 1936. It had turned cold and they took all the woods crews and all the double teams out to the main highway to hook on the boiler. They had to haul it up the mountain and the ground had froze. The usually had the mill set up before the snow come. Years ago they didn't operate in the woods in the summer. This loggin' business was winter work. When it begin to break up in the spring they had to give themselves time to get the mill out before the frost come out.

The boss said to me and this other fella, "You two go back in that corner and cut some of those big hardwood trees there." There was a little swamp place we didn't log when we started in on account of it bein' wet. So we went back and sawed down this big yellow birch. It was twenty-eight feet up to where the limbs branched off, and straight. The bottom part of it was about eighteen inches from the ground; the limbs were holdin' it up. We sawed part way down through it with a crosscut saw, down far enough so we could get a wedge in the top so it wouldn't come together. As we got sawin' down close to the bottom, we shortened the stroke of the saw up a little bit so the tree would drop. But when it dropped, it come sideways and struck me and knocked me down. It bounced and broke that leg off, both bones.

The young fella run up to the butt where the peavey was standin' in the ground and pried and pried and got the log up enough so that I could pull my leg out. I knew it was broke because I felt the shock go right up through me. He helped me set up on the log. I put my hands on the log, raised up and went to put some weight on it and when I did my leg buckled right sideways. I weighed a hundred and seventy-six pounds and that young fella carried me over a mile out to the camp on his back.

The best operations that I was ever in was back of Round Hill in 1942 and 1943. They cut almost eight million feet in there over two years. It was all done with crosscut saws. I never worked in the woods where they used chain saws. There were eight sets of choppers and I was the saw filer. I wore out a lot of files and a lot of saws. Before that, when I worked in the woods for Culp, I filed saws, and when we worked for Tom Fortière out to Lake La Rose I filed the saws, and in back of Tupperville too. I didn't file all the time because they wasn't required to be filed every day, maybe every other day. In between I'd go chop. Back there, Round Hill, Roscoe Potter [the woods boss] had a couple of spare saws. I had to go around through the woods where they were workin'. I carried a saw on my back and when I'd come to a set of choppers I would give them this saw to work with while I was filin' their saw.

There was one particular crew there, two old fellers, and they had worked in the big lumber woods out West. They knew when a saw was cuttin'. Whether it was a little better grade saw or what I don't know—they were all Simond saws—but I'd come along to them to file their saw and they'd say, "There's nothing you could do to our saw to make it cut any better," so I'd go onto the next bunch.

It takes quite a little while [to file a saw]. You don't carry any vise or anything with ya; like if you was in a camp, you'd have a vise to put your saw in to hold it. But goin' around through the woods, you'd have to get a little tree about four or five inches in diameter and saw it off about four feet above the ground, then saw a notch down into it with your saw and turn you saw upside down to put in it so your teeth are in the air. You'd get a little stick to stand under the end of it so it wouldn't wobble around sideways and then a little wooden wedge in your filin' box to drive down along the side of your saw to hold it tight in this little place you had sawed. That's the rig we used in the woods.

If their saw hadn't been on any bad knots or anything and their point's gone, it wouldn't take too long to file it. In the winter when the wood is froze, your saw don't require much set, much clearance for goin' through. But when you get a thaw and the frost comes out of the wood—you see the softwood trees a shinin' white-like when the frost's comin' out—I've had my troubles that day because the saw didn't have enough set in it. I'd have a busy day that day. When the frost comes out, the wood was soft. You have this big lever instrument in your filin' box and you drop it down over your teeth and pry the teeth out further—put more set—to cut better. You have a gauge, just put in whatever it requires. Now that might be all right for today and tomorrow when the wood is soft, but then when it turns cold agin and the wood is froze, your saw is cuttin' a little too wide a road. It works the best when your saw just has enough clearance to go through.

Hemlock cuts harder than spruce with a saw; the bark will dull the points of a saw more than spruce will. Pine is an easy wood to work with. And when you go to limb a hemlock with your axe, you got to be very careful; they'll break the bits of an axe. They sawed hemlock four feet across the stump with a five-foot saw. You had to cut the trees fairly close to the ground. You couldn't leave a stump two feet high; you're losin' too much wood. The biggest tree they cut when I was in there [Round Hill] was a hemlock four feet on the butt and it took two yolk of oxen to haul the butt junk on a trailer sled over to the bank. The tree scaled seventeen hundred feet; there was three logs in it. And to saw it down with a five-foot saw, you had only a foot clearance, but they did it.

Round Hill was the last place I worked in the lumber woods and the best. When Roscoe got them men in there, he said, "I'm goin' to have a hotel cook and I'm goin' to pay top wages." Well, if you got a dollar and a half a day in the woods then, and your board, that was good wages, but Roscoe paid two dollars. He paid once a month. He would go out to the bank and get brand new twenty dollar bills in a white cotton bag, right off the press that had never been folded. I was in there almost two years and when I come out of there I had fourteen hundred dollars and boy, that looked good. The food was so good, oh, hotel food and a hotel cook. Willis Potter from Clementsvale cooked at the Sea Breeze hotel in Deep Brook every summer, a beautiful cook. You could only eat so much. I've worked in the lumber woods where you'd look at the food a long time before you'd eat very much of it.

The woods crews, the fellas that cut the logs and the teamsters, had their camp up a little bit from the mill. The mill crew had their own camp. They were made out of logs and a board roof. They'd be probably twenty-five by thirty feet and double bunks, one above the other, and each bunk big enough for two men. They didn't have mattresses, they had ticks filled with straw. Double sinks to wash and shave, and lines between the bunks where you could hang clothes to dry. Great big forty-five-gallon drum in for a stove. Man, it would get hot in there. I know in the summer it was hot, and I took a tent up and four or five of us stayed there all summer. The cookhouse was about fifty feet from the bunkhouse.

I'd come out about every weekend 'cause I had a car and I brought out a bunch of fellas. Then when the snow got deep and we couldn't get back in Dalhousie with a car, we would take the Acadian [Lines] bus to Round Hill and walk back the Spur Road three miles to the camp. He hauled in pressed hay and hundred-pound bags of feed, and supplies for the cookhouse. A truck would bring it out to the end of the Spur Road in West Dalhousie and the ox team would meet it there.

At nine o'clock the lights went out. That's the law in the lumber woods. After supper some of the fellas might have ta put a patch on their rubbers where they drove a stub or something through it. Might be two or three sets of choppers that would want to grind their axe. They had a big grindstone outside and they'd light a couple of lanterns and go out. Sometimes some of the choppers would make an axe handle after dark in there by the camp. We had no entertainment much. I had a gramophone here that took the big flat records and I took that back there. Boy, they just about wore that out. Quite a while after we was there them little battery radios come out, so we all chipped up two dollars apiece to have the radio in there. That was good. When the operation was over, Roscoe took it home.

My, the big pine and spruce they cut back in there. Some of the prettiest timber I ever saw. Pine there must've been sixty, seventy feet long. They brought their portable mill down from Kennetcook up in Hants County, moved it through the woods with teams, and built camps. That was a diesel mill [Harold Anthony owned it] and, boy, could that saw lumber. The biggest piece of lumber they sawed was three by eleven, twenty-two feet long. Two and three inch is classed as "deal" and most of that went overseas—hemlock, pine, and spruce. The lumber was all hauled out to Round Hill and shipped by boxcar.

All that timber was browed on the side of Round Hill River with horses. Two men, that's all they did was cut out along the river to make these big brows of logs. They rolled 'em down over the bank against trees that grew on the side of the brook. When they started to drive, they would take augers and bore holes in the butt of these trees, put in a half a stick of dynamite in each hole, and break the trees off at the ground. Down would go the logs.

Above where the woods operation was goin' on, there was a big meadow on the Dalhousie Road, Buckley Meadow, and they had a dam at the foot of the meadow. They even flooded the main highway. Transportation, food and supplies, had to come across the bog by canoe. We'd probably drive enough logs down in one day to keep the mill for three days. The whole crew would be on the brook. Three or four fellas more or less stayed in this little territory.

One day, the logs was goin' and there happened to be three of us

"They rolled 'em down over the bank against trees that grew on the side of the brook [note sawed-off tree holding brow of logs to left of photo]. When they started to drive, they would take augers and bore holes in the butt of these trees, put in a half a stick of dynamite in each hole, and break the trees off at the ground. Down would go the logs."
(Creighton Balcomb)

standin' side by side. The boss come along. I said, "You caught us standin' here loafin'." He said, "You know something? When you're standin' on the side of the river here and the logs are goin', that's when she's payin'. They're not payin' when you're out there on a pile of logs and got a jam in the brook. When you break that jam, the logs all go in a pile, go on down further and jam agin. When they're goin' one behind the other, that's when she's payin'."

Two men went along that river in the fall before it froze up, and rocks that was stickin' out in the river, that would be in the way, they drilled and blew 'em when the water was low. There was lots of whitewater. I fell in different times and come up the other side of the log. Can't swim either—only straight down. They always said to grab the log and hang onto it. It was nothin' to have a log strike the end of a rock or something and you turn the end of it a little bit, then jump on and follow the log maybe twenty feet and jump off on another little point. Yeah, that was fun, especially a big pine log that would float high.

We had these long pike poles with a pike in the end to keep the logs straight in the water, like on a turn, or keep them away from a rock. If we got a jam, we'd have to get out with our peaveys. Boy, you talk about a pile-up of logs quick. There'd be two or three truckloads sometimes in one jam and all that water behind. It was quite a big river. The water would rush back in the woods four or five feet deep, just like a lake in no time.

We were all given a peavey when we started in the spring—we had to pay two dollars for it—and if we lost it through the day, we had to remember where. We'd go borrow one or use a pike pole the rest of the day or stay with someone that had a peavey. When they shut the dam, course the water run right down out of the river. We'd know where we lost our peavey and we'd go down and here'd be the stalk stickin' up. The weight of the peavey would stay down and the handle would be up and we'd get it.

Boy, did they hawk the salmon out of there when the dam was shut down after supper nights. Fellas would come up the brook with these high waders and dip nets. There'd be practically no water in it, only the deep holes.

Down by the mill was a little deadwater, maybe three hundred yards long, and they put a dam about three feet deep on that to hold a little more water back. When we drove the logs down, that piece of deadwater would hold three days' sawin' when it was full. My gosh, some of 'em was fifty feet long, beautiful, great big trees.

They bring 'em up to the end of the mill at the haul-up and these

Rolling a brow of logs
into the river to start a
drive. "We had these
long pike poles with a
pike in the end to keep
the logs straight in the
water, like on a turn,
or keep them away
from a rock." (Lillian
Scott Perry)

fellas cut 'em up with a crosscut saw. Then they have a cable with a
chain on and they pull it out. It's wound up on a pulley and they put
it around these logs, then pull a lever and that pulls 'em right in
beside the carriage. There's a man there they call a canter. He rolls the
log on the carriage with a little canter peavey. The sawyer puts his
dog down on one side of the log and the canter looks after the other
end to hold the log on the carriage.

There's a rig on the carriage. If your log is fifteen inches on the butt
and ten inches on the top, you pull your log's end out a little bit to
allow for when it's split up. They take a slab off of one side with the
big saw. When the sawyer shoves his lever to shove the carriage back
after they've taken the first slab off, the canter flips that log right over.
Then they put that sawed side up against the carriage and they saw

agin. That's when the sawyer has to know his wits what to do. He has a guide right across there with all the inches marked on. It's a board about six inches deep and about four feet long. It's fastened right on the carriage with a couple of little stakes and the inches marked right on it. When he goes to split that log up, he has to know where to pull his carriage out so he won't have a board an inch and a half thick and the rest of them an inch. He has to know that scale.

It's split up on the big saw and goes on rollers over to the edger. The edger man lines it right up in through the edger and pulls this lever down to raise the rollers so the end of the plank will go in. Then he lets go of that and the weight carries it right through. He has a long tight string on one side and he lines up one side of his plank with that string. The other one, whatever the inches are across this little board—if it'll make a board six inches wide, he puts his lever on six and away she goes through. If it's eight, then he'll put it on eight.

There's a fella on the other end. All he does is pick up those edgin's 'til he gets an armful and carries them right out and throws them down over the bank at the tail of the mill; that's the further end where the lumber comes out. He has to throw them back far enough so it will take in the whole day's sawin' and still they'll be out of the way of the end of the mill. The night watchman[2] has to keep fire in the boiler and his job is to burn that big pile of slabs, and it's a big pile. They use them to fire the boiler, but they don't use that much; he just burns them up through the night to get them out of the way in order to have space to put the slabs and edgin's the next day.

It goes through the edger and then if there is a foot or two feet on the end of the board that's got some bark on it, the trimmer pulls a lever and cuts that off. But if the edger had 'ave made his board maybe an inch narrower on each side, that bark wouldn't 'ave been there. If he's only got a foot or so that's got bark on, they'll cut it off and throw it in the slabs. But if he's got four or five feet with a little bark on each side, he'll get 'em to bring it back and edge it an inch narrower and no bark on it. It's up to the edger.

The trimmer trims the end of the board with a big circular saw to make it square to start. Then they shove it up on through and there's a measure, a board on its edge with the feet marked on it, and wherever it stops, he looks and cuts it right off square. The tally man is right on the other end to mark it with a lumber chalk. If it's ten feet long by six inches wide or if it's a plank two by six by twenty feet long, he marks it on there. He has his tally boards on a rack out in front up over his head and he just reaches there and puts a little mark with a lead pencil. When he gets four, he draws one down across; it's easier to figure up. They're a pine board about two feet long and a foot deep. When you get it full of lumber, that's all tallied in a book. You take the plane and plane it off or sandpaper it and start over again. After supper, he figures up how many thousand feet they sawed that day and he can tell you in fifteen, twenty minutes.

They started cuttin' pulpwood here and shippin' it out when I was goin' to school in the 1920s. Pop said, "That's the end of our woods. They're cuttin' stuff that they should be leavin' to grow." They're ruinin' Nova Scotia. This summer operations, that's what tearin' our woods to pieces. They're cuttin' the wrong time and tearin' the woods up with these big machines. There's nothing left, just barrens. We're goin' to have no game. And sprayin', sprayin', sprayin'.... You see these loads of pulp goin' through and half of it's brush, yeah, brush draggin' right alongside the side of the log. And rocks and mud and stuff, well, I'm tellin' ya. It ends up now, some of this wood they're takin' is about like a Christmas tree that you would cut; take one stick and trim it out eight feet long. It would maybe be four inches on one end and two on the other. That's in this mess of pulpwood they're cuttin'. There's lots of pieces of pulpwood in that eight-foot wood not big enough fer a little fence stake to hold cattle in a pasture. Oh, it's a shame.

Ralph Burgoyne

Ralph Burgoyne, 87, lives in Springfield, Annapolis County. A veteran of sixty years in the milling business, he remembers well when the largest sawmill ever built in Nova Scotia sat near the shore of nearby Springfield Lake.

In 1903 the American Lumber Company purchased all properties of Bridgewater-based E.D. Davison & Sons and renamed it the Davison Lumber & Manufacturing Co. Ltd. Included among its acquisitions were two large water-powered rotary and gang sawmills in Bridgewater and two hundred thousand acres of timberland which held an estimated six hundred million feet of spruce, pine, hemlock, and various hardwoods as well as eight hundred thousand cords of pulpwood.

Davison Lumber, with its head office in New York and regional office in Bridgewater, soon began an ambitious expansion which included the building of a huge steam-powered sawmill at Springfield. A direct result of this was the birth of two communities: Crossburn, named for logging superintendent J.W. Cross; and Hastings, after company president John Hastings. Included were the company-built Springfield Railway, company-owned locomotives, and a number of curiosities for the times: two Clyde loading cranes, a steam hoist skidder, a Rapid Bernhart crane loader, a Lombard steam log hauler with caterpillar treads, and a Bucyrus steam shovel.

Davison Lumber produced an annual average of forty million feet of lumber, most of which went to New York and New England. Large quantities were also exported to Madeira, the West Indies, Cuba, and South America. Bridgewater was the main shipping port, and in 1906 alone the company chartered ninety vessels to handle production. After 1916, most U.S.-based exports went by rail. Shingles, hemlock bark for tannin, sulphite chips for pulp, box shooks, and laths were among other products. The lath mill alone produced fifty thousand laths a day.

Davison Lumber was in financial trouble in 1919 with the decreased demand for lumber following World War I. By 1921 the company was bankrupt. Hollingsworth & Whitney bought up its assets in 1922. Rail lines were torn up, lumber and machinery was sold, and houses were moved or torn down. A fire in 1928 destroyed what was left of the mill and buildings in Hastings. All that remains today are the memories of a few survivors like Ralph Burgoyne.

When the company started down here in 1905, my father moved from Berwick out to Hastings where the mill was. I was only one year old. That was the winter what they called the "deep snows"; it fell seven feet of snow in one snowfall in March. They had roads tramped down over fences and everything. He had a horse and he got as far as Lake Paul and that played out. He stayed there overnight and traded with a fellow and got as far as Dalhousie the next night. There was a house empty there and the fellow that owned it said he could stay there until spring. Then he moved down to Cherryfield, then to Hastings.

They called it Hastings after the superintendent of the Davison Lumber Company. It was part of Springfield and part of Falkland Ridge. They started to build a railway in 1903. It started just down here in that hollow, the station was right there, and they kept adding on. They put all the logs in a lake and run a railroad to the lake and loaded them from there. They went from one lake to the other as they cleaned up one piece of land. They done most of their logging up here and some down in Caledonia and some out Alpena. The biggest part of it was up in here, in from Dalhousie, in that country. They had about forty miles of railroad to take up when they failed up. It went clean up as far as Crossburn, ten miles. The mill business was run from here and the lumber business was run from Crossburn. They had five of their own locomotives and they kept everything up there.

There was a little steam engine with a passenger car—it held about twenty—and that's what travelled back and forth from Hastings to Crossburn.[3] There's where they had their head office at first until 1914; then they built ten new houses [at Hastings] and moved some of the bungalows and everything from Crossburn down to Hastings and ran everything from here. Crossburn was a small community, but there's nothin' there now. It's all grow'd up in trees.

There were forty-two big houses [in Hastings], then they had some bungalows and a big cookhouse that would hold about a hundred and fifty men. They were all plastered and fixed up. They had a clubhouse, two bowling alleys, pool hall, dance hall, all in one building. They had their own electric lights over there. The generator was right on the crank of the steam engine. As soon as it begin to get dusky, they'd start the lights. They had lights everywhere 'til half past ten unless the mill was runnin'. Twenty minutes past ten, you flashed them to give ten minutes either to light a light or get the hell to bed. Sometimes they'd get a big order or somethin' [to saw] and maybe then they'd run them until twelve o'clock.

They had their own school and teachers. The teacher [in Crossburn] had around forty, just the one teacher. She taught right up from the time they started goin' to school 'til grade twelve. Today, they get four or five, they think they got a helluva lot to teach. When they

Davison Lumber Company transported many of their logs with a company railroad that included five locomotives and forty miles of track. In the background is a Bernhardt loader. (N.S. Museum)

moved from Crossburn, they built a piece onto the schoolhouse and divided it up then; had two teachers [for seventy-two pupils].

The company owned the houses. You paid a dollar fifty cents a month for lights, a dollar a month for your rent and a dollar—single fellers paid fifty cents—for the doctor. The doctor did every damn thing from pullin' out slivers to deliverin' babies. In the wintertime he had to make a trip around every week. They had twenty-five camps in the woods, I think, and about forty-five men to a camp. Some of the camps, when they was haulin' with trains, you'd just jump on the train and go. They had two veterinarians that travelled around to the camps all the time in the winter. The company used all their own horses [about 160], but when they started haulin' logs in the winter, they hired teams from everywhere.

That was the biggest mill that was ever this side of Quebec and I don't know at that time if they had one that big in Quebec. It was built for two hundred and fifty thousand a day, but the best they got was a hundred and ninety thousand in nine hours. There was a double slab chain that went up to the burner that burnt the waste wood and that was so loaded with wood one side broke. They was all night gettin' that fixed. It broke five o'clock and they had a hundred and ninety thousand.

That smokestack was one hundred and sixty feet high: forty feet of brick and the rest was steel. It was eight feet in diameter. The waste

wood burner was one hundred and twenty feet high, and twenty-four feet in diameter. It had a water jacket all around, up forty feet for water, to keep the hot pond open in the winter when they sawed and for the boilers if they needed it. The water tank was one hundred and forty feet. All the timbers inside the mill, and there was a lot of them, was hard pine from Michigan. It was the prettiest stuff you ever seen. It cut like glass; it was really hard. Most of the machinery come from over there too. Roops had a mill settin' where the station was and they sawed all the inch boards and stuff [to build the mill]. There was a long sorting shed and that had about fifty trucks—a tram with three wheels on it—sittin' around there at all times. As soon as one went out, there was another one put in. They could put about a thousand and a half of lumber on each one. Then they'd hook a horse on, take it down, hook on it empty, and bring it back. I don't know how many log cars they had.

Everything was done by steam. They had forty-two steam cylinders in the mill. There was a six-hundred-horsepower engine. That was the main engine. Then they had a four hundred just run the gang. They had a sixty horsepower that run the lights, and thirty horsepower in the machine shop and twenty horsepower up in the filin' room. They had another eighty-five horsepower run the planer.

They took all kinds of softwoods except hackmatack. Most of their stuff was sawed in inch lumber unless they got an order for timber. The gang could only saw inch lumber. If they were buildin' a wharf or somethin' they wanted some heavy timbers for, they'd saw them

Davison Lumber Company's mill at Hastings. "That was the biggest mill that was ever this side of Quebec and I don't know at that time if they had one that big in Quebec. It was built for two hundred and fifty thousand a day, but the best they got was a hundred and ninety thousand in nine hours." (N.S. Museum) out. That's the only way they sawed anything more than inch and two inch. About eighty percent of it was inch. It would go up to twelve inches [wide]. The logs were hardly ever over sixteen feet unless they got an order. They had to go through the single band; they didn't go through the gang.

The twin band saws was supposed to keep the gang goin', but if they couldn't, the single band would make some. The twin bands, one saw was stationary and the other one would move. The single band was stationary. The only two inch they sawed was what was sawed on the single band. They couldn't saw two inch on the gang because it would be too much waste.

When the log went through the twin bands, it just took two slabs off. Both slabs went to the re-saw for whatever they could get out of it, then come back to the edger. There was two edgers. The centre of that log, whatever it was—six, eight, ten, twelve inches through—went to the gang. They piled them up about three feet high and pretty near four feet wide and that would go through the gang in about four minutes. There were forty-one saws. When that load come through the gang, there'd be five hundred boards.

There used to be a railroad just back here—the Halifax & Southwestern—that run from Bridgewater to Middleton. They must have had a short piece of railroad down Caledonia because they had runnin' rights on this railroad. They could run from Bridgewater to Middleton or Caledonia. Boats used to come in and they'd load a lot in Bridgewater, but a helluva a lot went to Halifax. The last goin' off, if this train couldn't handle it all or if they couldn't handle the lumber when a boat come in, they had one engineer, he could take a trainload right to Halifax.

There was a hundred and thirty [men] around the mill and the office and the cookhouse. The men from Cherryfield and North River walked anywheres from six to eight miles up here and piled lumber. They'd go to work seven o'clock and leave at six to go home. They only ever had one woman hired. McKillam was the mill boss there for a while and his daughter was the book-keeper. She was the only one that was ever hired. It was all men in the camps. Choppers would get about eighteen dollars a month and their board. Camps were all boarded in and they had springs in them, two men to a bed.

When they was in the woods, they usually had a thousand people. There were people there from all over the world. Oh, my God! A lot of them was there from the States, England, France, Belgium, Germany, Sweden, Norway. There was one little short feller there from Bucharest [Romania]; but mister, you talk about a worker. There was some from down the southern parts. Wasn't too many coloured people, a few but not too many. There was quite a lot of Swedes one winter. They had their skis with them. That's the first time I every seen anybody on skis. They was here from at least, I know, twenty different nations, some of them I can't think of right now. There was lots of work here and I suppose maybe the wages was a little higher than they was in most places.* Christ, they'd get more here in a day than they used to get some places in a week.

The most of them could speak a little English, enough to get by, and there was no trouble. You hardly ever heard tell of a fight or anything like that. In the summertime, it wasn't that many. They'd be stayin' in the cookhouse and the houses. It was in the winter they used to load up, when the woods work started along about the first of October. From that 'til the last of March, middle of April, there was a lot of 'em. There was some comin' and goin' all the time.

The cookhouse was a helluva building. I imagine it was a hundred and twenty feet long and it was three storeys. One end [the main floor] was living quarters for a family—a cook with a wife—and there was a damn big kitchen and pantry and a dining room that would feed about a hundred and fifty at once. The other end was a big smokin' room. The next floor was all partitioned off in rooms. Anybody wanted a room for themselves, it was only a dollar a month. Then you go up to the next flight, it was all in one, and they just had the beds about three feet apart. These rooms was full most of the time with bosses and the top part was called the ram pasture.

They really fed their men good. They said they fed the men for thirty-nine cents a day, and the horses, forty-five cents. There was an old feller out here used to raise about three acres of cabbage for them every year. They used to call him old cabbage head. In the cookhouse, you could be livin' in one of their houses and go in there every day and eat your three meals and it wouldn't make any difference. They didn't know who, they never asked. I know there was one family, he never worked. He was from down in Cherryfield. He had an old horse and he used to go down there about twice a week and they fed him. He ate two meals a day at the cookhouse for years.

If Springfield right today had the food that went to waste in the cookhouse, it would feed the whole damn outfit. See, they didn't know how many men they was goin' to have. Maybe they'd cook for fifty, sixty men, maybe only thirty-five, forty come in. Well, that stuff had to be throw'd out. They had no way to keep it then. I went in there one day and the cook was swearin'. "I don't know why in hell they don't let us know from the office when they're bringin' a bunch down

*Men in the lumber-yard could earn a dollar and thirty-five cents a day, but the sawyer was the highest paid, at seven dollars

from the woods." They had a pan about as wide as this table and they was fryin' eggs. There was one feller breakin' them in one end of the pan and the other feller was takin' them out of the other end. They was just slidin' them right through; they had about four inches of fat in it. When they was done, I imagine there was five dozen eggs just throw'd right out in the pail.

My father always kept a couple of pigs. He was down there one night. The cook said, "I can't tell you to take it, but when it gets dark, dig down the bottom." Lots of times he'd get a roast that wouldn't go in his pail and bring it home for the pigs. He used to raise two pigs every summer and all the feed he ever bought was the last month's; they feed them cornmeal. Outside of that, just from the cookhouse.

There was one feller got killed. The carriage run by steam; there was a forty-foot piston rod on that and then that had to go into a cylinder. Cold mornings, the men would get there early and they'd sit on this cylinder. It was all cased in, but it was nice and warm. There was two big cylinder cocks on it, and Jimmy Deveau—he was drunk half the time anyways—was supposed to open them up before he ever touched his lever. There was one in each end of the cylinder to let the water out. The cylinder would condense steam overnight—there'd be barrels of water in that cylinder—and he was supposed to open them up and let the carriage move slow to squeeze that water all out. But this morning, he just opened 'er up and he blew the end out of the cylinder and a Wentzell from down Wentzell Lake got killed. He was settin' on the end of the cylinder and it blew out. He didn't stay in one place.

I only spent one day behind the edger and I seen a feller get killed. A piece of board dropped on top of the saws instead of goin' through under the rollers. It went up on top of the rollers and then dropped down on the saws after the other wood went through and it split in three pieces. One went right through him.

Them was the only two that was killed here in Hastings, but there was a feller murdered, Dan Veinot, from Northfield. They was going to build a railroad over to another lake and they was cutting a right of way. He broke his axe handle just before dinner and the boss sent him down to get a new handle to put in his axe and he never got there. They got lookin' around for him. He was leanin' up against a rock. He carried quite a bit of money on him and he was kind of braggin' about it and somebody, I guess, wanted it. They said there was men at the camp could point the finger at the one that done it, but they wouldn't.

That Jimmy Deveau I was tellin' you about, he cut one of the belts one noon; he was too drunk to saw. He went down and slashed a belt that was two hundred feet long, thirty-two inches wide, and about three quarters of an inch thick, solid leather. They had about a ton weight on all them belts to keep them tight so they wouldn't slip. I don't know what he used for a knife, but he cut one enough so, when the mill started, the belt broke and it took 'em three days to splice it. He went over to New Brunswick and worked in a mill over there and he couldn't get along with the filist. He used to take a pair of pliers and bend the teeth a little bit so it would scar the lumber. Then they'd have to change the saws and they'd fire the filist and get somebody else. When they caught him, they were goin' to lock him up, but they gave him a choice. Either go to penitentiary or work for a dollar a day for as long as he could work. He took the dollar a day. I don't know how long he lived afterwards. That was a long time ago.

I went to work in the mill [at Hastings] when I was eleven. A French feller from Quebec used to come to our place. He said to me one day, "I got nobody to pick out No. 2 lath." They sawed lath out of slabs. They come through the machine so fast they could only save the No. 1's. The seconds would have some bark on and one thing or another, but the No. 1's had to be clear. "Why don't you go down and pick out No. 2 lath for me?"

My father said, "He can't go down and pick out No. 2 lath."

He says, "He can. There's no way for him to get hurt at all." They was payin' a dollar seventy-five cents a day; that was seventeen and a half cents an hour. That was the average rate for the men. He said, "I'll give him a dollar a day and ten cents a thousand," and I made as much as my father and I was only eleven years old.

When I was thirteen, I kept thinkin' of the money I made and I quit school. I went down and carried water in the lumberyard for the men for about two months. My God, you carried it over half a mile—two big, sixteen-quart buckets—and then half the time they'd waste it. They'd take a pint full out, drink a little bit and throw it away. I got laid up and the doctor said, "He can't do that anymore." So I went over to the mill one day and went in. Hughie Pulsiner was the mill foreman. He said, "Are you lookin' for a job?"

"Yeah."

"Well, go up behind the gang." That machine had fourteen saws in it. There had to be a feller on each side, so if a slab of somethin' fell off, you had to get it out of the way.

I did that for about two hours. They had to shut down every two hours and a half and crawl down in that darn thing and fill all the boxes up with tallow. That's the only thing they had that would last [for lubrication]. It was red hot down there. The old feller that run the gang was an ugly old bugger. I looked down that hole and he said, "Get down there and tallow 'er up!"

I said, "If that's where you want me to go, I'm goin' up the steps!"

I went and started to go down to the lower part of the mill to go out and I met the chief engineer. He said, "Where are you goin'?"

"If I can't get somethin' to do besides behind the gang, I'm goin' home."

He said, "I don't blame you. Go down and pile wood into the fire room for me." They'd haul wood over and dump it and then had to have the fire room filled with slabs for the night. I piled in wood about three months and Wilbur Sherrard come along one day and said to me, "Ed Wiles, the head night fireman can't come to work tonight. His wife's sick."

Well, I thought the other feller that was on knew what he was doin'. I was only thirteen years old. I went up. He was an old French fella. "What do we do now?"

He says, "I don't know. You're the fireman."

There was six of them big boilers side by side. They was as high as this room here. When they stopped nights, them boilers would start blowin' off and oh, my God, they had the deadliest roar. You had to keep blowin' water out of 'em and fillin' 'em up with cold water 'til you got them cooled down; take about two hours. Oh boy, look a here, I was a nervous wreck. I was only a kid doin' this. When they shut down in 1921, I'd worked in the fire room four years. I was only seventeen years old yet. I worked three shifts [in a row] lots of times and them was twelve and thirteen hours. I knew steam.

They started the mill in 1905 and they blew the whistle the tenth day of July 1921. The last three or four years they only run in the summer. They was gettin' too much lumber. That didn't happen all at once. It kept buildin' up over the years. They failed up in the fall of 1920. There was thirty-five million feet of lumber in that yard when they failed up. They loaded four cars a day and they was two years loadin' it out. Then they started sellin' the machinery. Some of it went to Quebec and some went to New Brunswick.* I think they owed the bank around two million dollars. That was a lot of money at that time. I can't understand them puttin' up an outfit like that early in the 1900s but it was really somethin'. I'd just liked to had a movie camera and have a picture of that outfit runnin'.

* All the rails were torn up and shipped from Halifax via the Panama Canal to British Columbia for use in their lumber woods.

Harry McCurdy

Harry McCurdy, 87, lives in Middle Musquodoboit, Halifax County. "There's hardly anybody around here much older than I am." He spent very little time in the lumber woods, working mostly in sawmills doing "pretty near everything"—wheeling sawdust, firing boilers, carrying deal, tallying lumber. "We were happy then and gettin' a bite to eat. I think I got along as good as a lot of them."

I spent my first winter in the woods when I was about seventeen years old right here in the district up in Glenmore. That was for Hollman and Archibald; they had a portable sawmill. From then on for a number of years there was a lot of sawmills. There was an awful pile of lumber shipped out of this station right down here. The depot was just at the foot of this hill here. The majority of it would be three-inch deal.

They had a mill right over here by the bridge alongside the river. They sawed millions of feet of lumber there. At one time you could get up on the hill here somewhere and you could see seven or eight smokes from the sawmills in the district, five or six miles in a circle from here right out around. They'd be all steam mills; that's the times before diesel. There was Brown's, Creelman's, White Brothers, Roy Archibald, different ones. That was in the early twenties. It was after the railroad was built here, and it was goin' in '17. And it's all gone now, tracks tore up. There'd be probably up towards a million feet piled up in the deal yard down here waitin' to get loaded onto cars. Everybody workin' and not gettin' anything for it. I never got any wages worth beans all the time I worked in lumber.

In the twenties the pulp business was big out here. That was in '27 'cause I drove a truck and that was about the first time trucks come in. I drove trucks for a Portage fella a while that fall. No trucks were haulin' pulp in them days. I was drivin' to haul provisions. The roads

Interior of mill, circa 1900. "At one time you could get up on the hill here somewhere and you could see seven or eight smokes from the sawmills in the district, five or six miles in a circle from here right out around." (N.S. Museum)

all through this country went out here sixteen, eighteen miles and they went from there down into the woods. They'd take them with horses to get the rest of the way. It was all horses at that time. That year I trucked, I used to leave here in the morning with my load and go to Musquodoboit Harbour. I'd stop at the hotel and get my dinner for thirty-five cents. My goodness. When I think of it, what a change in a lifetime.

I was out West to Saskatchewan on the harvest excursion in 1924 and 1925. You never heard tell of that, I suppose. That was just men goin' out there to work the harvests. There's darn few of them livin' today. They was very shy of help gettin' their grain cut and all that in the West. I don't know how many years it went, but I think the last one was in '28 or '29. They went there probably seven or eight years, every fall.

A harvest excursion train left Halifax and it went right to Winnipeg. That train just run for that one purpose. We'd catch the train anywhere along here and they would have a load, three or four hundred, by the time they left Truro or Moncton. It was the old-fashioned Colonist cars. A lot of them had cushioned-up wooden slats [for seats]; they were good. I think they used to take us out for forty or fifty dollars. Course, you had to take provisions to eat on the way. You were about five days anyway gettin' out there. We went out on the CNR and come home on the CPR.

You only went on faith. Everybody said all the way out, "All you have to do is get off the train and they'll be grabbin' for men to get their grain cut and in." There was fifteen of us from right this district, between here and Upper Musquodoboit, all together in that one bunch and we went to the same place by the name of Hodgeville in southern Saskatchewan. We got off there in the night. Lots of them only had two or three dollars left, but you could get bacon and eggs at any restaurant for twenty-five cents them times. Next day, the farmers come in lookin' for help.

Lots of them that had no money, that was really broke, would snap up a job from the first fella that offered. I was one of the last ones gettin' hired. I was a little bit [fussy]; I wasn't goin' to take a job that I didn't want with some old fella that might be pretty rough on you. Another fella and I hired on with two young farmers, Harold and Bill Ashton. I went to the same place, same guys [the following year]. They had two places; a rented farm from their uncle and another one right alongside of it of their own. A farm out there would be about a square mile. Everything was measured off in sections [640 acres], mile squares. They had a section and a half.

They boarded you and everything. There was three of us hired on with these fellas. One went and stayed with the old folks on their farm. Course we all worked together because we were only a couple miles apart. The house on the one where we were was a great big barn; it was all the same. You went in the barn and here was this living quarters. It wasn't that bad. That end of it was fixed up pretty comfortable.

They paid you good money. We got four dollars and a half [a day] for gathering up the sheaths and stooking the grain, and six dollars a day for threshing. I always had thirty or forty dollars in my pocket, which was a lot of money. A dollar was a lot of money then. I had twenty-five or thirty dollars worth of new clothes; I had to buy a winter mackinaw coat and that sort of thing. I sent home a hundred dollars by money order. Some people knew you was comin' from the West, comin' home, they'd try to get your money. They wouldn't really hurt you, but they'd pick it off you if they could. I figured I made that money, I was goin' to send it home.

I went some time in August and arrived home the seventh day of November on my twentieth birthday. I weighed one hundred and twenty-two pounds when I left home and five weeks later I weighed one hundred and forty. I had four meals a day and worked ten or twelve hours every day, hard work, so it didn't do you any harm. I had a wonderful experience for two or three months.

The winter after I came home from out West, my brother-in-law said, "I want somebody to wheel sawdust in my sawmill. I'll give you two dollars a day." Well, that's twice as much money as anybody else was gettin', so I went out and tried it. That was supposed to be the poorest job on the outfit but in my opinion it was the best job I ever had around a sawmill, the easiest. The mill had been there the year before and they'd had a blower on the mill someway to blow the sawdust out and it was up a steep hill. I had to wheel it up over that. All I had to do was take it from the big rotary saw and I just played there. Some time later, I had to stay home a week and he had two men tryin' to do my job. I don't know what was the matter with them. It was an easy job.

Slabs was terrible. I wouldn't do that. It was crude you know. They just shoved those old slabs out of there and a man had to pick them up and lug them out onto a fire. But I don't know why everybody hated the sawdust. Yes, it kept you busy; you had to keep up to it. You never wanted to let it get ahead of you at all. There were about eleven men run a sawmill them times. Everybody knew their job. If everybody worked together, you got along great.

I believed in looking out for tomorrow, always did. For years there when I was young, I didn't have a steady job, but I always had that quarter. I lived up the road here about a mile, and I had nothing to do today, I'd start down to the village. Before I'd get hardly to the crossroad, somebody'd come along. "Hey, what are you doin' today?" "Nothin'." "Well, come along with me." And I'd get a day's work. May only earn a dollar or a dollar and a half, but that's the way things went. I've always said I couldn't borrow and pay interest. Buyin' on time and pay interest, I wouldn't do that; I never did. I can safely say I don't ever remember of a time that I couldn't put my hand on a dollar if I had to have it.

Gerald Day

Gerald Day, 76, of Jeddore, Halifax County, is a veteran of forty years in the lumber woods. During that time, he worked as a teamster and chopper and loaded pulpwood boats. His father, Isaac, was also a teamster who "never feared a horse," but according to Gerald probably died prematurely as a result of being kicked by teams on numerous occasions. A self-proclaimed jack of all trades, Gerald has worked as a floor layer, carpenter, and guide. He guided sportsmen trout fishing for thirty years, but never hunters. "They can't hurt you with a fishing rod." Today, he doesn't consider himself retired. "I'm stopped."

I first worked in the lumber woods when I was sixteen. That was up in Ship Harbour woods with Byron Mitchell. He was a subcontractor for Mersey. He logged Ship Harbour Lake and here in Salmon River and the combined lumber was shipped from here to Liverpool. I had to work all the time. Your job'd run out in one place, you went to the next lookin'. You usually got one. All these loggin' companies knew one another all over the province, so you got a man leave their job, he had a reference to go to so and so.

If you wanted to survive you had to take what you could find. There was lots of times you travelled a long ways. Kennetcook, South Maitland, Sheet Harbour, Upper and Middle Musquodoboit, Meaghers Grant, Porters Lake, Tantallon, Stewiacke, Pictou, Rossignol—I can't think of them all, but there was a lot more than that. Most of them we had to walk to and from, course, we thumbed some and the odd time you might be fortunate enough to have a couple of dollars to go by train. If you wanted the job you walked to any part of the country in Nova Scotia. I worked all the time [during the Depression], but there was a lot of people that didn't because they didn't push too much for it. If you were a good worker, if you went and looked fer it, there was no trouble to get a job.

Working in the lumber woods was a good healthy job. You worked hard, ate well, and slept a lot at night. I wasn't too much older than sixteen when I went to Rossignol. We'd go down in May and stay 'til the peelin' stopped, say three months at a time. I didn't work in Rossignol in the wintertime. I worked out in back of Tantallon in through where Mersey was cutting. If they wanted extra help they put ya to work on camps instead of in the woods. Most of the time when I worked for the Mersey, I worked piece work other than when they hired us on to do labour work. The first year [early 1930s] we got a dollar and twenty-five cents a cord and finally, the last years right after the war, we got six dollars.

Some of the Mersey camps I worked with up at Tobeatic Lake and Lake Rossignol, there'd be about a hundred, a hundred and forty, but they wasn't all in the one building. There was nobody that was too fussy about buildin' camps at that time. We was only there for maybe a season or two. Why should they build a nice big camp? At that time, they was called fairly comfortable. There's a lot of people wouldn't put up with it today. They had to either take it or leave it at that time, so the majority of us had to take it.

I've crawled into the bunk with the water runnin' right out of the ears. Everybody was alike on a river drive. As I said before, you worked hard enough that you went to sleep when you went to bed

Camps came in a variety of sizes and styles. Sleeping accommodations could range from perhaps a dozen men or less to a hundred or more. Pictured is a river driving 'shanty', Dalhousie Road near Gully Brook, circa 1892. (N.S. Museum)

whether you were wringin' wet or not. The only thing you'd take off is your rubber boots, if you had rubber boots on. Mostly had calked boots. Usually two men slept in a bunk, but if there wasn't enough bunks for all of you, maybe four men slept in a bunk. Kind of tight. There was more sittin' up on a bench than there was sleepin'. You put up with it because every man was alike. There was never any arrogance, like troublemakers. He wouldn't last very long.

There's a way to cure [snoring]. Whistle in his ear if you slept close to him. Oh yeah, that was done. I just about choked a poor ol' feller in the woods up here. Scared me half to death. He laid on his back and he just snored both ways. I happened to be sleepin' next to him. There was a pole between the two of us. I laid my head right over and I must have been five minutes gettin' ready. I whistled and it was right sharp. He was drawin' in about the same time and he coughed and gagged. My father was sleepin' on the other side of me. He says, "You done it this time." He scared me then. When he come to, we had the light on and he begin to turn purple; he was chokin'. It didn't scare him altogether. It was just the whistle you see and him asleep and he took a gulp. Some of the other men had put me up to it. I'm tellin' you, I never whistled in anybody's ear after that.

Sometimes accidents happened back at that time in the woods.

They'd get in a hurry. If they were cuttin' piece work, cuttin' by the cord or by the thousand, they'd tear right into it and they wouldn't pay attention to what they were doin'. And that's what happened, they'd get hurt bad. This man down here, he had his jaw broke, his shoulder was broken, and his ribs was caved in. He was actually smashed right up. It was just carelessness. A big hemlock jumped sideways. When it would strike the ground, it would bounce, the butt would come up and go sideways, especially when it went over that end of the stump. My brother and I was choppin' and not five minutes before that, I said, "He's goin' to get it this mornin'," because they were just tearin' right in to get so much on an average every day. Sure enough, that tree come down and hit him. Men that was workin' on wages, gettin' so much a day, they took their time as long as they done a day's work. Very few people got hurt. The odd person cut his foot or his finger or somethin' like that.

We had one chap drowned up here. They called it the High Falls on the Salmon River. I wasn't on the drive that spring. Nobody saw what happened, but they judged by what they found upriver where he was tending that he went out to break a jam. Part of the jam was still there. They figured he went out, the front end of it broke clear, and he got caught up into it. He had about a ninety-foot drop. The water carried him right downriver before he got where Frank Ritcey seen him below the falls.

The nearest time I ever was to death was from a cold in the lumber camp. It was pneumonia of the worst kind that I had. There was two other fellers in the camp that wasn't so bad. I thought I was in another world altogether for days. My brother was there in the camp workin' and he come in about every hour. When they was fifty yards from the camp they could hear me rattle, or breathin'. The cook and her husband would come and put a mustard jacket, a poultice, on your chest. Some of them were right close to the camp and they'd shove their head in the door to see if you were breathin' or not. I must've been layin' there ten days 'til I couldn't stand it any longer and I had to get out. I went back to work. I wasn't gettin' paid layin' in my bunk. I was right weak like an ol' dish rag. Stoop down to pick the saw up, you didn't know if you were goin' to keep goin' or not. Course there was men who passed away at the camp from colds. Bill Hartlen died in the woods; Roy Myers died in the woods camp from sickness. Go to the nearest undertaker and if he had a horse and a wagon, or ol' truck, they'd get into the camp to pick 'em up.

Jeddore men could load a [pulpwood] boat faster than any crew in the country. All done by hand. Picked out of the water, put in a sling, and take it up with a winch on the deck. It was spilled in the hole and stowed right in, right up onto the decks. There'd be about forty men and about three days at the most [to load a boat]. Each boat would carry on an average about twelve hundred cords.

Up in Merigomish, a big slingload of wood broke open and come down on top of Roy Jennings, but he lived. His jaw was broke and he had broken ribs. A cord of wood, ol' soggy wood that had been in the water all summer, was just like greased eels as soon as the bark let go. You had to watch and be ready to jump overboard. Oh yes, not the first time we had to jump overboard. Down in the hold, they had more of a chance. There was a sling tender up above; he signalled to them to get back. Well, there was nobody goin' to stand near that load comin' down.

There was one chap died up there at Salmon River. He laid down to get a drink of water and the next time they looked, he was still layin' there. They went over and he was stiff, stone dead. Course he'd been scalded bad years before and it was due to that.

The ol' chap that was runnin' the winch over here on the boats loadin' pulp waited 'til the men was on the deck. Milton was goin' down over the rail to go to the float—like a raft in the water where they loaded the pulpwood up in a sling. There was six men on that. Two men on each end pikin' it out of the water into the sling and a man on each end with a pike pole keepin' the sling into where the men could load it. I had just tied my end of the float to the rail and had just got down off the rail and the ol' feller turned 'er over. It was run by steam. An open exhaust, boilin' water runnin' from that winch that shot right out of about an inch and a half of pipe. The mouth of the exhaust was between me and him [Milton]. He got it and I didn't.

It was just like stickin' a pig when it struck. Right up his back it went. I caught him before he fell over the rail. Well, he was done up in healin' wax for weeks, months. Took all of the flesh off his back to the bone, right from the hips to the shoulder blades. Somebody sloushed cold water on him. They said that was the worst thing that could've been done: cold water on hot flesh, the shock. They took him ashore and let him walk home; he had to walk two miles. That's how well a man was looked after by that crew. It was the ol' *Tilley*, that was the name of the boat. It was upwards of two years altogether before he could do anything. I guess the company paid him some. The doctor told his mother that he could live ten days, ten months, or ten years. And it was exactly ten years to the day when he died.

Ralph Baker

Ralph Baker, 80, lives in West Jeddore, Halifax County. He comes from a seafaring family; his grandfather, James Baker, was a noted schooner captain. Ralph left school at fourteen to wheel sawdust at a mill in Middle Musquodoboit. "I was the only boy amongst the men there." He has lived a varied life from working the woods and loading pulpwood boats to working in construction, at a lobster factory, at the Halifax dockyards, apple picking, running a boarding house, and managing a general store and, most recently, tourist cabins in West Jeddore.

Lumbermen were looked at as a certain type of people. It reminds me of a story that I heard one time. A little girl was walking along with her mother and she saw these fellas. They were just coming out of the woods and they had on their mackinaws and heavy breeches.

"Who are those fellas?" she says.

"Oh, they're lumberjacks."

"Do they eat hay?"

"No, no," she says. "They're part human."

I was involved in loading pulpwood up West Jeddore. The *Liverpool Rover* used to come in. She wasn't a big ship. This was for the Mersey. The captain came from the next harbour, Ostrea Lake, which a lot of seafaring men came from. His name was Captain Ralph Williams. He had a brother who was captain of another ship, the *Markland*, that sailed up around Liverpool way.

It was an awful lot of hard work. We'd have to row from here up to the harbour, and then when you were done loading, row back at night. It must be five miles up to the head of that harbour. There'd be six or eight of us in the boat; it was a fair size, fifteen feet or something like that. We would meet along the shore. Then there'd be probably a couple go in their own boat further up or could be one man go in his boat, all according to how handy he was. We were rowing right from here up to Salmon River Bridge. It wasn't that far the boat laid off from Salmon River Bridge, no more than a couple hundred feet from the shore.

It was just the odd car was in here then. And more than that, who do you get to take you? Then after you got up there, you'd still have to get out from the main road to the ship in a boat. It was a hard row and if you had the tide rising with you when you were ready to come home, it really made it hard. If you had the tide falling, it would carry you along pretty near without rowing. We done that for a few summers; it didn't carry on for that long. There was nothin' in it much, just a matter to get a few dollars.

What you would do when that come aboard, you didn't pile it right up straight. You had what they called skinning the ship over; you put a tier across, keeping them all coming up the same level all over. They'd watch it, men that really knew down in there what to do, to come up so far. You couldn't keep doing that because you'd block yourself off. Then there was in underneath the decks that wood had to come up. The slingload couldn't get in underneath that; all the sling could do was come straight down within the centre of the hold. The wood had to be picked up then in your arms when you got up so far and carried back and block those places off, that old salt water and old dye in the wood and everything running out of our clothes. From underneath the decks you blocked out to the square of the hold. Then we used to scramble out on the deck because if you didn't we'd get hit with a stick or a load of pulp and that'd be the end of ya. They'd just give you time enough that you levelled that off right up full to the edge of the hatches.

Another contractor out of this harbour, we went aboard one of his boats and people were gettin' dissatisfied with twenty cents an hour and working so hard. We said, "The next time we go up, we're going to kick for more money." So we got up there and the hatches were lifted off, opened up ready to go aboard.

"You men can go down in the hold where you were the other time," he said.

"For that money?" we said.

"Yes, for that."

"We're not going to work for that."

"If you don't do it, somebody else will."

That's all there was to that. There was nothin' to go to work and strike and say I don't want to do it. There was no unions. All we got out of that, we rowed home and lost that two dollars. A terrible thing.

When I cut pulpwood on my land back here, they said, "You got to cut that pulpwood four foot four." I said, "Why the four foot four?" "Well, that'll allow for the bark." Four inches don't seem like much, but to every twelve cords it means another cord of wood. So I had a hundred cord of wood, I had roughly probably eight cord extra. If you're talkin' in terms of five thousand cords like Byron Mitchell was contracting, there'd be about four hundred cord extra. I understand when it went out of the hold of the ship up in Liverpool, it went out, even four feet. Now, I was told that. In the woods we were putting it up four feet four inches and when it went out up there, they took the scale at four foot.

There's somethin' on that one. I went down into Moshers River and I cut wood in sap peeling. The woods boss said, "You got to pile it four foot, six."

"Four foot, six?" I said. "Answer me this, will you please. Where I come from in the Jeddore area, I had to cut and pile it four foot four and I was told it was for the bark. What's this for?"

"For shrinkage," he said.

I said, "I heard it all!" Four foot six for shrinkage. That ended it.

Jack Anderson

Jack Anderson, 72, lives along the banks of the St. Mary's River at Sherbrooke, Guysborough County. A retired merchant, avid sportsman, and history buff, his family involvement in lumber dates back to the early years of this century.

My grandfather, C.W. Anderson, was in the logging business. He was owner, president, managing director—call him what you will— of Scotia Lumber Company. That was the big lumber outfit on this river at one time, in the twenties and thirties.

Right after the [First World] war, they were startin' to build sailing ships hand over fist. They had quite a fleet of their own. Eventually, he got a couple of Americans and another local person here and they formed this company. He built his own ships too. He didn't build them personally, but he had shipbuilders come in and they built the ships on the river here right by the mill. They didn't build them all, they bought some, but they built a bunch of 'em. They were good sized, all wooden schooners, threes and fours [masts]. A lot of these places, they'd just build one ship. It wouldn't be a shipyard per se. They'd bring in two or three people, usually a boss shipwright. The last ships he built would be around 1930, I imagine.

They eventually went from the lumber into laths and from the laths to pulpwood. They shipped a lot of pulpwood to the States; the odd bit went to Europe. The lumber takes you back to the days of the sailing ships. I was born in 1919 so I don't remember anything much before 1924, 1925, but we had lots of ships then. There's hardly anybody left in Sherbrooke that could actually tell you now. That was all long lumber then and practically all shipped to the States. That's when they were building Staten Island. Staten Island was apparently built at a crazy rate when they started and just went boom, boom, boom, boom; they built her up in a hurry. I seen shipload after shipload, just nothing but lath wood going out of here to Staten

Scotia Lumber Co. Plant
Sherbrooke
Nov 28 19

Island. The old system of building was you put up your frame and it used to be usually studded off in two-foot centres. Then that was all lathed with about half or three-eights inch space between each lath and then plaster that over.

There was another one here the same time known as the Canadian Lumber Company. One of the principal owners in it was the Dickie family from outside Truro somewhere.[1] They had a mill down in Sherbrooke here below where Scotia Lumber Company had theirs, about a half mile below. It was an older mill because Scotia Lumber Company had circular saws and this Dickie lumber company had the gang saws.

Sherbrooke, you're nine miles from the ocean and the crooked'st damn channel that you ever saw. When you leave Sherbrooke and go down to hit the ocean you're workin' three points of the compass out of four. It was quite a thing bringin' them old sailing ships up there, you know. You'd see them come in lots of times with a junk of green limb off a tree hanging on their main mast where she was dragging along the trees one place down the river at the narrows. I even saw one day, a feller came up there and he had her headed about halfway up and got her swung around too far in the wind. She turned on him and he sailed her up stern first. He had her all heading out when he got her up to the dock. Smaller ones, they'd come right up to the end of the street in Sherbrooke, but the big schooners we loaded, they came up to within about a mile where the village office is there. The

"My grandfather, C.W. Anderson, was in the logging business. He was owner, president, managing director–call him what you will–of Scotia Lumber Company. That was the big lumber outfit on this river at one time, in the twenties and thirties." (N.S. Museum)

Competition. The
Dickie Lumber mill on
the St. Mary's River.
(N.S. Museum)

worst problem in the river, the shallowest part, was goin' out to the
ocean just at the bar.

They never lost a man all the years they sailed them, but they had
an awful lot of close calls. I remember one ship went out of here with
a load for New York and didn't even get past the mouth of the Bay
of Fundy and she sunk. By God, every one of them got saved. On one
trip they got into a storm and Sam Pye, who lived next door to me,
washed over one side of the boat and the next sea washed him back
on board again. Somebody grabbed him as he was goin' across the
deck. Another time, he was up on the mainmast, right up on the top
riggin', in a big blow. They were tryin' to get the topsails off 'er and
he fell right off the very top. He came down and hit in the belly of the
sail and he just slid down right out on the deck on his feet like nothin'
ever happened. That's a long way up on those sailing ships.

I can't ever remember them shipping pulpwood by schooner. We
loaded pulp on the steel boats; they were motor. It was vastly
different from the days of wind and sail. Pulpwood was after the
Norwegian freighters come in here. Our buyer was principally
Bucksport, Maine. They'd ship all over the world too, but it went
principally there.[2]

There was another company, the Sonora Timber Company, that
was shipping some pulp out down at Sonora. This was at the last end
of it; they quit before we did. They came here, a bunch of Russian
aristocrats, that skinned out of Russia and got some money out at the
time of the Russian Revolution. I'd say there was seven or eight of
'em. I can remember, even tell you the names of a half a dozen of

them, and I was only a kid. They come in here, pooled all this money together, and formed this pulp company. They knew there was a great market for pulp at this time; they were smart enough for that as a means for making a pile of money. But the local people, I don't say all of them, but a lot of them, stole them blind. For example, a feller would go in the woods and cut a road full of pulpwood. They'd get the guy to go in and scale it for them and the guy would get paid. So then he'd go back and take the saw and he'd saw all the chalk marks off of the wood, pile the brush over on the other side, what was the backside of the pile, and get scaled again. And I have heard of even getting paid three times. They lasted a few years until they spent their money. They got involved in a few other little things too. One of them had a store in Guysborough and some more things.

This river here, in the spring after the ice went out, was full of woodsmen. I don't remember too much about the long logs. That was pretty near over when I started. I can remember as a small, small kid the log drive in the spring. My home was right by the bridge down in Sherbrooke. The log drives were always a great reason for all the kids gettin' out [of school]. Seeing these big logs coming down the river end over end in high water and there'd always be two or three fellers ridin' them too. I can remember three names in particular, fellers that were really supposed to be good on the logs. Len Rhodenizer, he was from up the shore a little ways and there were two other guys from up the West River here, Ike Demmons and Freeman Smith. Freeman Smith was a little bit of a man but, my God, they could handle those things. The logjams, blow the odd one, but most of them, some of these old fellers run so many darned log drives that they would just walk down the shore, have a look at a big jam and pick out two or three logs that would take it out of there. Other times, you'd have to pick every damn log off it.

A lot of the logs were cut in the camps, but a lot of them were also cut by the farmers up along the river. They'd all have their own land so in the wintertime they'd get a few logs out on the bank of the river or on a brook somewhere. Every farmer up along the river would cut some logs. You'd pay them at a certain time when the drive was going to come and they'd dump them in and away they'd come. It seems to me that the camps were more interested in the production of pulpwood rather than they were logs because you could get enough almost from the local farmers. Sometimes we'd cut here along the river just for lath wood. You'd try to get long stuff, cut it maybe twelve, fourteen, sixteen feet, and six, seven inches [in diameter]. A lot of the laths were cut from the slabs.

The St. Mary's River. "A lot of the logs were cut in the camps, but a lot of them were also cut by the farmers up along the river." (N.S. Museum)

I can remember [grandfather] telling me when they were driving pulpwood down West River, up on the cross brooks which is almost to the Pictou County line—it wasn't too big, around eighteen, twenty thousand cord—bringing it down the river and putting it up in the cove at Sherbrooke for ten cents a cord. Sonora Timber Company was too at the same time. And the other outfit from Truro was driving the river too. Used to create a little bit of a problem. My grandfather was one of these old codgers, you know, "I'm here first and to hell with you guys!" They'd fight continuously, mostly verbally.

If I remember correctly, the most we ever paid for a man in the woods cutting pulpwood was two dollars and fifty cents a cord. This was peeled and all piled and you had to have sound wood, no stained wood. Now, with power saws, they get twenty, twenty-two dollars for cutting it rough and just throwing it down. Ours had to cut roads for a horse and sleigh, a far cry.

Most of my work was done in the early thirties and things were tough. If we wanted men all you had to was send a truck down to Mahone Bay or somewhere down that way, put a sign on the truck "Men Wanted for the Pulp Woods" and, dear God, they'd come in droves. We'd go there because down that way you'd get good men. Excellent, excellent woodsmen. Never any problem, some of the best. A lot from down Lunenburg County come up here. We had whole families that would come. I can remember some of these fellows, sixteen years old, goin' in the woods in the spring up the river here ten or fifteen miles and stayin' right through, maybe come out for a couple of days at Christmastime. There were five guys in one family up there. Three or four of 'em stayed here, married and had families. They're all dead now.

I've seen we've had them in here, for example, a bunch come from Prince Edward Island. A rabbit cut more wood than they would, you know, all of 'em. They worked their asses off but just couldn't, didn't, have a clue. We could get pretty near enough fellers around locally anyway.

Part of the year, they'd put 'em in the woods cuttin' the stuff. Then when this boat would come in, maybe they'd have a couple of camps reasonably handy so at daylight they'd have a load of men, say fifty or sixty from each camp, down there to work these boats. They shipped a pile of pulpwood out of here. That was all manpower except for the winches. They had a real bunch of specialists there. They'd come here from all over the world tryin' to find out how they were loadin' pulpwood so fast.

We used to number our camps and we had something like thirty. This is not all operating at once. Guysborough, Antigonish, and Pictou counties; we also shipped out of Guysborough municipality; that's sixty, eighty miles from here. That would be shipped out of Country Harbour. These camps we had were practically all built of logs. They were mostly big buildings, sixty, seventy men in them; some were fairly small. Usually you'd have a covered walkway, no more than four or five feet, between the cookhouse and the bunkhouse.

To keep them clean was a job. Some of these guys would bring in a bunch of fleas or somethin' like that. A hot camp and forty, fifty, sixty men, it soon spread. There'd always be a few of the old cronies there and if they found a new bunch of guys come in and brought some little friends crawlin' over 'em, they'd clean up right quick. We tried to keep them [the camps] clean; mostly soap and water, a little creolin, Lysol, or somethin' like that. Slosh that around. That [burning sulphur] never worked; made a hell of a stink.

I often wonder how these cooks did it because we run camp after camp with fifty, sixty men and one cook and cookee. He did it all. There was no buyin' bread, cookies or cakes; you baked it all. I'm tellin' you, these cookee jobs were no picnic—washing dishes alone and peeling potatoes. We had two or three of the cooks that used to [make liquor]. It was a taboo thing. I remember one camp we had up Caledonia right beside the main road. Old grandfather was pretty sharp. "Jesus," he says, "you fellers better go up and find out what the hell they're doin' with all the raisins." We had a store in Sherbrooke too and when you delivered a grocery order they always got a couple cases of raisins. Well, there'd be a hundred and twenty-six pounds of raisins in a box. The old man spotted this. Two of us scalers went up and we started rooting around and, geez, we found five or six of these big old molasses puncheons boiling away with a bunch of brush over top of 'em, that much flies on the top.

In terms of drivin', we would drive from Trafalgar, that would be forty, forty-five miles up there; and the East River would be the Garden of Eden Lake—I guess that would be thirty, thirty-five miles. There'd be a lot of these other little brooks around. I know an old fellow lived next door to me down home there; if he was on a log drive, come Saturday night, thirty-five, forty miles, he'd think nothin' of walkin' home. Walk back up again Sunday. Some of these fellers come in, get up to these camps, and get one scale a month; they were pretty horny to get out of there. Get over to Antigonish or New Glasgow and get a bunch of that ol' Bright's Catawba wine; used to be green, gallon bottles. Gee, that was a big thing to get into that stuff after you'd have a payday. The fact that they're up the river thirty miles didn't mean anything. They'd go out the road and walk.

They never had enough money. A lot of them did well to average a cord a day. You had to pay for your own saw blades and they broke lots of them. And they'd have an account to buy tobacco and matches or whatever. So, Jesus, a lot of them at the end of the month, money would be pretty scarce. Scalers would usually deliver the pay around the camps. I've handled lots of envelopes at the end of the month with three or four dollars in it for a month's work.

Frank Burns

Frank Burns, 74, lives a short distance from Sherbrooke in Sonora, Guysborough County. While he never worked in the woods, his account of sailing aboard the pulpwood boats that frequented Sherbrooke in the 1930s lends a unique perspective to the overall story. A man of many talents— carpenter, bricklayer, lobster fisherman, tugboater, and dory builder—he spends his time today constructing large-scale ship models, some of which are on display at historic Sherbrooke Village.

Those vessels, the three-masters, didn't come after the 1930s, that was the last. I remember when they used to sail in here. When I was a young feller we used to run out to the edge of the shore and watch them sailing up the river. They took lumber from here over to the

States in the summer, and then the wintertime this place would be all froze up and they'd have a trip down south, maybe Barbados for a load of molasses. They used to sail down around the Turk Islands in the West Indies in the winter and bring up a load of salt. A lot of them comin' up around Cape Hatteras didn't survive it. I guess it was kind of a bad spot there. They didn't have no motors in them and when they struck a storm a lot of the times the sails blowed off of them and they went ashore. A lot of them vessels didn't live too long.

Around about 1936 or so, jobs were scarce. There was nothin' much to do on the land. At that time everybody thought if you got a job on the water that was goin' to be the comin' thing. I was seventeen years old. There was pulp boats in and there were other fellers that went from here on them and liked it good. That's how I happened to get a job onto it. I was kind of anxious to work as a mate to get the sea time in, so I stuck at that about four years.

They were around four thousand ton and three hundred feet. There was one I was on, she was pretty near five thousand ton, but that's only a little ship today. They were mostly Norwegian. I think they got the Norwegian ships cheaper. Another thing, Norwegian ships would go up in places where perhaps Canadians wouldn't send their ships. The Norwegians were good seamen. I know down in South America they'd go up them rivers and they'd be right on the sand. They'd keep chewin' away, running the motors and, by and by, they'd wash the sand away and you'd get up a little ahead. Course you'd get stuck again and wash away the sand—it was loose sand, just a matter of the propellor washing it away—and you'd get up to the dock.

The Norwegians were good fellers to work with. Most of them could speak pretty good English and after a while you'd learn a lot of their language. Accommodations were very clean; Scandinavian people are very clean. I was on one Canadian ship, but I found I'd sooner be on the Scandinavian ship. They didn't seem to have the system to the work like the Norwegians had. The Norwegians and the Canadians got along pretty good together.

The first ship I went on was the *Aristo*. I went as a cabin boy [at fifteen dollars a month]. There was another feller from home here went on as an ordinary seaman; he got twenty dollars a month. After a while the wages got higher. Then I went on the *Sierdel*; I was on that for six months. Then I went on the *Gudvin*, and the last one was the *Pollux*. My brother was on with me too; there was about six of us from here. They just had Norwegian officers on it, the mates and the captain and the engineers, and the rest was all Canadian fellers. My job was a sailor on deck and steering. They'd teach you to steer and like that.

They'd ship about forty thousand cords a year I think; that was one of the big years. They'd carry about twelve hundred cords here in a load, but if it was down at a place at deeper water they would carry maybe sixteen or eighteen hundred cords. We find on a new moon or a full moon the tides make higher and they could carry a little more wood then. On the dark of the moon, the tides don't rise as high and they'd have to put less wood aboard to get them out over a bar here across St. Mary's Bay. Lots of times they'd drag goin' out. There was kind of a little trick into it. The pilots would open them right out full speed, but just before they get to the bar they'd close the engines right off and then the ship would lift up a little and she'd slide over.

They'd have a big boom across just up here below Sherbrooke and that would hold all the wood. This place where they were loadin' at Anderson's had like two coves; a cove here and a cove here and right in the centre the ship would lay. They would bring the boom right around the ship. They could feed out of here when the tide was comin' down the river, and then when the tide would start to come in they'd get the wood from the lower cove comin' up. They always had wood there.

About eighty men loaded. Each slingload would be about half a cord and there'd be four of them slings goin' aboard all the time. A feller that was on the raft, if he was a real good strong feller like my cousin up here, they give him thirty cents an hour. Cyril Burns, oh, he had arms on him. My gracious, he was a big, strong, able feller. That's what they'd do; they'd pick out the good able fellers and put them on the raft. They knew the wood goin' aboard, the fellers down in the hold would have to work then. The fellers that worked in the hold got twenty-five cents.

There was a feller that used to carry water. I think he only got twenty cents an hour. He had quite a hard job. One feller carrying water for about eighty men, so every feller would just take a little sup. Them days, everybody chewed tobacco and if you didn't chew or smoke you'd be kind of standin' alone. Everybody drank out of the bucket. There was no mugs or cups or anything. And them fellers chewin' tobacco, there'd be a scum over the water. Still, nobody ever got sick, nobody ever went to a doctor then. Today, I imagine, if they were loadin' one of them ships, before dark there wouldn't be a feller left. Every feller would be up in the doctor's office. They would never stand that work. A hundred cords of wood goin' aboard every hour, that's a lot of wood.

It'd take around a day and a half, two days [to load a boat]. We'd take it over to Bucksport, Maine. They had a big pulpmill there that Scott Paper Company owned.[3] It'd take us about two days to unload. They had four cranes on the wharf and they unloaded it that way. Up here we had to run the winches because there was no unions, but over where there was a union the stevedores done that, so we got clear. It'd take about two days to go over in the summertime. Scott Paper would have her chartered for maybe five months and after that they'd get under new charter. In the winter we went to the West Indies and South America to haul bauxite and bring it this way. On the *Sierdel* in the winter we were into the sugar trade to haul sugar from Cuba up to Brooklyn, New York, and to Saint John, New Brunswick.

We used to go down to Guysborough and load wood. They put a deckload on, a huge load right up to the bridge. When the ship got outside and there was any sea on, the ship wouldn't move at all. We used to be glad sometimes to have a big load aboard of 'er. But if you struck a storm you were just as liable to lose the whole deckload. They run a cable, put it to the winch, and they'd heave it tight and that cable would hold it down. When they loaded the ship she was kind of canted in, but if the sea happened to get in underneath of it, once you get loosened up, away it would go. There was lots of storms. But when you was young like that, a feller never said anything too much, but after you get older you realize those storms wouldn't be too good.

"There was a feller that used to carry water. I think he only got twenty cents an hour. He had quite a hard job. One feller carrying water for about eighty men.... And them fellers chewin' tobacco, there'd be a scum over the water. Still, nobody ever got sick, nobody ever went to a doctor then."
(N.S. Museum)

Leonard Taylor

Leonard Taylor, 83, lives in Afton, Antigonish County. He first went to the woods at the age of five with his parents; his mother was a cook in the lumber camps and his father a teamster. When it comes to woods work, he has done it all.

Pulp didn't come in most areas of Guysborough and Antigonish counties until around the early 1930s. It was mostly mills and sawlogs until they started. At that time most of the mills they took in was steam mills and they would log a million feet. That was a fairly good-sized cut.

Some choppers knew what they were doin'; they were lumber-jacks. They'd pick up farmers to go in. Well, some had a knack of the woods and some would never have, like cuttin' and fallin'. Quite a knack in it, all right. Some people can build a camp [cross-pile trees] if they didn't know what they were doin'. But if you put your notch in and don't saw your corner off, you can put them back pretty well where you want them.

The story goes that this fellow went to look for a job and the boss asked him if he was a good faller. "Oh yes," he said. "I'm A-1 at that. Put them anywhere that I want them."

"Well, what would you do if there was a big fir leanin' one way and you want to put it the other way?"

"Oh, I'd fall another big tree into it and let them both go down."

"What if there wasn't any other tree?"

"It'd be a hell of a lumber woods," he said, "only one tree."

It's the same thing as sawyers. Some people would keep a mill in good shape, running good, and make good lumber. Some were pretty poor sawyers and didn't keep their mill up in shape.

I started when I was sixteen, sniggin' logs out of the woods in Lincolnville, Guysborough. The company was Hickey and Reed. We had three horses, so they hired my brother's team and I drove a snig

horse. We went there with the truck wagon and the sleds loaded on. It's a big heavy wagon and we had double sleds to transport the logs out of the woods. There was about forty-five men. The cookhouse and the bunkhouse was all one building, a partition between. We had big, heavy dark wool blankets and the toilet was a tree outside, as far as you wanted to go. Every man washed in the same basin and if you didn't get there before the bell rang for breakfast, you went without washing. In the winter when they brought the rations in with horses they threw the quarters of meat as handy the cookhouse as they could and the cook used to go out with an axe and cut frozen meat and bring it in.

The lumber woods in the wintertime was a good life, but in the summer it was terrible. Flies and all that sort of thing chased you back and forth. Go to snig and the horse would be switching his tail in your face. So much cleaner and everything in the winter. If you got a big snowstorm, there was twenty-five, thirty, forty men movin' around and everything was pushed down in short time. I worked up in Pictou County around 1938, '39 and there was seven or eight feet of snow. You couldn't load; there was too much snow. Used to have to shovel a road into the trees where they were cuttin' to get the horse in. It wasn't very profitable. But we don't get snowstorms like that now.

I done everything: horseshoeing, cooking, dynamiting, teaming, sniggin', chopping, building roads, everything that you could do. I

Portable sawmill, circa 1911. "Most of the mills they took in was steam mills and they would log a million feet. That was a fairly good-sized cut." (N.S. Museum)

learnt to blacksmith when I was in the forests in Sherbrooke with my cousin Lester McKean for about two and a half years. Wages wasn't that good. I only got four dollars a week and my board, so I stayed 'til I learned quite a bit about putting on shoes, shapin' 'em, and stuff like that.

Some camps had a portable forge and coal if a shoe on the sled bent, or a reeve. A bunk [iron bar] goes across the sled and sits on the runner. There's a cradle that they set in. The snye bills are two bolts that come up through holes in the runner and the bunks set in between them. They're about an inch or an inch and a quarter iron; it all depends on how heavy the sled would be. A reeve goes over the top of the bunk and bolts to the sled. If they bent you'd have to straighten them. If a runner broke, then it generally pulled things and you'd have to straighten the whole thing.

I had to fix everybody's sleds that broke. You'd have to do that at night. If a wooden runner broke, you'd have to put a runner in. You'd go in the woods and get a piece of birch and block it out with an axe. Birch are subject to have turns in it. Some people made them out of rock maple, and beech is pretty good too. About four hours time we drilled the holes and got it together. You wouldn't have to do it all by yourself, you'd have help. The steel shoe [on the runner] would practically never break unless you had runner chains on. If you were going down a steep hill you'd put a runner chain on; that would help hold your load back.

I got caught one time with a team comin' down a hill and I had four runner chains on. I had a big load on. They let go and my team come down the hill. Boys, I went flying too. At the end of the road there was a pile of logs that high [five feet] and they were all froze. It was just as solid as a brick wall. My two horses went up over that, my sleds struck square on, and I went over. My horses went end over end and I went airborne, horses and everything, into the swamp. The only thing I broke was the pole out of the sleds; never hurt the horses a bit.

I've hauled on hills that you'd have to make another road to get your sleds back, it'd be so hard to haul up [because] of the manure.* It was very good, but the trouble was, if you had heavy sleds and the hill was very steep, it was like haulin' on a bare road. Now over here on Glen Road where they had the pulpmill there, they used all ice roads. They had a tank on sleds and filled the tank full of water and when it was cold, it was just the same as sprayin' the road for dust. They had a very good place to make them. If you have a good level ground, an ice road is pretty good. If you get hilly country, an ice road is a pretty hard thing to make. If you're goin' down any kind of a hill,

* It was common practice to spread manure to slow sleds on hills.

it's not too hot. Places I've hauled, we had to put a rope around a tree and fasten it to your sleds and two men would hold the rope and let you down that way.

In the summertime when there isn't any sleddin' they generally had drags made to pull the logs into the mill. They'd have birch runners put together the same as you would a sled, but no iron shoes on them. They'd slip along over the roots. Some places they had just one [sled] and they tail-dragged. They'd pile logs up pretty high into the horse and just let the small ends drag. If the runner wore out, you'd just take your brace and bit, bore holes, put wooden pegs and another runner on top of it, the same as puttin' a patch on a tire. A lot of times, if the mill was handy and they had a piece of hardwood that would be three inches thick, you'd take that, taper it at the end and it'd be all ready. You wouldn't have to chip it out or anything. The first one you'd make [the original runner] would be almost eight inches thick so it would last. If you put it on good and thick it might last you all summer.

They didn't river drive in this area, but they did over in Sherbrooke. The drive we were on come down to Aspen Lake, then went to the St. Mary's River and down to Sherbrooke. That was in 1929, I think. I remember the woods boss was Wash Harnish from Lunenburg. The first time I went we had catamarans [two or three logs fastened together] on the lake and we'd have to get rocks from the shore and sink these floating islands before we started. It's like moss and sage that comes up [from the lake bottom] and they'd be above the water. Instead of them logs catching and not moving down the brook when you open the dam, they'd sink them. There'd be quite a few and we'd do that periodically when they got in the way.

I used to do road work: drill and blow rocks on the highway. When I went in there they wanted a dynamite man and I had the experience. It was an easier job than driving them; you didn't get wet every morning to the neck. You can't river drive without getting wet. The brook hadn't been prepared for startin' the drive. We cleaned it and blew it before; we were about three weeks on that. But when they opened the dams they'd always create another problem; you had a river then. If it washed out under a big tree on the corner, the water would be running under there and naturally would take the log under. The end of the log would hold up on a root and then the other part of the log would swing around with the pressure of the water. That would make a dam to stop the rest of them and the more that come down, the further up the river they'd back up. It would take a lot of work and manpower to get that cleared out. You could blow it or the men come down and they'd take their peaveys, break it, and let it go.

I'd strap my dynamite to a long pole about thirteen or fourteen feet long—generally used haywire—and put my fuse up the pole. I'd shove the dynamite as far as I could get under the water, then light the fuse and strike for the woods before it went off. You'd see trees going up in the air. Course dynamite under water, there's a lot of pressure because it's airtight. Anything like dynamite has to be airtight before you get any power to it. In the ground, you pack the hole with mud so instead of the blast coming up, it'll go down and do a lot of blowing. It'll just puff up the other way.

Mostly all dynamite caps were the same size, about an inch and a half, two inches long. It's called a fifty-pound cap. You make a hole with a sharp stick—the cap is very soft—and you shove the fuse down into the cap, like into a shotgun shell after it's fired, and then you crimp the cap together. That would hold the fuse from pulling out. You open the dynamite at the top of the stick. If your cap was two inches long you generally bury it that deep, then bring your flaps around your fuse and soap around that. The fuse is waterproof. The only thing you wanted was to keep the water from going into the dynamite. You could use grease to make it waterproof. I used to have Sunlight soap; cut that up and have it soft, put it around, and keep your cap dry.

Your fuse was white and you could coil it up same as a small piece of rope. It was only about as big around as a pencil. Whatever length you wanted, you just cut off your coil. If your fuse was eight feet long, you'd consider, well, I can get far enough away before it goes off. It'd be ten minutes anyway; you could go a quarter of a mile. At the end of your fuse you'd cut it with a knife, there's powder in it, and light it with a match.

You wouldn't use less than three sticks at any time. You'd use your own judgment. If it was a bad corner and you wanted to get it out of there, you put eight or ten sticks around the pole. If you put enough dynamite to throw the logs in the air, you'd break too many. If you got it in good behind you wouldn't break too many logs. When that charge went off, it would generally let them go without breaking too many. You break more logs takin' it out with peaveys, the pressure would break a lot of them in two.

I was in one camp, that was Anderson's pulp camp from Sherbrooke. I had my double team in there. There was lice and bedbugs and they also had the itch. I seen lice as big as grasshoppers. I remember I come home and I bought myself clean underwear. I went back and the next week, boy, they were just matted with bed lice, great big brown lice. Take a bath and burn your clothes in order to get rid of them. No way to get rid of them [in the camp], have to put up with 'em or try to put something in the bed—sprinkle sulfur in the bedclothes to keep 'em away from ya. There's one thing. If you get enough of the smell of horse on ya, you can pretty well get clear of the lice. A horse has quite a heavy smell they don't like, I guess. Put your clothes over the horse's back and put the rug on 'em. I had a big horse; he used to lay down and I used to lay on his back. No time, you're clear of the lice all right, but you got a great horse smell on you.

I pretty near set a camp on fire one time in the woods above East River. The bunks and everything was peeled [poles] when they built them. The heat opened the cracks and the bedbugs was in there. You could look up in these cracks and the bedbugs was just piled in the poles that held the bunks up so I threw a little kerosene on them and lit it afire. I pretty near got the bounce for that. I got it out though.

They should never've had pulpmills in Nova Scotia. I don't believe in clear cutting. It's the worst thing that ever happened. I don't know what's goin' to happen in Nova Scotia. They're raping it. The forests that are growing now that these people are planting, they're like a miniature compared to what it was back in the 1930s. From the start, we had mixed timber like spruce and pine and hardwood. When you had a base ground, that would be thick with leaves and things. But today, if they're going to plant spruce, they're not going to have any base unless they fertilize. The few needles that drop off a spruce are not goin' to make the bed you have in a mixed forest. Never, never be the same.

I got three hundred acres up here, mixed timber, and I've got some beautiful stuff. I wouldn't take one of them great wheelers in and make ruts that if you went to walk, you fall down and never get out of 'em. That's something, I can't understand it, ruination. To drive through and see all these artificial forests growing up; later on, it's not goin' to be today but days to come. With these mills operating they say, "Oh, we're puttin' twice as much back as we're takin' out. We're doin' this and we're doin' that." But they're not puttin' the beautiful forests in that we had before we started and they never will.... If man has anything to do with it, it doesn't grow right.

John A. Nicholson

John A. Nicholson, 95, lives on Gairloch Mountain near West Middle River, Victoria County. As a child he would cut three or four pit props for local merchants in exchange for candy. During the First World War he served in the U.S. Navy aboard a sub chaser. A fourth generation mill sawyer, he still works around his shop at home.

When I went to school, I remember log drives in the spring. They came from the upper settlement, the headwaters of Middle River, all the ways down to Nyanza. They were tough, tough people. I worked one day; I'd be fourteen. I was put out to keep logs from the boom in the lake. The lake was frozen over and I had to break the ice away from the logs to get them moving. I was out on one of the logs and it rolled, I guess, and I fell off it. I went under and came up between two logs. A bunch of Frenchmen were laughing at me for falling off the log. I crawled ashore and I never went back. That was my experience.

It was a hard life. I left home at sixteen and went to Massachusetts. I spent eight years [in the United States]. I first worked in a wood-work factory making looms, spinning frames, and textile cotton mill machinery. I was always hungry; I couldn't earn enough to feed myself. I was taken up with watchin' the workers in lunchrooms and how easy it was for them to fill up and get along so I finally worked around until I got a job in a lunchroom. I wasn't there long when I joined the navy. They asked me what was the last job I held and I said lunchroom. Automatically, I was put to cookin' and I wasn't pre-pared for it. I think I was nineteen months overseas. I came home, down to Cape Breton in 1920, and I'm still here.

There was a sawmill over here about a hundred yards from this door, a water mill. It was built in 1899 by Jim MacLeod, an old settler. First he built the dam and dug a trench fourteen hundred feet in the side of the hill bringing the water down. And there was about a thousand feet of race they call it—sluice, same thing—made of

"First he built the dam and dug a trench fourteen hundred feet in the side of the hill bringing the water down. And there was about a thousand feet of race they call it—sluice, same thing—made of boards supported on trusses to take the water from where it come in here down to the water wheel." Pictured is a sluice of similar construction in use at Gully Brook near Bridgewater, circa 1892. (N.S. Museum)

boards supported on trusses to take the water from where it come in here down to the water wheel.

I finally got workin' there and I wasn't there longer than a couple of months and I bought it. When I run this water mill I built this house in 1926 and I sawed every single stick that went in it. I had a shingle and board mill. The shingle mill was upstairs and the sawmill was downstairs. It was a beautiful workin' outfit. A circular saw, forty-two inches. Used to get some big logs. They were drawn from a radius perhaps of some three or four miles by teams. Just two men. He [the helper] took away the slabs and piled the lumber. First, in MacLeod's mill, it was all put on a little trolley and pushed out to the end of the mill. The slabs were thrown over and piled back. They didn't last long: disappeared for firewood.

I took a third of whatever there was. If there was three hundred feet, I took one hundred. Course there was a cash payment too, perhaps five dollars a thousand at the best part of it. It was just a bare living, but I had lots of fun, I enjoyed it. I suppose seven or eight hundred feet would be a good day. It wasn't fast but it was cheap. The world wasn't movin' very fast at that time. John P. MacLeod & Sons were merchants in Baddeck and they would take all the lumber. Eight dollars a thousand, I think, was about the limit we got there.

I operated that mill for nineteen years and then I went into a portable mill for ten or fifteen years. I had to give that up because it was infringing on my health—heavy lifting and heavy work. So I went into windows and doors on the west side down about three miles from here. A shop with a planer, saws, drills, a morticing machine, and band saw. I worked at that for twenty-five years. I wasn't making too much money. I made a lot of foolishness, windows and doors mostly.

My portable mill I bought brand new. It was a rotary, an edger, and a trimmer, a machine to take the slabs away, and a chain to take the sawdust away. You got rid of two men there. The first diesel I got I paid six hundred, and the second one I think it was thirteen hundred; it was a bigger one. I was burnt out one year, lost everything. A mysterious fire. I always thought it was set, but I couldn't prove it.

I guess I shifted it twenty-five or thirty times from one place to another—Big Baddeck, Bucklaw, Middle River, Hunters Mountain. The most I ever had was nine men; that's not a big camp. They'd have to have at least a hundred thousand before I'd bother settin' up.

There was years in Middle River when there was five and six mills. I suppose my great grandfather, Donald Nicholson, had the first mill, a water mill, in the settlement. He came from the old country off the Isle of Skye. He likely built it and my grandfather, Sam Nicholson, and his brothers run the mill. I don't think my father ever worked there. I'm not too sure what kind of a saw it was, but I imagine it would be an up and down, just like a whipsaw. In them years, they wouldn't bother with a log that I'd saw. Their log would have to be perhaps two feet.

The first whipsawin' I seen done, the platform was in two trees, perhaps three or four trees. It was built high off the ground. You lifted the wood up there and there was a man above and below. You could easily stand under it. It [the saw] would have to be nine or ten feet. They were much heavier than a crosscut saw. It wasn't hard to operate. It had two handles. The one below didn't have to be an expert, could be anybody. The man above, he'd lift it up. You'd have to follow a chalk line and you didn't go off that, not an eighth of an inch. You'd hew two slides of them to begin with. In those days, a hewer could be just as good as a sawyer. Father was good at it. He worked on a vessel at the Grand Narrows building it. He was a good adze man, which was very important at shipbuilding.

You're setting at a table my father made that was turned out of the ground and whipsawed. That was in the twenties. It was a big birch, likely a windfall that was buried. We were breakin' new ground and turned this log out. He took it and hewed two sides, then I sawed it with him with a whipsaw, the bottom of it. I was below and he was above. We made the six by six and the two-inch plank. When he built his shop, he built it so that he could take the wood in upstairs, open a hatch, and saw from upstairs–downstairs.

My father made his living at carpentry, a wheelwright, a carriage maker, and a builder. A farmer would give him the job of makin' him a sleigh. He might furnish some of the stuff himself and he might not; mostly hardwood—birch and maple. I whipsawed runners with him. He'd hew two sides, perhaps three, and then whipsaw. The curve in the runner would have to grow that way. He had a big turning lathe [operated by a foot pedal] for turning hubs for a wheel. That was a big job. Mostly birch for that; I don't think they ever used maple; oak if you got it, but there's very little oak in this country.

He went to serve his apprenticeship when he was sixteen with a carpenter. He worked seven years, the first three years for nothing and the next four years he got twenty-five cents a day or something like that. After seven years he got his carpenter papers, but that's what you had to do them years.

Duncan John MacAskill

Oxford Paper Company from Maine operated in Cape Breton from 1919 to 1931, having negotiated an extensive crown land deal with the province known as the Big Lease.[1] All told, they controlled over five hundred thousand acres in Victoria and Inverness counties. During their thirteen-year tenure, Oxford Paper Company cut nearly 325,000 cords of spruce and fir pulpwood for export. They employed 885 men in their camps and 136 at a debarking mill. Following their departure, much of the Big Lease holdings were expropriated for Cape Breton Highlands National Park. The remainder was cut over the years by Mariana Timber Company, Bowater Mersey, and Stora Forest Industries.

Duncan John MacAskill, 73, lived at Timber Brook, Victoria County, for forty years and cut pulpwood for Mariana Timber Company and Bowater Mersey. He was too young at the time to have worked for Oxford Paper Company but remembers it well. Oxford was a godsend for many as the plaster quarries at St. Ann's closed in 1918, throwing hundreds out of work.

They were the biggest company ever here in Cape Breton. All in the Highlands, they had dozens of camps out there. They were drivin' the wood down North River right through to Murray. They generally built the camps near a stream—the East Branch, the North Branch, and the Middle Branch. Camp Thirty-one was the last one; it was right on Timber Lake. That was close to the North River. It was only a very few feet between the lake and the road, but they put a dam in to back the water up the lake to drive the wood down through Timber Brook.

I remember I was livin' on the meadow side of the river then, what they call the Meadows Road in Oregon. You could hear the racket comin', the roar when they'd open the dams, five or ten minutes before you'd see any wood. They used to have trouble at MacLean's Pool. There was no bank on the river and the wood was goin' into the woods. They'd have men there throwin' it back into the river. They had to build breakwaters. There was one above MacLean's Pool, one below, and one near the North River Bridge on the main river. The Bishop Company had the job of building those. They were great big logs and were filled up with rocks; some of them would weigh half a ton. There were big drift bolts in those logs. You can still pick them up in Oregon if you ever go out to MacLean's at the old crib work. There was another place below the North River Bridge in Morrison. The wood used to go in there too and a bunch of men would be there for weeks throwin' it back out in the stream.

There was a boom across in Murray. The wood was all stoppin' there at the mouth of the North River. I believe it was cedar planks and it was bolted through. You can see some of the pieces in Murray yet. The old blocks are still there. It was big enough you could walk it from one side of the river to the other. I walked it dozens of times. The God damn thing must've been three feet wide. It was made in twelve- or fourteen-foot lengths and there was chains holdin' them together so they'd be able to open them to let the wood through when they'd be ready for it.

They had the pulpmill in Murray, across from St. Ann's. There was an endless chain and an old fella there with a pickaroon. It was put on the chain and it'd go in through to the tumbler that was taking the bark off. It was goin' out on a conveyor way the hell out, from here to that house up on the hill there, and dumping in the water in a boom. They were cuttin' it in half then, makin' it two-foot wood.* They left it until a ship would come in and then they'd load. It went everywheres. These were great big ships, three or four thousand cords.

I remember the time after the drive was over, they had sixty-five thousand cords in this boom I was talkin' about. It broke and I forget

* Pulpwood was cut there in two-foot lengths until 1929, and in four-foot lengths thereafter.

now how many cords they lost, but they lost a lot of it. It was full, stone packed, right from this boom up to North River Bridge. There was so much weight on it they couldn't stop it. They claim there was some picked up in Newfoundland.

It's not that wide, but it's a rough, rough river. Once you come down below Oregon, below Matterson Pool, it's really rough until you come way down to the Little Falls. It's all rock there about fifty feet high on both sides, just like a tunnel comin' through. You'll see some of the old pulp logs still jammed in the rocks tight, up what they call the Twin Falls. I guess they'll be there 'til they rot and fall out.

They'd send the men out with pike poles. One fellow up North River on the Meadow went out on a jam and he just moved one block. He didn't realize it was goin' so quick, one block, and away she went. He drowned; Dan Montgomery from the Meadow. That's the only one that I can recall.

My father, Malcolm MacAskill, and my brother used to work out there. That's a long time ago; I was only a young fella then. They used to work the mill in the summertime, and all fall and winter they'd be out in the camps way the hell back in the Highlands. Most of the crews out there were from Victoria and Inverness counties. They were walkin' it from Inverness. I remember my father comin' home on weekends from back there; come home Saturday evening after work, back Sunday afternoon. Must have been sixteen, eighteen miles. They were there the year round. It was in the summertime they were cuttin' most of the pulp, then when the snow come they'd haul to the streams with horses and pile it. Come April, they'd throw it in the streams, and if there wasn't enough water to take it, they'd open a dam. There was a lot of men there.

My father was with the Oxford all the time they were there. Them old fellas had it tough. G.S. Harvey from Baddeck was the manager. I heard old Harv say lots of times that my father was the toughest man he ever saw goin' out there. He was as skinny as a rail. That's the reason he was so tough, there was no flesh on him. He was generally choppin', then to get a reprieve he'd go to this camp in Oregon to get it set up for the men on the drive. He'd have to put the straw in the bunks and the cook was makin' ready for them. They'd be there for a week settin' up. I remember the cook's name was John Joe Gillis.

One building all made out of sawed lumber. It was big. There was three floors, hold a couple hundred men upstairs sleeping. The cooking was done down below on the first floor. It was a big project to get all that wood through to Murray. I was there lots of times with my father. We were just goin' along to see what we could get to eat. The cook used to give us a fist full of them big raisins they used to have, great big black buggers.

After the drive was all done the camp was closed. When they come into Murray there was a big boarding house there for them. There was three floors in that place. They'd start loadin' the pulp onto ships. It would generally take two or three weeks. Some of them would go back; whatever they needed they'd keep. A lot of people who come to North River headin' for the lumber woods, they'd stay in Murray for a couple of nights there [at the boarding house] before they ever go out there.

Camp Nine was the main depot. That's where all the supplies were goin' and they were distributing from there to the different camps. The camps were big because you got an awful bunch of men in there, a hundred or a hundred and fifty, but generally they had one big enough to hold them. The walls were made of logs on end and chinked with moss. The roof you lumbered to put the tar paper on. They had the cookhouse separate and a barn for the horses.

I remember those teams, we used to watch them goin' out. There'd be six or eight horses to a team draggin' twenty-two-foot blue sleighs. They'd have three, four, maybe five of them, one attached to the other loaded with supplies. You'd leave Murray in the morning and be at Camp Nine at dusk and that's only halfway. Then they got a big truck with solid rubber tires on it, but that would only go as far as the top of the mountain, not anywheres near it, because the road wouldn't stand it. There were corduroys in areas there it would go right through. It would hold the horses, but it wouldn't hold the truck. They had a warehouse on top of the mountain to store them [supplies] when the truck would go up if there was nobody around to take them.

I guess, where the Oxford worked, the flies were wicked. Some of the men workin' there used to go out and get a bunch of fern or somethin', take the lids off the stove, and stuff this in to make smoke to clean the camp out. They got hundreds of stuff on the market now, but that time there wasn't such a thing. They used to mix lard and pine tar, that was the best. We used that lots of times workin' in the woods home. That would stick with you all day; they wouldn't come near you, but it was always dirty stuff. The lard, you're right greasy and black. You'd have to get hot water and get it off in the evening. There was no such thing as jumpin' in a shower or bathtub. You had to go in a big wooden tub; wasn't such things as galvanized tubs.

They were cutting' big puncheons in half. That was at home. There was nothin' like that in the camps.

There was a lot of good stories about them old people in those camps. The camps I was in had little mattresses, poly-asses they called them. The manager went out. Seavers was his name, and he looked around the bunkhouse. He told us, "I'm bringin' out a bunch of poly-asses." Well, nobody knew what the hell he was talkin' about. There was a MacEachern there and an old Morrison from Tarbot. That Philip MacEachern said, "I don't know the hell what he's talkin' about." "I believe," Morrison said, "he's goin' to bring out a bunch of whores."

The Oxford had the best of the wood out there, but they were damn cheap. Anybody on them drives in April, the water cold and ice in it likely, a dollar a day and soakin' wet to your behind all the time. And the teamsters, a dollar a day. It was grim. They were gettin' the pulp for little or nothin'. The best I ever heard of two fellers cuttin' and pilin' out there in one day: my Uncle Johnnie MacDonald and his nephew, John Huey MacDonald, fourteen cords. Of course they were just sawin' it on what they called a landing; it was hauled into them and they were sawin' and pilin' it in four-foot lengths. That was a lot of work.

There was a lot of logs too 'cause there were several sawmills around. They were just as damn cheap. You wouldn't get nothing. You'd get about ten dollars a thousand for the best of pine roadside. G.S. Harvey used to buy it but, Jesus, he'd take about fifty logs to make a thousand feet of lumber. He was gettin' twice that out of it. And the spruce logs, red spruce or fir, eight dollars, sometimes six. Oh, yes, I know, we've done it. We had to in order to live; either that or starve. Since then you get the government scale; you'd scale your own logs and figure it out and know exactly how much you get. Once this started, they all quit buyin', they didn't want to pay it. We had three hundred beautiful pine logs in the old farm in Oregon. That ol' Harvey took them for ten dollars a thousand, and fifty to a thousand. I wouldn't sell to the old bastard because I knew better what he was tryin' to pull off, but my father did. Seven or eight of them logs would make a thousand feet of lumber, sure they would.

In the thirties, everything went flat in the Depression time. Cutting wood on our own properties, that's the only livelihood we had. And damn little for it. We'd get four dollars a cord roadside. You'd get sixty cents a dozen for pit props. You couldn't make a livin' at that. We used to haul hardwood from the mountain down to the road, cut it up in stove lengths, split and pile it all along the road: four bucks a cord. There was no chain saws then either, it was all crosscut saws. But you had to do it in order to live.

Walter MacDougall

Walter MacDougall, 78, lives in McKinnons Harbour, Victoria County. He chopped and drove team, then worked for a number of years at Chappell's mill and factory in Sydney making tongue and groove. Following World War Two, he spent thirty years at the steel plant in Sydney.

That's all every young person was doin' at that time was workin' in the woods when you got big enough to handle an axe, a saw, and a horse. I suppose eight or nine years old, somethin' like that. That young? That wasn't young at that time. You wouldn't be able to do much at seven or eight, but ten, eleven, and twelve you'd be workin' there. My father, Jim Alex, was cutting pit timber and we'd be helpin' him.

The biggest thing was pit timber in the early days. Then the pulp took over. I can remember back as far as 1920 and at that time pit timber was goin' out of here on vessels hand over fist for the coal mines down below. Sydney is where all the steel was made and of course the mines were down there.[2] They used to come up Washabuck River and take it on the vessels.

There were three merchants buyin' them. There was a fella in Washabuck had a store, John Dan MacRitchie, and a fella at Nyanza, Murdoch MacRae; he's dead now, but the old store is still over there. The other merchant was John MacNeil down at Washabuck Centre. They'd take orders and you'd fill them. You'd have all winter cutting and in the spring of the year there'd be three or four or five vessels come in, one right after the other, cleaning 'er up. And they'd be comin' every once in a while all summer whenever you'd have a load. That's what the people were makin' their livin' on. You wouldn't see no money; all you were getting was groceries.

A pit prop had to be six, seven, eight, eight and a half, nine feet long, and they were supposed to be five inches on the small end. Props could be fir, spruce, or anything at all, it didn't make any difference. Along with that, there were booms. They had to be all black or red spruce. A boom is a size or two bigger, perhaps fourteen or sixteen feet long. They generally twixed them out with a horse and traces. There was the odd man around here that would put them on

Two unidentified youths with tools of the trade. "That's all every young person was doin' at that time was workin' in the woods when you got big enough to handle an axe, a saw and a horse." (N.S. Museum)

his shoulder and carry them out. You were cutting them on your own property, then you'd haul them out and they'd be put on a vessel. Once they went over the rail of the vessel you were clear of them. The captain and his men would have to look after them after that.

There was ties, a sort of railway tie, that would be used in the mine, I think. They'd be four or five feet long. Just hew two sides down. I cut and hewed them. You'd hew a hundred of them and get fourteen dollars for them. That was the best pay out of the whole bunch. They were better than props and most of the people would try and get them if they could. They were supposed to be all spruce. If you cut in the summertime, you could cut fir, peel the bark off, ship them to Sydney, and you'd never hear a word about them. Now that tells you what was down below there when they couldn't tell a piece of spruce from fir unless it had the bark. As young as we were, we knew.

They had some kind of strike at the mines down there around 1924. It lasted a long time, but in the meantime there was contracts for pulp. When the pulp come in you would get cash for it if you waited long enough for it. There was no such thing as a scale like you do now, and when he's done, write the cheque out. Perhaps you'd wait for months and months 'til they'd send the money down. Mersey Paper Company was a good company. The way you used to ship pulp up to them was in [rail] carloads.[3] I sold pulp to them myself. A car would take about fifteen cords. Pile it in, ship it up, and they'd send you the cheque. They seemed to be a good honest company. There was another company, the Oxford, that was down north. They cut clear through to Margaree. They were down there for years.

The only pulp company that was around here at that time [1920s] was the Atlantic Pulp Company. Their headquarters was up in Annapolis Royal and their head office was over in Nyanza. They could get it for what they wanted, and the people were so poor they had to take it if you wanted to get a cent at all. They were out here on Highland Hill. They cut all the wood and drove it down the Washabuck River, loaded pulp boats, and shipped overseas. The Depression was just comin' on the time they were done.

The Depression times, there was wages for nobody. Pit timber wasn't goin' because the mines wasn't working. You were too young, you didn't go through them, and a hell of a lot more besides you didn't. I'll tell you what eased it up a little bit was that Angus L. Macdonald went in and he paid the old age pension: six, eight, twelve dollars, the highest was twenty. If you didn't have a single solitary thing, not a mat on the floor or a floor to put a mat on, you'd get the twenty. Helped out a bit? Oh, they were all rich then, everybody was gettin' into the money that was old. You had to be seventy years of age to get it. The Depression started to work away in 1936, '37, and it wasn't too bad. At least you could get work in a sawmill. Mills had started up [again] in the middle of the thirties. The Depression never really got over until the war started. As soon as the war started, you could work any place then you wanted to.

In the older times when the steel plant started first, they leased different pieces of land where there was good lumber. Then they hired fellas with sawmills to lumber the piece. The big deals and everything was all going to the mines or into the steel plant. A "truck" was hardwood and is probably three or four feet long and sawed about six by six. They went to the mine for blocking up. Anything at all as long as they weren't popple. Down at Gillis Point, they'd load it in boxcars and ship into Sydney. They'd be workin' all summer over at Nyanza and Baddeck, shipping it in vessels. There were two or three factories in [Sydney] buying a lot of it. They used to ship some of it overseas. When the Depression was over, then they had trucks and they'd take it to Iona and load boxcars and ship it off to Sydney. There were four men over there regular loadin' lumber all the time.

I spent different winters in the lumber camps out from Sydney.

They'd be about nine miles out on the Morrison Road. A car could get to them. There was a man there from New Brunswick, Ford Duffy, that had the mill. That was about 1936. He also sawed this cut down on Gillis Point. Everything was hauled into a big field, logs upon logs upon logs. There'd be a frog pond, they used to call it, at the end of the mill. It'd be about the width of this room, eighteen feet. It was built with two by fours, one on top of the other and caulked. They used to put hot water from the boiler in there to take the ice and mud off of the logs, what they could get of it, before they could saw them. They'd be draggin' the logs through the mud and there'd be so much on them, a saw wouldn't last no time. In the fall of the year, they'd freeze up—ice on top of them—and they'd put them in there and get kind of a half-decent washing.

When I was working down Sydney, he never had no frog pond. The ground was different, hard and dry, but down here at Gillis Point it was all mud. You'd walk through it and be mud up to your knees. Trucks were hauling all day long from 1936 up to the time the war started in 1939, [then] they couldn't get men, they went in the army. They'd saw it and take it away to the mines generally in Sydney or Glace Bay.

Anybody that ever worked in the woods, all the old people, you asked them, how many winters did you spend in the woods? The answer was supposed to be fourteen winters. I don't know why. You'd ask a feller, could he chop with the axe over both shoulders? Perhaps if you were choppin', you'd put the axe over one shoulder, but when you're workin' in the woods, you won't be there very long when you can put it over the further shoulder just as good as you can the shoulder that's automatic.

You went to the woods with the idea you cut a thousand for each chopper and a thousand for the yarder. That's what they say the lumbermen used to look for. You'd see what the rest would be doin', and we were as good as the rest when it came to cuttin'. Chain saws didn't come until after the war. There wasn't even a dozer until after the war. Ford Duffy had a tractor but not a dozer, treads but no blade on the front of it. He only had one, workin' with horses, and he bought it in the winter of '38, I suppose.

You were all right workin' in the woods if ya were workin' with a good man. That's all you needed, a good honest owner. That's what Ford Duffy was, the very best. Mostly anytime at all, you could go in the cook room and have a bite. Your place was at the table and you'd take your cup and get tea at ten o'clock if you wanted to. The cook left and a new cook came in his place. After he was there about a month, he figured he was goin' to put a stop to this. It was goin' to be three meals a day.

They were puttin' out some lumber at the mill and I come in with a load. I went down to see what they were goin' to do with the cook. One fella went up and told the foreman. He says, "No lunch today. The cook give us orders not to have anymore." "Yeah?" He waited about two minutes. "Now boys, we'll all go down and see what the cook got." So he went in and there was a great big bowl of doughnuts there. "What are these for? To eat or hang on the wall?" He walked over to the table, got hold of some mug—he didn't have a place—and filled 'er up with tea. Everybody went and got theirs, two or three doughnuts apiece, and out they went. We never heard anymore about it. Lots of foremen wouldn't do that; they'd go along with the cook, I suppose, to save something. I always figured a feller couldn't work on an empty stomach. The cook was a damn good cook. I think there was somebody in the day before and spilt tea or something on the floor. Instead of findin' out who, he was takin' it out on all hands. There's always somebody will spoil anything if they get a chance.

I was there another time and I saw a truck comin' in from town and he had a bunch of mackerel on. It was just there that day. The next day the trucks were goin' to Sydney and the cook come out. "Get that barrel out of here. Take it the hell back; don't want any of that stuff out here!"

"How you goin' to get it up on top of the wood?"

"Well, if you can't get it up, there's lots of men around here will put it up for you."

It was supposed to make you lousy. Did you ever hear that? Yes, sir, bye! Salt mackeral, if you eat any amount of it. No, it wasn't an old wive's tale. When the barrel of mackerel come in, they were watchin' to see what was goin' to happen. That barrel wasn't long before it was sent back where it came from.

Robert Kincaid

Robert Kincaid, 74, lives in Eastville, near Upper Stewiacke, Colchester County. He was born in Leeds, Maine, the son of a Presbyterian minister who came to the area when Robert was fifteen, ministering to churches in Dean Settlement and Musquodoboit Harbour. During the Depression, "Dad moved to Truro and I didn't like town that well, so I drifted back out here and got in the lumber woods." He also spent thirty-five years at the Halifax shipyards, eventually becoming a general foreman. Not a management type, he passed on being superintendent. Today he lives in the original manse for the old Presbyterian church. Officially retired, he still cuts ten cords of firewood a year. "I split them by hand; it's good exercise."

I always liked to be around the woods, but to go in, have a job, earn your keep, and make a few cents, it would be 1937 when I first went. First camp I worked was at Fall Brook up here on the Lansdowne Road with a contractor for the Canadian Lumber Company, Byard Ogilvie was his name. The company was in Lower Stewiacke and was owned by Rufus Dickie. I went on the river drive that spring; it's good fun if you didn't know any better and we didn't. The last drive, just guessin', was in 1945.

For some reason, they used to [always] start the drive on the tenth day of April and there was lots of ice and snow around those days. It'd depend on the spring of course, if it was pretty hard goin', I've seen it the twenty-fourth of May when you'd be at Upper Stewiacke and other times it may be the middle of May. We'd get finished somewhere down around Upper Stewiacke and there'd be some other men that would take it down to Lower Stewiacke. You get more deadwater then and it takes less men and it's easier. Most of us come home and helped somebody put in the crops or somethin' like that.

It's not a long or hard river to drive, doesn't have any nasty waterfalls and real swift water. It's a good river to learn on. The drivin' made a good channel, but now it's flattened out quite a bit.

Pembroke, now, had some spots on it that was tricky. It flows in [the Stewiacke] about two or three miles below here, a separate river with two dams on it. Narrower, smaller, it's really a brook, but with the dams behind it they could make a river out of it. They had about a ten- or twelve-foot falls up near the head and sometimes those logs would jam right down over the falls. The Pembroke I would say was a harder, rougher river to drive. I can only guess, but I'd say they'd drive that eleven or twelve miles. They'd usually bring a drive so far here, then Pembroke would come down with a drive about the same size. When they got to be close, two crews joined together and took them from there down to Stewiacke.

Dickie had mills that cut lumber in the woods too in the winter-time, but this was all sawlogs he drove. I'd say they'd take down maybe a million and a half on the Stewiacke and perhaps the same amount in the Pembroke. What they would do if there was a contractor puttin' logs in the river, they would be scaled, get the number of board feet, and then that feller would have a paper to show what he had put on the river and he would be paid for that.

The drive would start at Fall Brook up here ten miles, pretty well at the head of the [Stewiacke] river. They had dams that kept your water up. Here at Logan Brook, they had Matheson Dam. That's the only dam we had 'til you got below Cox Brook. Then they had College Lake Dam and Cox Lake Dam. Course, Matheson Dam would still help you. They'd hold the water and give you a splash [a rush of water]. When you get here, you were at Walter's Lake Dam and Deyarmond's Lake Dam. That kept your water up and they'd time them [to open] at different times. You'd usually get a splash about every two hours. The Matheson Dam was right on the river, but the rest were in the feeders. There might've been another dam or two that I've missed, but those were the main splashes.

There was two crews, sixty, seventy men total. One they called a tending out crew. When the splash would come, you'd get busy and push the logs out in the river and try to keep them runnin' as much as you could and break whatever jams would happen. The bigger part of the crew would be what they call the rear. You'd be bringin' up the rear, rollin' the logs out all the time and breakin' jams. Tending out was the better job, of course. They didn't have to get wadin' around in the ice, snow, slush, and whatnot. You'd be on the drive quite a while before you'd get the chance to tend out. That was mostly the older men—forty-five, fifty—but at that time I'd be chasing twenty. They'd be stationed at spots on the river where jams usually

"You'd be on the drive quite a while before you'd get the chance to tend out. That was mostly the older men.... They'd be stationed at spots on the river where jams usually formed and they'd just keep it open." (Lillian Scott Perry)

formed and they'd just keep it open. We stayed on the back and did the dirty work.

I think we got up about four o'clock and got breakfast. River drivin', they'd have a great big pot filled with eggs; you could get a half dozen, dozen, whatever you wanted. Then we'd walk to the rear wherever that would happen to be. At ten o'clock, they'd bring a lunch, then you'd work through to two o'clock and you'd have another lunch. You'd work through 'til about five, five-thirty, and you'd have to walk back to the camp.

There was one [camp] at Logan Brook and a house we used up here at Eastville. The main drivin' camp was down near Crossroads. I'd say four or five miles between camps. That would take you to the village and most of the men went home. Once you got so far down, they would move from one drivin' camp to the other. Now Pembroke, they had a drivin' camp up at Burnside and I don't think they had another camp 'til they hit Crossroads down here. They had a long walk, maybe four miles down, then you'd go to the next camp and walk four miles up to get to the rear. These camps back here would be empty until after seed time, then you went to work in the summer as well. I worked summer and winter for about five years. They'd log in the wintertime and use the same camps. The first camp at Fall Brook, I think, was log, but the other camps would be made from lumber and tar paper. Logan Brook camp would hold maybe forty, fifty men. Some of his camps would be larger than that.

There'd be men, farmers and these older chaps I was tellin' you about, that lived along the river that would have a job tendin' out while the drive would be goin' through. In Burnside there was one old gentleman, so I understand, that used to go on the river drive while it was passin' through his property. When the drive got by his boundary, he went back home. I think they paid him every year. He did that for many, many years.

On the main river here when you go above the Matheson Dam, you had the ice cakes to travel from one jam to the other. You could hop on an ice cake, four or five of ya, and go downriver. When you got below the dam these ice cakes had to break up to go through the flume and then you had to find some other means, usually wadin'. Above the dam, it would be pretty well all rearin' and tendin' out, just the one bunch, because you were just gettin' started. The logs had to go through the gate. Some had double gates and each would be eight feet wide, maybe a little more. You had boom logs to sheer them in and you'd need a man there to keep them straight, but usually they'd go right through.

When the logs go through and they get jammed, they push out logs, what they call a wing, on the gravel beds. Well, when the centre of the drive goes through, these wings are all left on the banks. You had peaveys, some pike poles, and you'd go down, roll them in the water, and get them floating again. Then they had what they called dead heads. They were usually ol' pine or big cat spruce that would get kind of waterlogged and they'd always be layin' behind. They'd just go from here down a few hundred yards and go ashore again. You'd have them picked so bad there'd be hardly any bark left on them. You'd roll them out, get the big end out into the current in the channel, and it would go a little piece and then decide it wanted to go ashore again. You'd have to chase that feller; got to know him personally. They didn't see the mouth of the river. When they got down that deadwater they just, *woosh*, go to bottom. There's still logs down there in spots.

If you was out on a centre and a splash come, well, you're out there so you'd be pickin' the centre off, but you'd be lookin' to see a couple of logs that you could get on to get ashore with. You could walk out on the centre quite easily while the splash was down. Usually fairly shallow, sometimes there'd be seven or eight feet of water. When the splash come you got another three feet of water and everything's startin' to float. You pick off whatever's holdin' that centre; they'd be stuck on somethin' like a rock. Some logs would be dry and float high and others of them would be three-quarters under water. Never jump on that high log; he'll throw you quickly. You get the one that's ridin' three-quarters down, then that feller don't want to roll so

Stanley Scott,
Barrington,
demonstrates his river
driving skills. "Never
jump on that high log;
he'll throw you
quickly. You get the
one that's ridin' three-
quarters down, then
that feller don't want
to roll so easily....
When the water's still,
your log's cranky, but
as soon as you get out
in the current, the log
steadies right down,
you can feel it freeze
[from] the pressure."
(Lillian Scott Perry)

easily. Another thing about logs that might surprise some people,
when the water's still, your log's cranky, but as soon as you get out
in the current, the log steadies right down, you can feel it freeze
[from] the pressure. The men tending out downriver would use pike
poles more, but usually you'd just take your peavey and dog it into
another log, pull that one alongside the one you're standin' on, and
it was pretty good, not too much problem.

The first jam that I broke was up at Fall Brook. I didn't know much
about it. The front end of a jam is solid, the back end is loose. A log
come, got in back of a root and this thing jammed. The boss come
along and he thought I knew somethin' about river drivin'. I had to
take an axe and chop this log that was caught. The jam broke. Course

I didn't know to stay in the front and run across to the home side—that's the side the camp's on. I was on the far side of the river. It was late in the afternoon so I was pretty anxious to get on the home side. It wasn't very wide. I took the axe and threw it across, then I started across and instead of keepin' up in the front of the jam where it's nice and solid, I got back where the logs are loose and I was in to my neck, pawin' and scratchin'. I got over but I got a good soakin'. You learn quickly.

I was up on Pembroke and a feller come ashore off a jam. He lost his balance and he had to drive his peavey down and he drove it right through my foot. Luckily it went right between the bones. Yeah, never hurt a bone and didn't bleed either. Well, my feet were so damn cold it didn't bother me. That was in the morning. I kept on working, but I knew somethin' was amiss. When I went up to lunch they put on a fire and my foot thawed out. I could barely hobble with it. I had to go home for a week, I think.

You get wet and come out, oftentimes the only place you have to walk is on ice cakes on the bank. Cold? I guess it was! Your feet would get so numb, there's no feeling in them. Feels like you're walking on clubs. But no one seemed to get a cold while the water was that condition. If you picked up a cold it was after the water got warm. It's funny about that. You had these Humphrey pants and usually Stanfield long underwear and a heavy shirt. You didn't take those off when you went to bed. You got in and put these wool blankets over you and in the morning your underwear would be dry. The outside of your pants would be a bit damp, but the heat from your body would dry that out. That's the way they did it.

One thing would happen to you. When the water starts gettin' warm, your feet get terribly soggy, but while the water's cold, your feet stay okay. When it gets warmer, day after day, your feet seem to want to squash out and get sore. Put on a pair of boots and your feet would be just burnin'. The thing on this river here was a good pair of lumberman rubbers. To be a big shot at first goin' off, you had to have the leather boots and calks. On some rivers you'd need them, but you didn't so much here. The younger fellers wouldn't know any better, but after you was on the drive awhile you didn't bother with that foolishness. We thought that was great fun, but after three or four years, you learned to ride the logs a little bit. You can get along on this river with a good pair of lumberman rubbers better.

Oh, you'd get dunked, sure. They'd play little tricks on you too. One year, the feller that was keepin' time was the boss's son, a big fat fellow. They got him down river showin' him how to pick the logs off the wings. This feller was just waitin' 'til he got in a certain spot, gave the log a flip with a peavey, and this feller went down. You'd get dunked. It doesn't matter what you do, you're wet anyhow.

One day down here just before the village, it was high, high water and there was three or four fellers from Annapolis Valley walkin' along the bank. The water was murky and they were wadin' halfway to their knees. First thing they stepped out, couldn't tell the water was deep, and away they went. They had a nice swim, a dandy. When they got back on shore, two or three of them quit right there and went home; no more river drivin'.

I got in what they call Esson Brown's Water Hole, kind of a deep hole. I guess it was the first year I was on the drive. Hugh Ellis and I went out and broke this jam. I wasn't too smart and didn't know what to do. Hugh went ashore and I stayed with the jam and got down amongst the logs and got a pretty good dunkin'. I got one log under each arm and when they swung sideways, these other logs would be comin' down. They'd be hittin' it and pretty near take the ribs off you. The boss, Ambroise Stuart, came down. He had a great big long pike pole and he reached it out. I grabbed the end of it and he turned around, faced up the bank and put it over his shoulder, leaned forward, and dragged me clear up on dry ground.

Two fellers were drowned up there in September when we had a flash flood. The Matheson Dam broke in high water. I remember that morning when we went to breakfast the water was just runnin' in the front door of the camp and out the back, just level with the floor. There was two camps, one where you slept and a place to go eat. When we come back, the water was up level to the deacon seat in front of the bunks. It kept comin' up and we had to get out. It went downriver. The horse hovel went a piece and got stuck. After a while, the cookhouse took off. This was the woods crew's side. There was a small back channel and the mill and mill crew was over there. They were right down on the bank of the river. They lost all their stuff. There wasn't much of it [the mill] left. It took all the small camps and the cookhouse—*bang-o!*—one after the other. Those people got up on a pile of hardwood lumber, be twenty or twenty-five feet high. They set there 'til the water went back down.

Two men didn't go over; they drowned. They could 'ave got there. A feller by the name Rhyno with one arm got over. I don't like tellin' ya, they had a little bit of beer and they didn't want to leave their homemade beer. So their camp went and they went with it. They had a wing dam, just where the mill set, to back up water when they bring the logs down. When their camp hit the wing dam, it went spinnin' around. They'd get knocked out for sure. They picked them up downriver somewhere.

That's the only ones on this river I know. I heard them talk about a man on the Pembroke that got drowned years ago, long before my time. I think they had a grist mill on that river and this man got below the mill in straight, rough water, and somewhere, I guess, he got in amongst the logs. They didn't get him. Like the people, they're pretty peaceful rivers, but there are some I hear of that can say they've lost a man for every mile.

I talked to an old fellow, Rube Archibald, he was an old man when I was a kid. He said they used to cut lumber, hew it in big pieces, make rafts out of it, and they'd put it in the river just down below here a mile or so and float them down to Maitland where there was shipbuilding. They called it ton timber.[1] The raft would be big enough, I suppose, for five or six men. When they got down to tidal water, they would go when the tide was out, and as soon as the tide would turn they'd anchor and wait for the tide to go again. He said they used to do that a lot. That was the first drivin' they did here, the ton timber. You'd be talkin' turn of the century and before.

You got big wages on the drive. You got a dollar and fifty cents a day and found compared to, if you were workin' in the woods in the winter, your top rate would be a dollar and twenty-five cents a day. That was quite a thing, an extra twenty-five cents a day. It went from that down to a dollar. Yarders sometimes would get a little less than the people choppin', depending on who you are, how long you've been around, what you know, and how much you can do. Everything adds up. Teamsters would get paid so much for his horses. Say he got a dollar and twenty-five cents a day; his horses were fed and you'd get so much a month for the horses.

Usually here, you'd be home for seed time, you'd get a couple of weeks off hayin' time and perhaps a couple weeks off harvest time. They always logged here in the summer. They got certain ground that works well in the summer. They'd put in a portable mill and log the same ground they got logs for the river drivin'. They had different contraptions. They made [log] rails just like a railroad track and put teams on. They did that some. At the last of it they were doin' quite a little bit of work with trucks in the dry places.

The last of September you'd go in the woods and be cuttin' sled roads and levelin' up a few bad spots up to Christmastime for the winter's cut. When they start sleddin' on it they usually had a man that would cut skids and fix it up if there was a bad slue spot in it or something so it wouldn't get any worse. After Christmas, they'd start cutting logs until the last of March pretty well.

I cut pulp out in West Loon Lake in Trafalgar, Pictou County, for Anderson on the St. Mary's River one summer. Less than six miles will put you on the headwaters of the St. Mary's. You have a watershed goin' into Liscomb as well back here four or five miles. They drove pulp on the St. Mary's and Sheet Harbour waters, but it was all sawlogs [on the Stewiacke]. You cut, peeled, and junked it four foot and you piled it four foot six. That was a cord of wood, and the bark off it yet, that makes quite a difference. God help you if there was one speck of rot of any kind. If they could see it, they'd dock you one-eighth of a cubic foot. It would add up to beat hell. That would just be a speck. Any worse and they wouldn't even accept it. Sometimes you'd get a tree with a hole in it. We'd cut another little tree, peel it, drive it in, and saw it off. I don't think you made any money time you cut the little tree and plugged it. It was just the fact of beatin' 'em. It wasn't much use to [complain], there was always someone wanted your job. And we didn't know any better. How the hell did we know any better? Today, people would know better, wouldn't they?

Logging was usually crosscut saws and axes. Pulpwood was usually with what they call a Swede saw, three and a half, four foot, one man. But two men could use a four-foot saw. I don't think the pole axe was ever popular in this valley. I could never understand how they could use them. They don't balance. A double-bitted axe, you always took the shortest bit for choppin' and your biggest bit for limbin'. Your choppin' bit's a little shorter than your limbin' bit. They had a balance to them, but the pole axe, I could never use one.

First chain saw I saw came in from British Columbia. They called it a Timber Hog. It weighed ninety-eight pounds and took two men to carry. Had handle bars like a motorcycle; that was the driver's end. Then they had a little bar come out with a handle on it for the feller on the other side. It was just for bigger lumber. Now a few years back that would have come in handy, there was terrific big lumber. We cut hardwood up back of Eastville here, it took ten logs to the thousand, average. We had six-foot crosscut saws. A normal crosscut saw is five-foot, but they got us big ones. Oftentimes you'd have to corner a tree when you got in the swell. When you sawed in to where you got to the larger part of the tree, one fellow would let his saw go back and one fellow would work for the corner of his notch and the other fellow would work for his corner. Then you'd jig the centre out 'til you got by the swell of the tree. They called it cornering, an easy way to get through the centre part of your tree.

The cook was boss in the cookhouse. You might say he was boss around the camp. Some cooks wouldn't allow you to speak at the table and others would. Course, you didn't ask for anything anyway. If you wanted anything, you just reached it, and if you couldn't, you got up over the table and grabbed it, no please or thank you. If you happened to shove your sleeve through another feller's plate reachin' across for somethin', well, that was too bad. You'd get a few arguments at the table sometimes. I think that's one reason why some camps didn't want you to speak because a feller could have a little bit of a grudge and it would start at the table. I've seen it flair up a bit but nothing serious. The worst times were when a wet day would come and if there were cars, you went to town and then got into the liquor. There'd be a little fracas from time to time, but it wasn't common.

Just like an animal, you had your boundaries and you kind of kept them if you could. They were a pretty decent bunch of men. There was an awful lot of people from New Brunswick and a few from Prince Edward Island worked for Dickie. I think they came down here because it was an easier winter. The harder you worked, the less trouble you had. If you were cuttin' by the thousand, you had a real quiet group. When you were out all day tryin' to get every stick of wood you can and never satisfied, it would be kind of a quiet camp, civil and tired out, when you came in at night.

I always worked by the thousand; I liked to get more money. First time I cut by the thousand, I think it was two dollars and forty cents a thousand for cuttin' it down, junkin' it into log lengths and snoutin' it so the horse wouldn't catch anything. When they talk a thousand, you were talkin' twelve hundred and fifty feet 'cause mills took twelve hundred and fifty feet, but they called it a thousand.

If you were within a certain radius you'd try to get home to wash and have clean clothes. I'd get home on the weekends oftentimes.

I never had them but, yes, you'd have some lice. I had a partner one time got loused up bad. When the sun would get hot, he'd open up his shirt and this heavy woollen underwear, and he'd be pickin' them off. They didn't know any better, I guess, that's what I put it down to.

You had good food, anybody that didn't mind grease. I don't eat pork and, my gosh, the beans would be swimmin' in fat pork. I used to have to pick that out. Breakfast and supper might be porkish. The cook and somebody would go out in the wintertime and they'd pot a moose. Nobody ever said anything about it, but you knew damn well you was eating moose meat. They got meat in a barrel they called red eye. I don't know what it was. My gosh, there'd be slabs yeah long and about an inch and a quarter thick. It was good. I always figured it was horse meat. There's nothin' wrong with horse meat, I've eaten that before. I don't like it warm and I can't hardly eat it in a soup or anything. I like it sliced, cold; it's somethin' like beef, only coarser. I ate a lot of whale meat. Boy, that's top notch. They used to bring the whales into Blandford. They'd sell forty-pound junks of clear steak for ten cents a pound. That's good.

Angus Graham, my wife's father, was quite famous in his day around here. He was a good axeman, well recognized. He hated a saw. He was just a man, I suppose, five foot six, but he was heavy set. He could chop! When he went into a tree, I don't know how he did it. He'd start by hitting two glancing blows down at the bottom and he'd start the scarf. You cut down on a slant, then cut fairly straight in the bottom of your notch; we call that your scarf. Then he'd drop to the far side of the tree and drive that axe right to the eye, pretty well up to where the handle starts. When he chopped, he didn't give you a chip like I would give you, he'd give a junk; it'd be a piece. He was quite famous. All their family were good axemen, but Angus was considered to be good and steady.

Now, the Depression, the winter of 1935, there was very few people worked in the woods. I think there was only one camp worked up in Burnside. Dickie set one camp up at the Mary Anne Creal lot and he put the lumber back there, but he never built the camp. Prices went all to hell. But there was one bunch on the Pembroke, a Mr. Wallace Gault and another man, they were about the only ones that ran in this whole valley. Angus and his brother Cy, he'd be gettin' close to sixty, were choppin' there that winter. Her father'd be fifty, fifty-five years old, yet they were askin' for him to go. I used to laugh to hear Angus's wife say, "Funny, you old fellows are workin' and all these young men haven't got work." They could put up lumber.

Angus come down here one time from Burnside to cut a wood pile for Luther Grahame. He was only seventeen years old. The man yardin' this stuff just laughed when he saw Angus comin' to the woods. Angus said by that night he had cut a year's wood for the man. I well believe it 'cause he could knock hell out of it. That was all axe too, a good-sized axe, and hardwood. He'd be using a Blenkhorn double-bitted axe. They'd go from about four pounds down to maybe three and a half; you seldom see a double-bitted axe go over four pounds. The fellow that made fun of him in the morning when he went to work was drivin' back and forth on the horse's back, yardin' out come late day. He had been walkin' back and forth and was played out. Angus told me the trick in splittin' wood with an axe was the way you held your mouth.

We're not just losing the woods, it's being ravished. It's clear cut to such an extent that it won't seed out by itself because it's too far back. If they cut in strips, Nova Scotia has a great regenerating power. It will seed out itself very quickly, but when you cut back too far the seed can't get over the ground. Not only that, I think you change your climate, certainly lose your topsoil. It's a hell of a thing.

You hear them come up with all different ideas. Small second-growth stuck pretty close together and you'll get as many cords off an acre as you would if it was mature wood. They come up with everything. Their last good gimmick over here was they would buy the wood by the ton. Well, that's fine if you can get it hauled the day you cut it or the day after. You let wood set out and it'll lose fifty percent of its weight once it gets dried right out. You read in the paper that their profits were higher this year than other years, then you know why. I would much rather give them four foot six on a cord of pulp than what they're gettin' by the ton. I'd think I was gettin' a deal then; twelve hundred and fifty feet to the thousand was a gentleman's agreement to what they're gettin' now.

There's no old-growth lumber left. A load went by here yesterday you couldn't use for skids we used to roll logs on. That stuff they're takin' now for pulp you've got to see it to believe it, that our country's gone down that they're takin' beanpoles.

It'd be a good thing, a wonderful thing, if we could have regulated it. Seems like they regulate themselves. We should have been able to, especially cutting up the streams, leaving a little bit on each side or around a lake. Keeps your wash down, keeps it cooler. Today, a trout, I don't know how they ever live with the water warmed up like that, with everything opened up. Trout wants cool water and shade. And there's bound to be a lot of topsoil [lost]. The minute you get a rain here it just turns brown. The water will stay up for two or three days, then drop right back down again. Years ago, a good rain, you could figure the river would stay up for a week, a week and a half anyway. You know what's happening? The ground's exposed, it's not sponging up the water at all. You've got to have trees. One thing common about woods, where there's lumber, you can usually take a rod and drive it down a foot or a foot and a half on the average and that's just a sponge. That'll soak up water to beat hell. It'll even soak up water on the slopes and retain it. But now, we haven't got it anymore, it's opened up too much.

And when they replant, they just want to replant something that will make pulp. They're not interested in the balance. Really, a good woodlot should have twenty percent hardwood on it; the animals need the hardwood. You take deer, they need hardwood to exist. They're sprayin' our hardwood to kill it, acre after acre, to make sure nothin' but what they want is going to grow and that's not good. They found in Germany they had to go back to the old mixture of woodland to keep the balance. There's too many animals that can't exist on just one type of tree.

So, I don't know, we're goin' to hell in a basket, I guess. They just want to make this kill and then I suppose they can pack up, but I don't know where they can go. They've got everything ravished here in Canada pretty well unless they go up to the edge of the timberline. Bad, bad stuff. The government, if there's anything comin' in that'll employ a half dozen people, they'll give pretty near anything you ask for. It would be a terrible thing, but we're going to be like the fishery. They're going to have to use quotas because our lumber is not going to last that much longer, it's gettin' down. We can either starve to death now or starve to death ten years down the road, whichever you want. Starve to death now, you'll recover maybe a little quicker.

I'll tell you what. You talk about manpower. With the machinery they're puttin' in the woods now, you don't have that much manpower connected with the forestry. They got these machines that snip the tree off, lay it down, knock the limbs off it. Then they have chippers that go right to the woods. The company's makin' a profit, of course, the contractor's makin' a little money, but the average man, the lumberjack, so to speak, he's gettin' it tough right now. If they want men working, they shouldn't be goin' so heavy on the mechanization should they? If they want people to be employed they're going about it funny. Machinery, they can turn it on and run twenty-four hours a day and they do. I guess it's greed, the fast buck. When the wood's gone, I don't know.

George Volans

George Volans, 81, lives at Pembroke, Colchester County. "I just drifted around from here to there." He worked on the railroad in the 1930s for seventy-three cents a day and board. He's worked construction during the summer, helped to build the first two ammunition bunkers on Magazine Hill near Bedford Basin, and worked in a shoe factory. His last woods work was at seventy when he cut a road for Scott Paper. "In the woods, I worked at everything you could work at. In the mill, I did everything but saw."

I worked in camps the lice would carry you away. They'd build them out of old green lumber and they'd dry out from the heat inside and the tar paper would lift up on them. You could look out and see the stars them cold nights, twenty-five, thirty below. Come a snowstorm, the snow would blow in on you and you'd cover your head with blankets. They'd give you the boards and stuff when you went to work and you made your own bunk. You'd go out to the hovel and get straw. You'd take about four bran bags, an old crooked needle, and binder twine, sew up a mattress and put the straw in that. They'd give you one old rough army blanket and you'd put it over that old straw tick, then you put two blankets over you.

You had no unemployment back in them days. If you couldn't have nothin' to eat, you got relief. Now a man, his wife, and one child in the thirties, they'd get about three dollars and twenty-five cents and you had to go out and work three days for that on the town or wherever you were. They'd put you to work. If you worked in the woods, they'd send you to them cullins where you'd cut hardwood and deliver it to the people that was on relief. Instead of that now, they call it welfare. That's how they worked it.

Years before, they'd cut a road and they'd leave a belt along each side, say twenty feet, all the big timber. She'd be closed right in and the sun wouldn't get in and take the snow off. They'd stay there pretty near all of March. They wouldn't cut that out 'til the lot was cut. If they finished the lot, they'd cut it out, and if they didn't, it would stay there for that road. Today, they can put roads anywhere. You don't get a horse in the woods too much now. They started going out in '65. I imagine from that on there was hardly a horse in the woods. The only ones would be an odd farmer yardin' up some stuff for himself. Those big contractors went into the machinery because they'd have to or they couldn't get a contract. That's why we got no wood today, those big machines.

When I first went to work up here in Riversdale for McLeod's, they had four big mills in there and they cut thousands and thousands of cords and shipped it out of here. They parbuckled their logs. They'd take a tree like that telephone pole there and they'd start limbin' it up. They'd put a pulley on that tree and dogs, like ice tongs. When you

come in with your logs, that grabbed them. You took your horse off, hooked it on your block and tackles, and he'd haul them up. They'd put brows up thirty-five, forty feet and they'd run 'em maybe a hundred feet and they'd never move them 'til winter. There'd be maybe five horses comin' into that same landing. They put skids in and bring 'em up and up and up, and they keep rollin' the logs back using the tree as a backstop. They would limb that tree as they went up. When they got them up so high and back so far, they quit, get another tree on another road, put another brow up. In the winter they'd cut them logs out and let them go down. I'm tellin' you, it was somethin' to see. Load them on their sleds and haul them to the mill.

There's a lot of difference in it for the last fifteen, twenty years; that's the only time that you ever made any money in the woods. You was gettin' three dollars and twenty-five cents a cord for fallin' and peelin' it. Then we got three dollars and twenty-five cents a cord for junkin' it. Now all right. When you got all done falling and we started junkin', you can't junk your own wood, but you can junk mine and I can junk yours. Why that was, if you junked your own wood and they scaled it out and you had your own scale what you got paid for and it was fifty cord over, you could come back at them and they'd have to pay you. That's true. Ah, terrible.

The mills will cheat you just the same, there's no difference. They'll cheat the ears right off you. They'll saw your lumber and every ten thousand, they'll gain a thousand. They'll take a thousand off you,

"You don't get a horse in the woods too much now. They started going out in '65. I imagine from that on there was hardly a horse in the woods. The only ones would be an odd farmer yardin' up some stuff for himself." (PANS)

but you'll never know that. If you want to check it, they don't think much of you.

You want to know about woods, I'll tell you somethin' about woods. I worked in the woods forty-five years and I know a little bit about it. You get in a crew of men, maybe thirty or forty men, and they're all ugly and mad. "I'm gettin' gypped so bad, we've got to do somethin' about it." They'll all get together and talk. One or two fellers will say, "All right, we'll go to the boss and see what he says." You walk up to the boss and the other fellers will walk away. They ain't got the guts to do it. Then you get in shit. The boss will say, "You're through. You're a shit disturber. You're done." That's what he'll say. It don't matter how good you are, if you're the best man there, if you try to lead them other fellers and they quit on you, you're done.

It was a helluva way of life, it was really. It wasn't a picnic, boys, years ago in the woods. You had to work. I seen some bad accidents; I seen guys get hurt bad. I seen a guy get his wrist cut off [in a mill], and I seen another feller, three fingers taken off on a slab saw. A lot of things happened around this place. Hugh Ellis cut his self on an axe. He come over to Maggie Graham's place and she sewed him up. Sterilized a needle and sewed him up with black thread.[2] A woman broke her arm right off up next to the elbow. A sled or somethin' run over it. They took her arm off into her house up in here. The doctor come up in a horse and sled, and Maggie helped him. That was sixty years ago. I heard that so many times.

I had a few close calls. I had a chip in that eye. Choppin', just an underneath cut on a limb. Drove it right in, and I pulled it out. I was sick pullin' that. Oh! I had five stitches right in that eye. I was twelve, thirteen days in the hospital with that one. Just another hair and I'd been blinded for life. I was workin' down the branch at Meadowvale. I had a feller pilin' for me. He took a swing at a big pine with a pickaroon, missed, and hit me in the ankle. Drove the pickaroon in her about that far, cracked 'er in three places.

Another time, I was yardin' for a feller back here. He was choppin' and the wind was blowin' hard. I was doggin' up a log somebody left there and I was goin' to pick it up. I stopped the horse and grabbed the set of side dogs. I drove the dog in and I just bent over like that, and just as I did, *Whew*, a spruce come right across this log, broke it in three places. I was like here and it hit right there. Wouldn't be a foot. Another foot over and I'd a had it. What a man goes through to bring up a family.

Vern Crockett

Vern Crockett, 78, lives in Eastville, Colchester County. His grandfather, John Crockett, and his father, William Crockett, were both teamsters who worked the lumber woods and also trucked supplies with teams for local merchants. In 1943, Vern and his two brothers went into contracting for themselves and did considerable logging for Dickies and Creelmans, both well known lumber names in Colchester County. During the 1950s, he bought stumpage for logs from Scott Paper. "We been around quite a bit. I quit when I was sixty-five. Yeah, it'd be about fifty years I was in it."

I didn't like school and of course at that time money was very scarce; and a big family, the sooner you got out to work the better. I was only about fifteen, I'd be no older. I drove a yard horse. I'd been brought right up with horses from the time I was big enough to walk. My father worked around the woods a lot, mostly drove horses. Didn't use oxen in my day, but I guess before my day there was oxen used. The oxen were so cussed slow movin', it took a long time to get anywhere; horses were much faster. On an average, a good big team of horses would be way ahead of a pair of oxen.

Back years ago they wasn't as big as they are now. Some of the last horses I had weighed about a ton. It must be the breeding, I guess, now. Years ago I can remember some of the teams wouldn't be over twelve hundred to a horse; thirteen hundred would be a pretty fair horse them times, way back in the thirties. For woods horses, they went lookin' for them bigger, so they used to bring in a whack of them from out West. A lot of them were partly broke but they wasn't all. I guess there was a good demand for horses and there wasn't that many raised around these areas, didn't seem to be. Them times, you could buy a pretty good horse for two or three hundred dollars. But now to buy a good big workhorse or a showhorse, they don't work them now, you'd pay maybe a thousand, I imagine.

There's the Percheron, the Belgian, and the Clyde horse. Them's the three big workhorse type. It didn't matter which was which because we've had different ones and one seemed to be as good as the other around the woods work or around the farm. Tried to match them up pretty good, but sometimes they wasn't; probably matched good for workin', but not in colour. Some people liked to have the same colour and the same type of horse. As long as you had a good workin' team, it didn't matter to us if they matched up too well or not.

If you got a good road, not too many hills or downhills, sometimes you'd put on a thousand and a half of logs, sometimes it'd be a lot less than that. It varied so much. Some horses you'd get wouldn't be that good to pull, so you had to be careful to not put on too much or you'd get stuck on a rock or something and have to throw some off. I remember one winter we had a little job over here. A great big hemlock. Boys, I'm tellin' you, that's a lot of rubbin' to get one of them off the stump. We cut a lot of them down, another guy and I. My brother, he had to yard them with a pair of horses together because we cut one there, I think it was sixteen feet long, there was seven hundred and ten board feet in that one stick. Again, ya cut that down off the stump, then junked them off sixteen feet. That was a lot of rubbin' with a crosscut saw.

I remember especially that one log. The snow was deep. Boys, he had these big pair of horses and they were rockin'. I thought, you're goin' to get hurt. He had to hold 'em and I had to hook 'em on. They were just rarin' to go, just a smackin' and goin'; they knew there was somethin' heavy. Strong? My gosh, they never stopped 'til they landed to the brow. We didn't take it probably any further maybe than a hundred and fifty feet, but you didn't want to take it any further.

There was some winters, my gosh, it was hard goin' for 'em. Especially when they got that crust on the snow; towards spring it'd come a rain and freeze. That'd be hard on their legs. Scrape the hair off their legs and sore them up some. I remember one horse I had, a gray Percheron, his leg got awful sore and I got some stuff from the vet to wash it with, but it really healed 'em right up. Some horses now, the Clydesdale, had a lot of hair on their legs. They could take that a lot better than the Percherons and Belgians. They had a lot of protection.

Some of them horses we had, my God, they were great in snow. We had one big fella there, weighed nineteen somethin', look a here, he'd wade that snow and drag a log out by God, boys! Some horses could cut themselves too, sharp shoes on. They'd overreach and put their hind foot on top of their front foot. We had them get cut pretty bad sometimes. A lot of times, they'd pull a shoe off, step and catch their front shoe and pull it off. Some horses would and other horses wouldn't.

My brother was quite a blacksmith. He used to do a lot of the shoein' to 'em. They had the shoein' gear right in there—the horse nails and rasp and hammer. At the last we used to have a guy come in the woods and do some shoein' for us. He'd get the shoes sharpened up at the blacksmith shop and bring them in and put them

on. They had quite a sharp edge on them calks in the wintertime. Had to be on ice, you know. They had a toe calk and two heel calks and they'd be sharpened right up. They'd last quite a while if it was just snow and ice, but they'd soon dull up if you was on frozen mud or ground. I remember them saying they were hauling lumber by teams over to Upper Musquodoboit—that was years and years ago when I was just a young fella, and that was the winter there wasn't much snow. By gosh, about every other day they'd have to get those shoes shifted on the horses.

Some fellas could do it right easy, but it wasn't easy to get that horse's leg up there and hold it. Some horses wouldn't put too much weight on you and other horses let a lot of weight on you when you pulled it up between your legs and held it there. Some of the blacksmiths had a sling and when the horse was hard to shoe, they'd put them in them slings. Some of them were pretty rough, especially a young horse first time.

I remember one big horse we had, I raised him; oh, gosh, he was a big horse. I guess he weighed a little over a ton maybe. Well, the first time we went to shoe him I didn't take him to a blacksmith shop. I got this guy that used to come up just in the barn. He said, "We'll have to put a rope around his neck and around his back and around his tail and put a pulley up and pull his hind foot up." Well the horse pretty

"If you got a good road, not too many hills or downhills, sometimes you'd put on a thousand and a half of logs, sometimes it'd be a lot less than that. It varied so much." (N.S. Museum)

near went crazy, scared him so bad, but we could hold him. I thought he was goin' out through the front of the barn. He didn't dare tackle him, afraid he might kick him or something, but that's the way we shod his hind feet. He got all right after a while, but it nerved the horse up bad. I think if he had picked his foot up and went easy, but he was a little bit nervous. The front feet was much easier; they never had as much trouble shoeing the front feet as they did with them hind feet, because they could give you an awful kick. I was lucky, I never got kicked, but there has been a few fellers got kicked. But I don't know, it seems if you was kind to a horse—a horse is a pretty smart thing—he seemed to know, but if you got too rough with them, they'd get a little rough with you too sometimes.

We never had any killed, but we lost a few horses in the woods gettin' sick. They used to call it black water. They take this inflammation and they'd stiffen right up. You take some horses, if you're feedin' them high on grain and then let them stand in the barn for three or four days not workin' that seems to be when they'd take it. Their water would get right black. Inflammation of the kidneys I suppose it was. Sometimes you'd get a vet out and get them survived, but other times I remember we lost a couple that way.

The last horses we used was about twenty-two years ago. Some of them went out of them before that. You couldn't get no one today to drive horses. They wasn't brought up with it. I don't know where you'd go around here to find someone to drive a pair of horses. They wouldn't know the first thing about a horse, wouldn't have a clue. He wouldn't know how to feed 'em or harness 'em or anything. To take care of horses, there was a lot of work involved. When you was going to work them hard, you had to take good care of them, because first thing you'd have them crippled up or something.

"They wanted you to get down within a reasonable distance of the root, but some of them didn't get down too far.... They didn't bend too much.
(N.S. Museum)

We never had it happen too much, but I remember lots of fellers you hear tell of they were cruel on animals. They had no mercy on them at all. They'd pound them around, half feed them, and try to get everything was in them. Oh, it was cruel. They got cruel usage at some of them places, the big outfits. Yeah, they didn't have any mercy on a horse at all.

I guess I done about as much [chopping] as I did teamin', but my brother now, he was all for teamin'; both brothers I had was all for teamin'. They didn't like to use the axe and the saw. You'd get some fellers on a crosscut saw, it'd be awful heavy. They seemed to put so much weight on, oh, you'd pull so hard. Other fellers could just let that glide through. You take a fella short in the arms, he seemed worse than a feller with good length in the arms. You got to make sure you pull, then let go when he pulls back; you don't want to be holdin' on it when he's pullin' back. Some fellas would be kind of holdin' and you'd be pullin' half of him through the cut. That's what it was all about. Some fellas was real good, by gosh, just get the right swing on it.

I had a brother-in-law, Lyman Grahame, him and I worked quite a few winters together. My God, he was good. Another feller, Charlie Reed, and I averaged two thousand and a half a day one winter with the crosscut, junkin' and limbin' it ready for the yard horse to take out. As a rule I heard them say about two thousand was a pretty good average for people. Some would cut a lot more.

We used the Swede saw a lot. We was cuttin' the tree down with the crosscut, then one fella would limb up and the other fella would take the Swede saw and junk it. It worked out pretty good that way.

Cuttin' down with the Swede saw was hard alone. Anything not too big we used the Swede saw. Oh boys, you had to get down on your knees pretty near. They wanted you to get down within a reasonable distance of the root, but some of them didn't get down too far. Especially a winter of real deep snow, I've seen stumps around the woods, my God, they'd be [three feet] high. They didn't bend too much.

I remember them sayin' about these old fellers before my day. There was an old feller up here in the mountain, Billy Brown, and another feller, John Robert McCool. I guess he lived up on the mountain too. I heard them say them two fellas cut, it was eight thousand anyways, I'm sure, in one day. Axed it all; great big trees. Could them old fellas chop with them axes. Didn't put them out a bit.

I heard this fella say this Billy Brown ground his axe up, took a whetstone and whetted 'er up. Thompson Cox, he was married to my father's sister; he used to be a great axeman too. He said to Thompson, "I'll shave your neck with that axe." My God, he took that axe and shaved the hair off his neck. It must have had a pretty good edge on 'er. In my day, it was all double-bitted axe. There were different makes. There was an axe named the Mann axe, it had quite a wide bit on it. Blenkhorn was quite popular around that time. Now it's pretty hard to find a double-bitted axe around.

That Billy Brown, he cleared all this little farm up on the mountain, big hardwoods. They used to have frolics. A whole bunch of men would go somewhere and help one fella clear land. They'd help him cut these big hardwoods down, then they'd have a dance at night. They used to do a lot of that years ago they said.

Them times, they didn't go up in the limbs too much. Lumber wasn't worth anything. They'd come to them big trees, they'd take two or three logs off, come in the limbs and let the rest stay there. But just to think, swinging one of them big heavy axes all day, morning 'til night. Jump up on that log and stand on it and chop in one side, turn around and chop in the other side. Yes, sir, them fellas was brought right up with it. You had to be rugged to take all that.

Art Mattix

Art Mattix, 99, lives in Londonderry, Colchester County. Born in Albert County, New Brunswick, he came to Londonderry sixty-two years ago, having worked in the woods throughout New Brunswick, Nova Scotia, and parts of Maine. Approaching his one-hundredth birthday, he moves yet like a man half his age. Having lived a most interesting and varied life ("I had to do everything to make a living"), he was known far and wide for his deal carrying prowess in the mills, and his animal husbandry skills were in constant demand. Opinionated on a variety of subjects, he looks unfavourably upon today's forestry practices. "At one time, you was allowed five trees to a hundred undersize. They had to be ten inches on the stump, nothing under ten inches you could cut. Well, that left a God damn big field of stuff in behind it standin'. Is that right? Wasn't that buildin' the country up or was it? The old people built this country up and this God damn trash we got now put it down so it'll never come back. You'll never see it back, you. Today, they cut everything off; they've ruined our country completely."

I never went to school a day in my life. I earnt my livin' from the time I was thirteen years old to this hour. I worked. I wasn't like you fellers and sit on my ass and wore my pants out. I was chucked on the side of the road when I was thirteen years old, same as you chuck a cat out. No home. The old feller died, my grandfather. My father, I never seen him. My mother, she was gone somewhere else. They took me in an old wagon and a horse and started out with me. "You don't want a boy?"

"No, I don't think I want a boy."

"Don't know where anybody would want a boy, would you?"

"No, I don't."

Go into one place.

"Do you know who'll take that boy?"

"No."

"Mother and Dad will take that boy." I sat in the wagon and said nothing. So we went over and drive in the Beeman Road and talked for a minute. "I got a boy, and your daughter told me you might take him."

"Well, how old is he?"

"Thirteen."

"Well, you better put your horse in and stay all night." So they did. I played around, got the cows—they had five or six cows—I drove them up, carried in some kindling wood, frigged around, stayed all night. Next morning, "Well, what do you think of him?"

"Oh," she said, "we'll keep him." So they did.

I was there three years. Now this is my work in the summertime: take a hen wing, an old dish, and put it under the potatoes, brush the bugs off into that, take it down to the old house and she'd scald them and throw 'em outdoors. I'd have to go down and pull chickweed for the old pigs, that was another job. Well, then, I had to carry the wood in, sometimes split it, and suppertime, I'd have to go get the cows. Didn't know where they was; had to listen for the bell. Brought 'em home, milked three of 'em, she milked the other three. Same thing over the next day. Calves to be fed; carry out milk. Winter come, I had the wood to cut, carry in, six cows to water with a dipper like this, dip it out of the well and put it in a washtub like that. Feed forty sheep, carry the hay on my shoulder, and put it in the pen. Two colts in the barn; I had to carry water down to them buggers. That was my day's work for then, snow on like this. A pair of men's boots on or women's boots on, whatever I could get on my feet; a pair of wool pants, no underwear.

The old bastard, she could cook pretty God damn good. Them hot biscuits, I liked them. I was only allowed one, just one hot biscuit. I'd take bread and pancakes, lots of pancakes. Soon as I got those down, go out and do the chores; had to have 'em all done before dark. No light goin' out to the barn. See, I might upset it or somethin' and burn the barn down. Soon as it come daylight, I made it for the barn again. That was my work. Could I go to school and do that? No, God damn right I couldn't.

Well then, Uncle Burl Bannister, that's grandmother's brother, he was a lumberman. Uncle Johnnie Wilson, he got kind of mad too, they went down and took me away from there. Uncle Burl took me to the woods. Used to have field beds, you know, at one time, four in a bed and just roll the blankets down and roll 'em up over you. Uncle Burl Bannister had field beds. I was a kid. I used to go in there and I'd get in amongst the men and sleep. The ones in the middle where's the heat was. We got along all right.

Now, this is my job in there. I had to clean the barn out for two cows and a heffer, milk the cow night and morning; he fed 'em. Well then, in the morning, the teams took the lanterns to the woods with 'em to load logs. I would say a half as far as from here to the Catholic church, they went down this road and then another road cut off this one and went down through the bog. Burley Bog they call it, named after him. This road went down like this from the camp and then turned and went down here. Now the lanterns set right along here, on this side of the road; left the lanterns there. Then these arms here went down and gathered them up and walked right up the road with them like this. Took 'em up to the camp and the girls, they had to wash the chimneys, fill 'em full of oil and then hook 'em on the outside of the camp for night. When the teams come in at dark, they had to have 'em to put the horses in the barn again. That's how I earnt my livin'.

I'm the only man that cut colts for seventy-eight years and never lost one. That's alterin' them, you know, stud colts. Havelock, New Brunswick, that's where I learned my trade. Jim Coates, he was the veterinarian and I worked with him. I'd be eighteen or nineteen years old then. I learned right, some off of him and I learnt some myself. When Jim Coates was cuttin' 'em we used a chain then for cuttin' the cords off. You had to be awful careful when you turned that chain. You put the cord in the chain, drop it in the chain, and then you turn the chain and the chain cut the cords off. If you turned it too quick and didn't shut the blood off you understand, when they cut it off, the cord'll go back and he'd bleed to death. I cut 'em with a different outfit now, knockulators; I got the first one that was ever out, the safe ones. But you got to be careful with it just the same, be a little cautious.

I made an average every spring of two or three hundred. I cut five hundred and fifty in one year; that'd be in the thirties. Seventy-some-odd years I've been doin' 'em. I left over town here and went to Presque Isle, Maine, and cut fifteen colts and come back to Woodstock and cut another one four years old. I travelled all over the country. Milton McKeen used to travel around some with me; we'd go in an old car. Ask anybody pretty near and they all know me. I've been in every barn pretty near from Presque Isle, Maine, to Halifax. I can tell you where every barn set. If you can find one colt from Presque Isle, Maine, to Halifax, up as far as Quebec and over on the Island [P.E.I.], or anywhere I've been that I lost, I'll give you a hundred dollars. There was the same lost as there was saved. Even the man I learnt from lost them.

I'm the only man that goes inside of a cow and cuts the calf up and brings it out in chunks and don't open the side up, and she'll have calves afterwards. And if you don't believe me, there's the phone there. All you got to do is call up in Lorneville.... I done one of his at eleven or twelve o'clock at night. They [veterinarians] got to split the side and a cow's no more good after you do it. But I do it from the inside. I've never lost anything that ways, bulls or nothing.

I carried a lot of deal. I carried deal in so damn many different places before I was married, I don't know where the hell I didn't. I could get a job carryin' deal when no one else could. Yeah, that's right. They'd hire me and fire the other feller.

While the mill's runnin, it goes out to the end of a pile out here. It's up there and you just back your shoulder right in on it and away you go and dump it off and give it a kick like that and come back and get another one. You got to move. You ain't got to stand there and look at it like that, you know, because if you do it piles up like that and you can't get 'em out. You put your shoulder under it and away you go with it. Then you come back and put your shoulder under it again. You just put your hand on the top of it to steady it. Three by ten, three by twelve, and boards. They'd pile the boards up about that high [a foot]; you just put your shoulder and go, throw it off like that, and give it a kick or two with your foot to straighten it out. When you fired it down, it would go kind of scattered.

A pad on your shoulder, a leather pad. All one shoulder. I carried on the side my heart wasn't on. Too hard on your heart to carry all off your left shoulder. The mill would saw about fifteen thousand a day. Some would stand and deal would pile up; they'd have an awful time with it. They was too scared to move their feet you see, their feet were kind of tied. You had to move. I had no trouble carryin' deal. I didn't stand and look at it. It's an awful job to get anybody to do anything today. They're so God damn lazy. I don't know what the hell's goin' to happen to the people if it keeps up.

I carried deal in the summertime and in the wintertime I done somethin' else. I worked in the lumber woods all my life. I was loggin' when Halifax was blowed up [1917], at Laverty Brook, in New Brunswick. I logged in Cape Breton too; that's sixty-eight, sixty-nine years ago. Nyanza, there's where I logged. I'm the man that put the mill in a dry river.

Charlie and Finn Founds, I know'd 'em well, they was the men that owned the lumber and I just took a contract to do it. They come up to New Brunswick where I made sugar. Harry Cain brought 'em up to the sugar camp. They got talkin'. "You log some, don't you?"

I says, "A little, not too much, but some."

"You don't want a contract do you?"

"What doin'?"

"Loggin'."

"Well," I says, "I don't know. Might."

"Well, we got one to give out."

No wonder they wanted to give it out. Hard job to get anybody to do it. So, anyway, we talked quite a bit and they says, "You better come on down and have a look at it." So down I went and looked it over. When I went up on Gairloch Mountain, the bank was high, my God, they're high. Just straight up and down and lumber all over these banks; never was cut. So I was goin' along up through there and I didn't say nothing, I just kept lookin'. The alder bushes up as high as that ceiling, there was grass on them, old grass in these bushes on the limbs hangin' there. I never opened my mouth because

I wanted to get a price out of it. Well, I says, "It's a pretty hard place to log, isn't it?"

"Yes," he says.

"What do you want to pay for gettin' this done?"

"What do you want?"

I says, "No, I want to know what you're willing to pay."

He give me a price. I said, "I wouldn't do it for that at all. Just might as well stop right now. This is a place that you can't get logged and you think you're gettin' a fool down here now to log this."

So anyway he says, "What do you want?"

I says, "Who's goin' to saw it?"

"Well, we got to have a mill."

I says, "I can get a mill."

A saw mill crew, circa 1900, with three deal carriers seated in front wearing their leather shoulder pads. Apparently, they were not as concerned about their health as Art Mattix was about his. "I carried on the side my heart wasn't on. Too hard on your heart to carry all off your left shoulder." (PANS)

"You can?"

"Oh yes. I know a feller's got a mill up there where I am." See, I was afraid they'd steal the lumber on me. I had to watch that. Them damn thiefs, you know, they're awful thick.

"What's he want for sawin' it?"

"I don't know. I have to bring him down and look at it. Then we size it up together; we'll know what we're goin' to do. But I want a price on it so I can tell him. He's got to move the mill down here and everything." So he give me a price. I told him what I'd log it for. He says, "You'll not just start it and not finish it?" I said, "We'll sign papers up and then I'll know what I'm doin' too."

So anyway, I went up and got him and brought him down. We cruised her. He said, "You're goin' to take 'er?"

"Yeah, I offered to log it for fifteen dollars a thousand and put it to the mill. They think it's goin' to be some job, but I got my mind set for this."

He said, "What have you got your God damn mind set for now?"

I said, "You're here. Are you goin' to saw it or are you not?"

"If they'll move the mill and give me nine dollars a thousand to saw it, I'll saw it."

You had to move it on railroad cars. Couldn't move it no other way. A big boiler came and the saw bed and the edgers and trimmers and everything had to come. So they rigged up the contract. We put everything on [the train] and I put my riggin' on too, camp outfit for men to stay in, blankets, dishes, stoves, axes, saws, harness, yardin' dogs, blacksmith outfit. You always had to have a blacksmith outfit. You can't shoe horses or weld chains without one. You had to have all that down there. I think I had six saws goin' there, and three horses yardin' in, seventeen or eighteen men there. So we loaded everything and went down.

There was no hardwood in it at all. It was all spruce and fir. We went up and looked at the lake up there. This river has a lake at the back end of it. It's a brook, a dry brook, just a little bit of water runnin' down. You could step across it anywheres, but in the spring of the year when the snow comes off the bank, you see, it makes water go higher than this ceiling. That's how the grass got in there. They didn't know what I was up to, they never dreamt of me ever doin' this. I said, "I'm goin' to put a drivin' dam in. We'll clear the river out, cut all the alders out of it, make a brook of it, and we'll just put them logs off the bank down and when the water comes, we'll dump them in and let 'em go down to the mill."

That old dam's in there yet, they tell me, rottin' down up the head of that river yet. We had to timber it in, logs and deal and spikes. Christ, you take half a mile of water up there, by God, that's some force, I'll tell you. When you open those gates and let that water through, God Almighty, wash anything you ever come to.

What we done, a God damn stupid trick too. I laughed about it. I didn't laugh at the time, I felt pretty sick about it, but after it was over with I laughed about it. We put in a boom and a dam down there by the mill to catch the logs so they wouldn't go through. I told him, "Make sure that's fastened solid." So he put the boom in. When I heisted the dam, the God damn logs went through and took the mill and all. Took the ass end of the mill and swung her around just like that. Here was the boiler settin' out here and the ass end of the mill sittin' in the brook. Well, we was some sick, don't you think we wasn't. We took the horses and yarded the stuff out, then we took the mill apart. We had forges and we made whatever we wanted and put 'er back in again and got it goin'. We yarded all them in and drove 'em. We sluiced every log, over a million and a half feet, off the bank right down into the brook. We didn't have to make no sluices, the log would go by itself. We were a little better than a year and a half there cuttin' it out.

Charlie Founds came up when we was cuttin' the brook out. He says, "What are you goin' to do, haul 'em right down the brook?" "No," I said, "I don't know what we're goin' to do. We're goin' to clear it out here." I didn't tell him what I was goin' to do. We got the dam all in, got the trips into 'er, that's the gates to hold the water. He said, "What the hell ever made you think of that?"

I said, "The day that Finn and you was here, I thought of it."

"That's what you was studyin' on was it?"

"Yes. I figured that I could drive these damn logs."

"I thought you was goin' to sluice 'em down here and put a road down the river."

"No," I says, "that costs too much money."

He says, "You drove them for fifty cents a thousand didn't you?"

I worked for the Barker Lumber Company of Bangor, Maine, two years. Young Johnnie Wilson bought a place in Presque Isle, Maine. He was a pretty good carpenter too. So he said to me, "Will you come down and help me build my house? You're done sugar makin'. Why not come down and help me build my house?" I went up. We had our Christmas dinner in it, had it plastered and everything. After we got the house built and New Year's come, I said, "I should go and get a job somewhere up here for the winter." Americans always paid more money than Canada. The pocketbook got bigger. When you was workin' for a dollar, you got two. "Tomorrow morning, I'm gettin' on the train and goin' down to Old Town."

So anyway, I got on the train. I had no papers or anything to be in the States; I stole in. So goin' down on the train, this feller come, "Anybody want to work for the Barker Lumber Company? Bangor, Maine! Anybody on this train wants to work for the Barker Lumber Company?" He's goin' up and down, up and down. This feller in front of me went in and sat down and talked to him. He was writin' down. I says, "You're hirin' men are you?"

"Do you want to hire on?"

I says, "Yeah, I guess I will."

"All right. What's your name?"

"Art Mattix."

"Where do you live?"

"Presque Isle, Maine." See, I daresn't say Canada 'cause I had no papers to stay in there. They'd chase me the hell out. I know'd enough to know that.

He wrote that down. He had a table out there. Back he come. He says, "You say you live in Presque Isle, Maine?"

"Yeah."

"Your name's Art Mattix ain't it?"

"Yeah."

"You know who you're talkin' to, do ya?"

"No."

"You know Tim Mahaney?"

"Yeah?"

"You know Jack Mahaney?"

"No," I says, "I don't. I know Tim well."

"Yeah, I guess you know Tim well. You worked on the river drive in Pollett River didn't you? You and him pretty near got drowned, didn't ya?"

I says, "How do you know this?"

"I'm Tim's brother. I'm Jack."

"What?"

"Yeah. Now all right," he says. He went out and wrote a letter and sealed it up. "Now when you get into the camp tomorrow night, you take that and go up to the wong'n box and give that to the boss." We talked awhile.

I said, now I'm all through right now, they'll put me the hell out of here, sure as hell. But I'll keep quiet and see what's goin' on. Up I went. We had our dinner at the halfway house goin' in. They paid for that, or somebody did, I didn't. Eight or ten of us went, team took us in. Dark as the devil when I got in there. I said, "Where's the boss?" "He's up on the hill there in the wong'n box." I didn't know what in the hell a wong'n box was. So I went and knocked on the door.

"Come in!" He had an old lamp stuck on the table. "What do ya want? Some socks or mittens or something?" Had everything just like a store, everything in there.

"No," I says. "Here's a letter for ya." Handed it over to him. He put his glasses on, read the letter.

He says, "You see that spring up there? Get that down." Oh, there was a heap of blankets that high in there, brand new blankets. Seventy-five or eighty men in the camp and he had ten camps in there. "Make a bed for yourself there. You got a suitcase?" "Yeah." "Go down and get it."

So I went down and got the suitcase. I didn't know what was goin' on. Come in and laid down. He kept on writin' and workin'. That was all right, I didn't say nothin'. I just kept my mouth shut. I went to sleep. In the mornin' we got up, went down and had our breakfast, come back up. "Well," he says, "it's time they turned out." I couldn't stay in that camp alone—my God, there was thousands of dollars worth of stuff in there—so I went with him. Went down to the camp, kicked the door open and the men started walkin' out. They wouldn't come out until the boss kicked the door open, that's the law.

This is something. "Now," he says, "you come with me." We walked down about a mile to the lake and the boys was all there. He says, "You got a new boss on here this morning." I looked at him. I didn't know what the hell was goin' on then. He says, "Boys, this young man, he's takin' charge of the lake this morning." So that was all right. I went on the lake. Wages was two dollars a day roughly seventy years ago, and I got two and a half.

He showed me what he wanted. The logs had to be three tier high on the lake and them was all sixty and seventy feet long pine. Every one had to be painted on the end, red paint on it. I didn't have to do this. There was twelve or thirteen men there rollin' 'em up and pilin' 'em and fixin' 'em up. The Great Northern and the Barker Lumber Company all come in one river. The logs all had to be painted on the ends, you understand, yours was blue and his was red. If any of them wasn't painted, I lost them. They went into a boom here and stayed there until we got done and they split 'em up: I took one and you took one. But if they were painted, it went out to this boom and if it was blue it went out to this one. You had to be damn careful with them.

There's an island for every month of the year on that lake. He had camps on this side and the Great Northern was on this side. They all come in this way and down the river.

This morning, it was a cold morning, *burrr*, it was cold. The wind comin' down that lake. I got an old peavey and I started workin' with the boys. I watched you to see you painted the logs. This old feller come in with a fur coat on, overshoes buckled up to there and a fur cap and fur mittens, walkin' along, lookin' around. He come up and stood, oh, I suppose maybe as far from that buildin' off of me. I was snappin' my peavey around, rollin' up logs, workin' around. He walked up. He says, "Who told you to use a peavey? Are you the lake foreman?"

I says, "Well, yes, I am." I didn't know who I was talkin' to.

"Two pins, I'd fire ya! Who told you to use a peavey?"

"Nobody."

"Boss didn't tell you to use a peavey?"

"No."

He says, "I don't want to see you with a peavey in your hands again. Do you know who you're talkin' to? Mr. Barker, the man that owns all this."

I says, "This is the first time I ever heard tell of a man tell a man he couldn't work. You hire a man, you generally have them work."

He says, "You can't look after this job and work. I want them logs all painted. You ain't supposed to take a peavey. All you're supposed to do is walk around and look after this job."

Now, did you hear tell of the like of that?

I river drove quite a lot. I'll tell you what happened up there [on the Pollett River]. There were forty or fifty men on the river drive. Tim Mahaney and I worked together. There was a jam come in with ice, backed up about a mile and a half. We were breakin' this jam of ice and pickin' it off. They wasn't supposed to heist the dam two or three miles up river until four o'clock at night. You take a mile of water back, about twenty-five feet; that's quite a lot of water come down all at once. So, anyway, we was down there workin', the men was all workin' and the God damn ice got shakin'. I said to Tim, "Geez, what's wrong?" We looked and here was the ice comin' right over top. We made for out and she broke. Tim went on that side of a junk of ice and I went down the river on a log. Charlie Turner stuck a stick out and caught me, hauled me in or I'd went over the falls. They got Tim out on the other side. It gave us quite a scare.

My grandfather on my mother's side was drowned. That's in Pollett River, the same river that I damn near got it. Left my grandmother with ten kids, a cow, a pick and a shovel, and a hoe, to raise ten of them. One of them bull-headed buggers, won't listen to anybody. They told him not to cut that log because if he did maybe he'd get drowned. He went and drove the axe in and, boy, she just went like that—*whack!*—and down he went.

Now here's somethin' a woman done over on the Beeman Road when I was a young feller, oh, I'd be thirteen, fourteen, fifteen years old. She was workin' in the house and she heard this man yellin'. She run down and the tree had buckled over and caught him; he was underneath this big birch tree. I saw the tree rotted there. How that woman ever done it I don't know. She got that log off of him and drug him out of there and took her underwear off, you know, slips and stuff, and made a pillow for him and went out and got help. When she come back, he was dead.

Charles Noonan

Charles Noonan, 86, lives in Hastings, Cumberland County. A master carpenter and cabinetmaker, he spent many years around the lumber woods, working primarily in sawmills. "I edged millions of feet of lumber for a dollar and a half, ten hours, and filed the saws at noon and night. Tough times but, by golly, you could take five dollars then, go to town, and bring home as much as you could now for seventy-five."

My uncles, William and Renerick Chappell, run a big stationary mill about halfway between Oxford and Oxford Junction, right handy the River Philip. They run there from 1919 until 1930 every summer. They were building contractors; they built houses all over the country and an awful dose in Newfoundland. They run a woodworking factory in Sydney making doors and windows and flooring, anything for building. They milled and had a woodworking factory in Tidnish before I ever was born. Then they had one in Windsor; my father run that after he married my Uncle Chappells' sister. They got it cut out, what was there, and went to where there was more lumber and more business. The last one was in Sydney for years.

This was the biggest and strongest mill around this part of the country at that time. A Robb engine 1414, around a hundred and forty-six pounds of steam. Now I want you to know, there was power. I worked there the last four years they sawed; I was only a young fella. When she was sawin' and you was out in the yard, you didn't know if she was sawin' or ridin' idle, she done it that easy. A forty-eight-inch circular [saw], same as they use today. There was no band saws then, they'd rip it up. She'd saw around twenty-five, twenty-six thousand a day.

The River Philip was over there and this tributary came in here that the logs come in on and the mill was between on a pretty big interval. Then down a little further there was a smaller tributary; they said it was man-made, but I don't know. It come in around and drove the

Oxford Electric Plant. It drove by water, and if the water got scarce there was steam to it. It was there for years. They shut the old power plant and [then] they got the power from Maccan.

The mill itself was sixteen feet up, and the boiler, engine, and drive shaft was all down below. This haul-up was a long slant from the water up. There'd be a fella there with a pike pole and a raft to stand on and he'd just point them on the endless chain. Every few feet, there'd be a square block with like three peavey pikes. Them would catch the logs and go up, no slidin' back or anything. It was a lovely place to work. A beautiful shed, shutters you opened, cool air from these two rivers. You never knew what a hot day was there.

My father, Albert Noonan, was a millwright for Chappell's. He done the filin' of the lath mill; he never had nothin' to do with filin' the rotary saw or the edger, they done their own filin'. He had the mill to look after. If a belt wanted lacing or anything wanted doin', he was there to do it. He canted when he was a young fella. He didn't like that job and told them he'd like to go on and fire the boiler; he fired for years.

They sawed a lot for themselves and sold a lot of the lumber, a lot of beautiful hardwood. Some years, maybe it would be half and half and other times it'd be more spruce, but always a lot of hardwood: rock maple, yellow birch, beech. Mostly, I would say, would be yellow birch. An awful lot of it went to Sydney. It was only a step over across to the siding. There was a short line that run from Oxford Junction down to Pictou and up to Sydney. The greatest place to saw lumber and ship it that I ever seen.

The logs come down the River Philip twenty-three miles; dam the River Philip from Williamsdale down to Oxford. I worked on that. Williamsdale is where we landed out, Second River where it runs into River Philip. They had loggin' camps up right around River Philip, Collingwood, and Williamsdale. Log all winter, and when it broke up in the spring, down they come. They'd bring down an average anywhere from a million to a million and a half.

They kept the hardwood out of the water and up off the ground all summer so it dried an awful lot and it drove easier. By doing that…[they didn't have to peel it]. The way they worked that, after the drive was done right around the first of May, they'd put a bunch in the back camp and they'd fall these hardwood and keep the butt up off the ground. Just fall it and not junk it at all, just leave it there. Then around about the first of October, they'd start to junk them and brow them in the woods. They'd dry there all summer and they'd be browed there all winter. You could tell that they dried a lot too, my

One way of transporting hardwood logs was to raft them out by means of the softwood as both were normally driven together. (Lillian Scott Perry)

golly, you bet. They'd float then just as good as spruce. The year I was there and helped pile those logs, I think it was seven thousand trees down, and there'd be three or four or five logs in a tree. There was a lot of thousands. My golly, there was some big ones, I'm tellin' you. They'd get up maybe to thirty inches, birch or rock maple. There didn't seem to be no pine at all or no hemlock, all spruce. Once in a long, long while, there'd be one or two beautiful fir comin', just white beautiful wood. It was a spruce and hardwood country.

That was wild country up there. It's all high mountain ground. Comin' down off the mountain, there's places up there that was solid rock on both sides; go like that, then drop right straight down for twenty or thirty feet, level off, and go again. That water comin' down there just white, white foam, roarin'. Logs goin' down on end. You talk about a wild lookin' place. That's up where they call the Second River. I seen a jam there, oh, I expect a hundred thousand anyway. Two or three of the old drivers, "Well, that's easily taken care of." Put three or four sticks of dynamite in there and blow it up. Blow three or four logs in maybe two or three places and away she'd go. There was a man killed the first two or three years they were there. I forget how it happened. They said it was kind of his own fault, just carelessness. My father was there. He come up from Oxford Junction to Amherst on the train and brought the corpse.

After they quit the mill in Oxford, my father went to Sydney and he done the filin' of all the band saws and sharpening the planers and everything until he was eighty. They had two mills in Cape Breton running for years. One was in Sydney River and the other was in Grand Mira, twenty-six miles out of Sydney. I worked out in the yard; my cousin was the boss. I liked it out there, great fellers to work with. Well then, they put me up in the factory. I said, "What am I goin' to do?" "I don't know. Do something." I used to start up a jointer and joint some of the lumber off and put it through the planer, what we were makin' doors and all that stuff out of.

After a bit I went over and I put a bowlin' pin in the turning lathe and I turned a bowling pin. My boss was right up in a room in the corner upstairs and he seen me. He come right out; "My God," he said. "Where did you learn to turn?" "Learn to turn?" I said. "I never even seen one goin' before." The man that had turned for years, he was old and had died a short time ago. They owned bowling alleys themselves, Chappells did. They were just about ready to shut down, out of pins, nobody turned them. My God, I turned thousands of pins there, thousands of 'em, rock maple.

Quite a few years after I was there, the old factory burnt and they built a new one. It was supposed to be the best and up-to-date east of Montreal. My uncles' sons, there were four of them, they're all dead and none of the grandchildren ever had anything to do with it. I don't know who owns it today. It's been a long while since I been down.

When I quit millin', I went to work as a carpenter. It would be about the time the second war started. Before the war started things had been commencing to get up. We started at a dollar ten an hour. We built a big building on main street, offices, the St. Charles School—about three hundred feet long—and a church and a house and a school or two. That was all done in Amherst. I said a million times, my father was the best carpenter I ever worked with. All I had to do was work with him. It just come natural to me. I stayed at carpentry and cabinet work until I was seventy.

Layton Smith

Layton Smith, 84, lives in Amherst, Cumberland County. His family history in the lumber woods goes back five generations. In addition to woods work, his varied experiences include forty years of farming, running a boarding house, and construction.

I was born in Shinimicas right alongside granddad's farm. That's the original farm that runs five generations back. The Shinimicas River runs right through the middle of the farm. They had four or five hundred acres there at that time and they were just loggin' their own land. They had the old water mill with the big dam just above the house there on the river. That broke down and then my father come along, that next generation, and he took over and had a steam mill on the same site. I remember when they were haulin' the logs up out of the pond into the mill, sawin' them, and the sawdust, slabs, and the edgin's all went into the river.

They had a big grist mill too, run by a water wheel. I was in the grist mill when I was a kid. Everybody grew buckwheat and wheat all around that part of the country and took it to the grist mill and got it ground. That was goin' strong and then it deteriorated. All these rivers had dams on them and water mills and grist mills to no end a hundred years back and before that. They started petering out seventy-five, eighty years ago, then the engines come in and took over.

Up above seven or eight miles into Leicester, that's where the lumber, a lot of it, come from. People up there would bring it right down the river. The Wallace River that runs up through Collingwood and into the mountains, and the River Philip, that's the only way they had of bringin' lumber down in those days. The tide come up that Shinimicas River within a mile and a half of where our farm is. We're just six miles up river from Northport. Northport at that time was quite a little village, and the big sailing boats would come in there. There was three or four sawmills on that river and they were sawin' logs all summer from different farmers. There was all kinds of lumber in those days, back a hundred years ago, all around that part of the country.

The lumber, not the logs, was put in the river and stream drove down to Northport, loaded on the schooner, and shipped out. It's a smooth-flowing river, no rapids. They rafted it, small rafts, and each guy had his name on the raft with paint so they'd know whose lumber it was. They had teams of horses, but poor roads to haul anything on, and that was the cheapest way of transporting in those days. They'd raft their own down, maybe five or six or seven men, and they had big long poles. The schooners set out in the bay and they took the lumber right out and loaded the rafts on the schooners.

Down Parrsboro years ago was a big shipbuilding place. Pugwash was too: schooners, wooden ships. The elm trees are awful tough and they cut a pile of elm trees down for ribs and the keels. Elm is twice as strong as any other kind of wood there is. It'll bend better than oak, steam out better. We don't have any oak around here.

When the steam come in and took out the water wheel, and the roads got better, then they trucked with teams of horses all the way to Pugwash, twelve miles, to load on boats. They had big special wharves built down there. At Northport, there's no wharf to amount to anything. Most of it was all shipped away: Pugwash by boat, and Amherst or Oxford Junction by rail. Advocate was a big lumber country then. There were lumber dealers here in town. Charlie Reed was one of the big shippers; he shipped to England, France, and the United States. Albert Miner was a dealer. Then they started bringin' the big steamers in from Germany, England, and those places and load pulpwood in the 1940s. Farmers would have a little woodlot and they'd want to pick up a few dollars on the side and they'd put out maybe a hundred cord of pulpwood. We was always logs.

Father, William Smith, had a portable mill and he went around to whoever had a cut they wanted sawed and he'd set up the mill. Then in the winter, we'd go in the woods and saw all winter. Those days, there was no trucks on the road so we had to load the mill on flatcars and ship it by train, then haul it into the woods on a scoot sled. You could make somethin' in just a couple of hours 'cause all it took was two logs about a foot through. That was the runner on each side. Put

Lumber raft on the LaHave River, circa 1900. This was practised on different rivers in the province, providing no rapids or other obstacles were present. (N.S. Museum)

about three bunks across to keep 'er from squeezin' in. Bore a hole through the front of each one, put a cable through, fasten it up, and have about six or seven feet to haul the sled with. It'd be about twelve feet long. You could only put on so many pieces, and when you got a load we'd take it in a mile or two in the woods, unload, and come out and get another load until we got everything all in.

You didn't lift the boiler, it was on wheels. You'd just jack up the front end, put a set of skids under for runners, jack the hind end up and let it ride on the two big skids that come back. Put four or five teams of horses on ahead and snig it through the woods. She'd set right there. You're only goin' slow with teams; wouldn't be goin' over two mile an hour. We never had any oxen that I ever knew of around this part of the country. You had to go down to Lunenburg and Shelburne County; down in there is where all the oxen were. It might have been back a couple hundred years ago, but not in my day or my father's day; it was always horses. In about 1943 we got our first crawler tractor and, boy, that was the answer. We didn't bother with any more teams. We'd just load 'er up, put a couple ton on and away we'd go with a scoot sled and the tractor; take the machine in wherever we wanted it.

He'd set his mill up along the last of November. Arnold [Layton's brother] and I would go in and cut the roads out where we were goin' to cut logs to draw to the mill so he could saw. We always had camps in the woods those days, in the thirties and mid-forties. It was only after the Second World War was over, between 1945 and 1950, that they started plowin' roads and you could go anywhere in the wintertime. Before that, the only way you went was by horse and sled. You went in in the fall after Christmas, you settled in for the winter and you didn't come out until the middle of March. That was it. Our camps would hold about fifteen, sixteen men for the mill. The loggin' camp we always had around thirty, thirty-five men. We used to have three or four teams of horses for haulin' logs and then we always had seven or eight yardin' horses.

Maybe once or twice through the winter a team would come out here to Amherst, take a day to come out and another day to go back, and get two or three tons of flour and sugar and an extra barrel of molasses and take back and replenish. They used to shoot the odd moose years ago, but you'd buy maybe a carcass. You take a good big carcass of meat dressed at five or six hundred; that'd last you for a couple of weeks. The farmer or whoever you bought it from, you let him know when you wanted another one and he'd kill it and bring it into ya. There was no refrigeration or anything; you never knew such a thing. Everything was froze at eight or ten degrees below zero.

Haul the hay in; pressed hay those days. There wasn't any such thing as baled hay like they have today. The hay was all put up loose, pitched on the wagon by hand and stored in the barns. Then in the fall this big hay press would come in and if you had twenty-five, thirty, or forty tons of hay, he pressed the whole thing and you'd sell what hay you wanted. They pressed hay into bundles that weighed around a hundred or a hundred and twenty pounds. This hay that you know about, they're only fifty, sixty pounds. It wouldn't be any bigger bale, but it'd be a tighter bale.

The press goes in on the barn floor. There's always a couple of guys pitchin' the hay down onto the table of the hay press. A man stands there with a fork and he forks the hay into the press. The ol' hay press just goes back and forth. When you put the hay in the hole, the plunger comes against it and shoves it right up in there. When it comes back, you put another big fork full in. That works steady all the time and you have to time yourself puttin' the hay down.

That was a business all by itself every fall. These marshes had hundreds of barns on them. They'd start about the middle of November and they'd press through to maybe the first of February. You'd have this big hay press and a gasoline engine to run the press and that was your business. You'd have a man with you. In grain, a lot of fellas that was runnin' threshing machines would take what they called toll: so much grain to thrash the farmer's grain. They pressed the hay so much a ton. That was big business in the teens and twenties, yes, and up in the forties, then it died out. These new hay combines come in and revolutionized all the farming.

I worked in the steam mill when I was sixteen, seventeen years old. Then around 1944, my God, the big steam dome on top of the boiler blew up. Jesus, just blew the old mill all to pieces and killed the fireman. My youngest brother Harold, he was surveyin' in the mill right within twenty feet of where the boiler blew up. He was scalded and was in hospital for three months or so, skin grafts and everything for years.

The mill was goin' right along sawin', they just nicely got started about half past seven and, my God, all at once, *boom!* The ol' dome blew off the boiler with about a hundred and forty-five, a hundred and fifty pounds of steam in 'er, just pulled the boiler apart and the hot steam flew everywheres and scalded two or three of the men. He [fireman] was right beside the boiler. The boiler just jumped right back and squashed him against a bunch of three-foot slabs they had for feedin' the boiler.

Just a winter shed, it would be closed in to keep the snow out—it blew everything to pieces. They had a big hardwood log on the carriage where they were sawin'. She was about halfway through and it just twisted her sideways. Did a pile of damage. Knocked the men down; the concussion from that pressure was terrific. The dome weighed about five hundred pounds, just like a big barrel only it's a big steel dome. By God, she blew way off, four or five hundred yards from the mill.[1] That was in back of Springhill at Mapleton. They felt and heard the noise in Springhill; that was six or seven miles from there. Yeah, it really shook things up. They just cleaned up the works, pulled the old boiler out of the way, got an engine and finished up the cut. That was about the time diesel engines was startin' to come in. After that, father always had a diesel engine to use.

I was up in Boston from 1930 to 1935. It was just one of those things when you're young, you like a little adventure and you start out. I was up there when the United States went bankrupt and closed all their banks. In 1933, when Roosevelt come in, the banks was all in bad shape and he closed every bank in the country. I had a chauffeurin' job for an old guy and went down to the bank that morning to get a few dollars and the banks was closed and a big crowd all around. They were closed for about a week before they opened them again.

The old fella that I was chauffeurin' for, old Mr. Walker, he lived in Maldon, Mass.; it's a little town outside of Boston. His son, he'd be a man at that time around fifty, fifty-five. The old man was eighty. I was only about twenty-two or three. I stayed right at the house seven days a week and got twelve dollars a week. That wasn't bad for up there when there wasn't no work and everything was flat. His son played the stock market a lot. The Walkers were worth quite a bit of money. Well now, when the bank closed, boy, things were in tough shape.

Right after the banks opened, Roosevelt called in all the gold. He knew there was a pile of gold the people had hoarded up. Your gold standard, now today, the way the gold went this last number of years, we're off the gold standard and we'll never get back on it again; I don't think we will. You take interest in the banks years ago, why it was the same from one year to another and you knew where you was gettin' off at. But today you don't know inside of twenty-four hours what you're goin' to get for your value. Why, it's up and down like a yo-yo. That's the reason the country, the world, is in such a helluva state that it is.

The old gentleman's son come home for a few days; he was out somewhere on business. He says, "Look, I've got to go into the bank in the morning and I want you to take me in." I said okay. Come the morning, he says, "They've called the gold back and I've got a bunch here I've got to take back." Well, you know, that young feller, that was just one sample of what was goin' on all over the country. There was a heavy fine [if it wasn't turned in]. "I've got six bags and I just don't know how we're goin' to get it in. We got to take it out of the house and to the car." We had a little coupe car. I says, "We'll just carry it out to the car and that's all there be to it. Put it in the rumble seat and drive into town. Nobody will ever know anything about it."

I was livin' there in the house right with them and the old saying is, "I didn't know putty from shit." I didn't realize how much money it might be. You know what the money bags are like from the bank? Well, Christ, I got hold of a bag and I'll bet you there was fifty or seventy-five pounds in each bag. All twenty- and fifty-dollar gold pieces, that's what they were. There was at least a million dollars worth of gold there. I helped him carry it out of the house and chucked it in the back of the old car. We went down in through Boston and drove up alongside of the Shawmut Bank—that's one of the big banks there at that time. I stayed right there in the car and he went in and brought a guard out with him. They loaded it on a truck and away they went.

If I'd a known and been smart like some of these other guys, I could have knocked him off and took the load of gold. It's like everything else, if you knew what was goin' on and how things was workin', I could have been a rich man, but I didn't. I was just an honest country boy, green behind the ears, just out learnin' a few things.

In 1935 when the wife and I come down from Boston, we went right in on the old farm. Not a damn thing to do. Everything was right down to where you could get a pound of butter for fifteen cents and you could buy a cord of hardwood, landed right in your back door yard, for six dollars a cord. So my brother Arnold and I and a friend of ours went back in the woods and we cut hardwood for stove and furnace wood. We cut a hundred cord in two months and brought it out. In the spring, we had a woodcutter come in and then we split it and hauled it to Amherst with the old 1929 Chev truck for seven dollars a cord. Now, can you imagine what we made, but we had a warm place to stay and lots to eat. That's all you thought about in those days. Lived and got by and enjoyed themselves a helluva lot better than they're doin' today, I'll tell you that. I can see the difference from seventy years ago until now. See, when you come into the work force everything was goin' for you. You don't realize what us old fellers went through.

They ain't loggin' anymore as we used to know it. They're stripping the country now as far as that goes. There's no more horses in the woods for yardin' or anything like that. There's no more labour work in the woods. We used to cut winter after winter with the old crosscut saws; that's what kept you in good shape in those days. Now, all he does, he sets in a machine and goes up to a tree, cuts it off and lays it down. They're ruinin' the whole damn country here. Now, you've heard that before, haven't you?

We have a sample right in there, the two big farms in back. We had about eight or nine hundred acres. Twenty-five years ago we said we'd never allow a machine in there. We seen what they were doing. We'd go in and cut what we wanted and keep on cuttin'. You just cut the big trees down that you wanted and the young stuff all grow'd up then. With a yarding horse you wouldn't hurt a thing. Your skid roads are in through the trees three or four feet wide and that's it.

Now the whole damn place is as flat as piss in a plate. Couldn't do anything else. The budworm was raisin' hell with us in this part of the country. The first thing we knew, there was big spruce trees there dead as a nit. They couldn't control it. That was our only alternative we had to get clear of it in two or three years. You'd have lost it anyhow, but where the budworm didn't hit, it didn't make any difference, that's the only way of cuttin' they had anyhow.

These big machines come in and cuts the whole damn thing, pulpwood and lumber, the whole works is cut down. When they get through with it, other than a lot of rubbish and junk, it's just as flat as that floor. When you go in with those machines, you got to take everything. It'll grow up in time, but it'll be a hundred years before they ever get a log off of it again.

Arnold Smith

Arnold Smith, 76, Layton Smith's brother, lives on their great-grandfather Thomas Smith's farm at Shinimicas Bridge. He began logging with his father in 1930 and worked in the woods business for fifty years. For years he used a mixture of loaders, horses, and chain saws, and he milled "pretty near all over Cumberland County."

It was all axe work in the late 1800s. In fact, I've heard my father speak about they'd be loggin' up here, it'd be in 1910, and it was mostly axe work at that time. There was hardly any saws; saws were just startin' to come in. The first saw was what they called an M tooth crosscut: two teeth in it, then a space, then two more teeth, like an M. I've seen them out here in the old granary. Then, after that, in my day, just before I was born, they come out with the crosscut saw that had drags on them. The M tooth didn't have a drag [tooth] on it, but the other had three or four teeth and then a drag. Supposed to be easier cuttin'.

You could buy different kinds of axes. At one time they had what they called the Bird axe. It was built here in Cumberland County. This would be around 1900. There was a blacksmith, a Bird, livin' in Leicester. His son built axes for me. They were a good axe: double-bitted, hand-forged. They tempered and shaped them and ground them and hammered them out. There was the Campbell axe and the Blenkhorn. They had the Blenkhorn and then the Blenkhorn Chief, ten or a dozen in a box. At one time, axes were about two dollars and fifty cents apiece. Not the handle. The handle would be fifty cents or a dollar. I've bought hundreds of axes, because every time you had a crew of men in the woods, usually the axes would get lost and worn. So every year you'd start in, you'd buy a box of new axes and you'd have the old axes for the yarders and stuff like that.

We never bought factory handles those days. You don't know what you're buyin' 'cause they could be cross-grained and brittle. The Indians would make handles and you'd buy them. They were a better handle. They would cut a certain size ash and they would split it right down and it wouldn't be cross-grained. Then they'd take a spokeshave and a plane and drawknife or crooked knife, and in an hour or so they could make you a handle.

We had Indians would come and go on our property and cut ash and nobody would say, no, you can't go. They would come in and put up a little camp. I can remember when I was just a boy, an Indian, his wife and two or three kids had a little camp up on the intervale here. They'd go through the woods and pick up good ash for axe handles and make a lot. He stayed there all summer one year. Then he'd take off and go somewhere else. They'd do that different places. Noel Paul down here around Oxford Junction, he made axe handles for me for years. He made a good axe handle and I used to go buy them by the dozens. They would sell them to the stores and anybody that wanted them. They'd charge around a dollar, a dollar and a quarter for a handle.

We always had two-storey camps. They'd be about sixteen feet wide and it'd depend how big a crew you were goin' to have how long you'd make them. You tore the camp down and took the lumber to build another one. You'd do that for two or three times and, of course, every time there'd be a few boards you'd have to throw away and get some new ones. The camp would be tar paper outside.

Sometimes in the winter we'd put two thicknesses to make it a little warmer. A roll of tar paper years ago, very early, used to be only a dollar and a half or so, then it got up to five and six dollars the last end. It would take eight or ten rolls and then you'd have to build your hovels and they'd be all tar papered too.

Downstairs in one end would be the cook's room and there'd be a partition across, maybe out seven or eight feet to give her room for her bed. You'd have two stoves probably in the wintertime, a big cookstove at one end and a "ram-down" we call it, at the other. It'd be a furnace about three feet long made of steel and it was round with a door onto it. It would take a thirty-inch stick or even a three-foot one. Where the table was you'd have two or three windows on that side and a window or two on the other.

Upstairs there'd just be a big window in each end and sometimes we'd put one in the ceiling you could lift up for ventilation. You'd have one set of steps up and you'd have it [floor] double-boarded and all papered over underneath so there'd be no dirt comin' down. That would be a heavy white paper on the floor. You'd have bunks on each side. We always had a quilt besides the blankets; lots of places didn't, but we always did.

My father milled all his life. He would saw about three cuts through the summer that people would log and he would kind of have the same circuit year after year. Then in the wintertime we'd put the mill in the woods. Up 'til 1930, he would usually saw down below Joggins and River Hebert. From 1930 there was two or three years lumber business was very slack and he didn't saw in the winter, but there'd be two or three brows in the summer that he'd saw.

Down at Lynne Mountain when my father was sawin' there, a yarder was killed. They felled a tree on him. That was pretty near fifty years ago. They didn't know that they'd felled a tree on him until they limbed the tree up and looked down and here the yarder was, layin' there dead.

Most of ours was what we call hot loggin'. Other than maybe twenty-five or thirty or forty brows that was browed up before the mill started or before you could haul, then you would haul off the choppers just as they cut it, right to the mill. That would save you handlin' them a couple of times and the logs was cleaner, there was no ice or mud on them. The mill man didn't like too much mud on the logs 'cause he can't make good lumber. All you need is one frozen, muddy log and your saw is dull. That's the trouble a lot of mill men used to have. When we logged for Wilson McCullen, father took the mill and I took the loggin'. He said, "This is the first winter I ever had any peace." Before that, every week, either the mill man was in there complainin' about the loggers or the logger was in complainin' about the mill man.

It's quite a hard life. I can remember in 1936, I'd be just a young fella, there was no money. You had to make every move count or you'd lose your hide. I'd have paths through the woods from one road to another. I'd know about when the teams was comin', so that when I'd get one team loaded, I'd run through the woods and be there about the time the other team got there. You'd work yourself pretty near to death to make a livin'.

Harold Trenholm

Harold Trenholm, 83, lives in Amherst, Cumberland County. Unable to afford a college education upon finishing high school, he studied electrical engineering through a correspondence course while working in the lumber camps. He eventually went on to M.I.T. where he furthered his studies in gas and oil engineering. His career has been varied, and he ended up in charge of construction, maintenance, and vehicles at Springhill Penitentiary. He was offered the position of warden but, with only two years before retirement, he declined. His father, Locksley, was a cabinetmaker who learned his trade with Chappell Brothers in Sydney. He left that and ran a sawmill for twenty years. "He never made any money at it. He was not a businessman at all. He just went from one place to another and some years he'd make money and other years he lost everything he had. He had the house mortgaged about three times trying to keep things going."

My first experience in a mill is when I quit high school. I was going into Grade 12 and my dad said, "I think you've got enough experience now. You can read and write, we need you in the woods." He was working in Southampton at this time and he had his portable mill plus a lath machine. These jobs would only last maybe two or three months. They'd be what we called farm cuts in the summertime. The farmers get together, they'd all have little lots and they'd get out maybe twenty-five, fifty, hundred thousand to the clear and come spring they'd haul 'em to a common area where a mill was set up and saw them in a field. A mill can't saw in the summertime in the woods on account of fire.

Of course, the first job in a mill they put you in is carrying slabs and it's an awful job. It'll test you if you want to work. You're carryin' those slabs and they're a big butt end; your sleeves are rolled up to your elbows and you get balsam stuff on the hairs of your arms and it takes the hairs and all with it. You had to carry that out into a slab fire and face that smoke every time you went out. Nobody liked it.

That fire, once it got started in on a cut whether it was spring, fall or winter, once the fire got goin' the first day, it never went out after that. There'd be enough coals there to carry it through to the next day. Sometimes it'd be maybe two o'clock in the afternoon before the fire'd really get going, especially if it was a wet, snowy day and the slabs were all wet and dirty coming in.

As time went on I was promoted from that to the lath machine. Edgings of any size come to the lath machine, and on the way they get cut into four-foot lengths and then go through a bolter—it's over a twelve-inch saw—and it gives you your thickness, the width of the laths, which is an inch and a quarter; that's standard. Then it moves over the table to the lath machine, which cuts as high as four laths at one time. It drops into a baler, which bales it up at a hundred to a bale. You're throwin' these laths—two, three, four—out into the baler and you keep count of them so when you get to a hundred, another fella there will grab them and take them away from you. You can't leave it there too long, there's more coming all the time. That machine goes pretty fast, you work pretty fast there, and you'll make as high as maybe three hundred bales a day.

I graduated from there up to what they call the skid man; he rolled the logs into the carriage where the canter takes over and puts them on the carriage and the sawyer saws them up. I moved up on the skidway and then I moved into canting. You got to learn that quick too, to turn them up right for the sawyer, because the sawyer knows whether he wants the round up or round down or round in or round out. The log is never straight, it's always crooked, so you have to put it one way to get the most lumber out of it. There's dogs on the carriage to hold it in place. I had to know which way to put it, and if I didn't put it the right way, I wouldn't be long being told either. You learn fast because that carriage is just back and forth all the time.

I worked my way all through the mill right down to the fireman who fires the engine that keeps the steam on and keeps 'em goin'. You have to carry about a hundred and fifty, a hundred and fifty-five pounds of steam all the time. I did find the firing of the mill was the easiest job in the end although you worked from five o'clock in the morning until maybe eight or nine o'clock at night. It was still not that big a job because there was nothin' really heavy and you was in where it was warm all the time, but to keep steam on, you had to know how to do it.

There was always little things going wrong all the time. You had an engine there to contend with to keep that oiled because it was working all the time. You had to keep the steam up and keep the water to it. The odd time, you'd blow your water glass, it would burst on you. Could be a cold draft hit it more than anything. There was boiling water inside of that glass, and somebody open a door at one end of the mill or the boiler room, that sudden draft would break it. That's what we usually tried to guard against because in the winter sometimes it went down as low as twenty below, Fahrenheit. If we could, we'd put the door around the corner so any draft that come in, the warmth would take the chill off. It [the water glass] showed the height of your water in the boiler all the time, and when that burst there'd be steam flying everywhere. What we'd do, they had a valve and you shut them off and try to remember how much water was in the boiler when you started so that you wouldn't let yourself get too low. Otherwise, you'd blow the whole thing up.

Then in the wintertime you'd have your problems when your water line would freeze up. You had an injector which worked from the pressure of the boiler, a siphon affair, which would suck the water into the boiler so far, then push it the rest of the way in against maybe a hundred and thirty, a hundred and forty pounds of steam. When that laid idle, say, for twenty minutes it would have a tendency to freeze up, and as the day went along it kept freezing up so far that you couldn't get hardly any water through it. Then the injector would refuse to take it. You had to watch your chance to blow that pipe back and you would reverse the injector. Instead of haulin' stuff in, she'd blow steam back out the pipe and that would free the pipe again. These were very touchy moments because, by clearing that pipe back, at the same time you made the pipe hot so it would not accept the water; the injector would refuse to work while that pipe was hot. So what you'd do, you always had a bucket of cold water in the boiler room to cool that part of it down as fast as you could so that she'd get your water back.

The same thing in your engine. It had six-inch bearings in it. The odd time you maybe forget to oil the thing, she went maybe half a day and, bang, all of a sudden she'd be bangin' her head off and burn out the bearings. If you caught it, so it didn't pound too much, you put the oil to it and sometimes you'd save it and sometimes you didn't. If it wasn't too serious, you could let it run 'til six o'clock, then that night we knew what we'd have to do. We had to take that thing apart and re-babbitt that bearing. A babbitt was made out of a combination of lead, zinc, and copper. Your bearings were a shell with the babbitt poured inside. So we had to melt the old babbitt out of the shell. You'd have a babbitt scrapper to scrape it shiny and take any roughings all off. Then you had your babbitt groove cutter; it's like a chisel. You'd have to cut grooves all in it for oil to run through.

There were things like that or a belt would break every once in a while and you'd have to stop. Course as a rule you were used to the mill stuff; you'd get so you'd know it was coming, you'd hear it flapping, so you'd shut down. If you waited 'til it went, the belt would go all over hell and tear everything to pieces; could knock half the end of the mill out.

Our main belt was about a hundred and ten feet long. You had to put clamps on that first and draw that up 'til they come together. You can't do it with the belt off the pulleys; it's too hard to hold it. You had a big needle as big as my little finger with a ring on the end of it. You had to punch holes in the belt and it was always double holes, two holes, one behind each other, and about five across, according to the width of the belt. You got to bring them up tight together, then lace it with a marlin spike. You put about three lacings in each hole so you can weave it back and forth, cross-weave it, so that you tension all ways. That'd take about an hour sometimes to do it.

Then we had what they called alligator fasteners. They'd go every once in a while. They were for smaller belts and something that was not going too fast. They were metal prongs and you put that over the belt and then you had a clamp you put in and squeeze them, lock them right in. When they were done, each end, you shove them together and put a rawhide thong through the centre and that held them.

Sometimes in a hardwood log, if it was in an old sugar woods, which we used to hate to do, oftentimes they left their spiles right in and they would grow over and you wouldn't see it at all until the saw struck it. When that saw struck, it was *urrrgh!* And all the teeth would fly out of it and the shanks would go and everybody would be swearing and cursin'. You'd have to shut down and put all new shanks in and new teeth. A shank is a spring-loaded control that you put in—I'm talkin' about rotary saws now—and it had a big circle which each tooth went in. The shank went in and hauled the tooth in behind it so there was a spring against a tooth all the time, and that would have to be all replaced. When the sawyer was facing the saw, there was always a wide board just down between him and the saw, so anything the saw struck, it would fly and hit that board or up through the roof. It was so close to him it couldn't get by without hittin' it first. Boys, when it struck, you knew it.

They had what they called dogs and they were just like a big railroad spike with a ring in it. They'd drive that in the side of the log close to the end, then the yarder would hook a chain in that, hook his team to it, and out he went. Sometimes they'd break those dogs off and they wouldn't bother choppin' 'em out and gettin' rid of 'em, they'd just leave 'em there. The saw would strike that once in a while. It would almost throw the log off the carriage, it hit so hard, and there'd be some swearin' go on then too. The teeth were all replaceable in a rotary saw. In the other saws, the edger and cutoff saws, they weren't, and we had to sharpen 'em. But very seldom you'd do it on those saws, the main saw would catch anything like that. There were always little things that happened that would slow you down.

I went away for four or five years. In my early twenties, after running around the country doing different jobs up in Detroit and Boston, I come home. I was up there at the time of the Wall Street crash, so I had nothin' to do. My father was operating a mill down in the Truro area. It just so happened he was moving into the woods for a spring cut and he needed a cook. Dad said, "I've got a job for you. I need a cook." I said, "God, I can't cook!" "Well," he says, "you'll learn." That was the answer. I had no alternative, so I went. The first month I cooked there was more went out the window than went on the table.

When I went down to cook, there was only about six men, the crew just getting things organized before the main crew come in. I didn't know what to cook or where to cook or what to put together. Her sister [his wife's twin sister] was cooking for the logging crew, which was forty-some men, and they were just getting going same as we were. Pearl said, "I'll help you out." Her camp was about a hundred yards from where our camp was and I had a pretty good path beat back and forth 'cause sometimes I'd go up and get some information on how to make cookies or somethin' and before I got back I forget about it. Then the trouble was to find things. I didn't know cream of tartar from soda. What a time I had.

Well, the first thing, I was going to make a good batch of cookies. I had no idea what to put together, and when I got done I had a great big bunch of dough. Her sister said, "You got to roll them out because they'll puff up." So I got the rollin' pin and I rolled them out thin and, God, they spread all over the table. I took a cutter and cut them out and put them in pans. I had about four dozen. The oven was about three feet square in those old camp stoves and I got the pans in the oven. They was lookin' good. So I ran up to Pearl and I said, "How long do I leave them in the oven?" She said, "About ten minutes." I thought they'd have to stay there 'til they was hard. I didn't know they're supposed to be just ten minutes and then take them out and they'll harden up as they cool. So I looked at them, ten minutes, and they were still soft. The next time I turned around, smoke was comin' right out of the oven. Out the window they went.

A little later, Dad had a barrel of salt beef there. He says, "You should have some corn beef and cabbage; be a change for you." I was makin' soup most of the time. Dad says, "You better get some meat goin'. The men are workin' quite hard." I took this ol' corned beef right out of the barrel and I put it right in the pot, cooked it all up, put cabbage in it and potatoes, turnips, and carrots. Oh, I had a great big potful. Dad come in that night, "What are we goin' to have? Smells good." "Corned beef and cabbage." "Oh boy, that's just what we want." Well that ol' corned beef was full of salt, saltpeter, and all that stuff; I never parboiled it at all. They tried to eat it. This darn brine went all through the vegetables too. Well, they had a very small supper that night. They filled up on bread and potatoes. Dad told me afterwards, "You should parboil that stuff." I said, "What do you mean parboil? What's parboil?" He says, "Boil it first and throw that water away; get that ol' saltpeter out of there." Oh, we had some hard times there. But gradually I learned. That put the bug in me and I've been cooking off and on ever since.

We worked for King Brothers most of the time from Oxford—Bob and Guy King. They owned thousands of acres of land and we'd do most of our winter cutting for them. That would be in back of Lynn Mountain, East Mapleton, and Westchester mountains. That's about the areas we worked in the winter.

We would get in and get the camp set up and get the cook in and gradually get our mill in. We'd go in the fall and locate our site. We always tried to find a place not too far from a brook so you'd get lots of water for the mill and the camp. Course on those mountains there was brooks running every direction. There'd be no roads where we'd go; you'd have to cut roads in. You had to cut roads wide enough to get your camp supplies in, get your mill in and all the gear. That meant you'd have to cut the trees down, cut the stumps out, and any big rocks, move them out of the way, level as much as you could with what you had to work with.

The loggers was another outfit; they'd have about forty-two men in their crew. They never come in until you got the road in and you got pretty well established, then they'd move in. It didn't take them long to get goin' because, although they had to cut roads too, they didn't have to be too particular because they didn't intend to haul too many logs until the snow fell, and that would be the middle of November.

It just so happened that most of the time wherever we went there was an old camp that had been left or one camp handy there. We would either tear it down and rebuild it or steal stuff out of it enough to get a shelter made to get into and then we would get organized. Course it didn't matter too much how rough it was or how cold it was, because you was healthy, you was rugged, and you was dressed warm. You had lots of heavy gray blankets to put around you and no problem makin' a good fire even if it was outdoors. The first lumber you saw would maybe be for a camp. We may saw for a day and shut down and build ourself [a camp] or renew the camp or make it more permanent. Once we got our camp established, then we sawed enough lumber to board our mill in. We picked pretty good stuff for that, so we got wide boards so we could close the mill in fast. In the springtime, you didn't worry. The mill always laid wide open, and anything for a camp to get into; the main thing was to have the roof tight.

You'd go in there possibly in September and you worked 'til the last of October before you'd get the mill in. That was a hard job gettin' that mill in. Many times we had to take the boiler for miles just with a block and tackle and have a team of horses on the end. The blocks would weigh seventy-five pounds apiece and the rope was about inch and a quarter and could be three or four hundred feet long because our blocks were always what we called a four and two block. There was four here and two here, so it [the rope] had to go back and forth three or four times before it actually went out, before the teams hooked onto it. We'd have to take that block and tackle, stretch them out and hook 'em to a tree or something, then let the team start. One reason why we had this was it moved so slow that if the boiler was starting to tip, you'd just holler for the teamster to stop. If it was a little quicker she would flop over before you got a chance to get her stopped. The boiler weighed about five and a half ton. We never had it fall over.

If you were on a hard road, two teams would haul it, but if you were going up a mountain road, it would take six teams. One time we moved up from Westchester Station into a place on top of Westchester Mountain called Twin Bridges. We were goin' up there for a spring cut in April and there was four feet of snow on that road never been broken. We had a team ahead of us just breakin' road, they wasn't tied in. The horses were breakin' through to the lower crust and it was hard enough to carry them, but that top crust was just like punching holes. We had four teams on the boiler itself and had a long pole fastened to the top of the boiler. Whenever the boiler come to a soft spot she'd tip right down and we'd have to swing that pole around the other side and two men hang on.

Between teamin' and runnin' up a mountain all the time you had to be rugged. It took us three days to go up there four miles. Teams could go only so long and then they wore themselves out and set right down; they couldn't move any further. We'd rest them overnight and back at seven o'clock the next morning and go at it again. You'd have one block tied to the boiler and the other block maybe fifty yards up the road hooked to the tree. The team would be tied to the rope about opposite where the last block was fastened, because if anything breaks, you wouldn't want to hit the teams or the man driving, because this happened sometimes.

I tell you, we had the block and tackle and we had one fellow lettin' the boiler down a sharp hill. He had three wrappings around a tree and was lettin' go a little at a time. For some reason or another, it let go on him. The boiler was slidin' and that thing was just singing around that tree. He was rolling, trying to get away from it. I happened to be handy and I seen it was pretty soon goin' to catch him so I grabbed an axe and cut the rope. It saved him, but that boiler went down and what an awful mess. And then I got hell for cuttin' this big long rope.

We used to splice our own rope and that's a job in itself, especially an inch and a quarter rope. You make about a four-foot splice and when it's done you can't tell where it's spliced. It takes a long while. You've got to use your marlin spike to weave that thing. You got to unwind your strands of rope and feather them out to nothing. If you didn't, you'd have double the thickness when you put the two together. If it's made right, the splice is stronger than the rope itself.

Another time we took the mill up from Folly Mountain, down through Londonderry into Londonderry Station and up to Westchester Mountain by Sutherlands Lake. This was another spring cut by the foot of Sutherlands Lake. This was April 9th 'cause there wasn't supposed to be any snow there, it was supposed to be spring up there. It was all prearranged maybe two weeks ahead of time. We'd get up there and build the camp and the hovel to keep the horses in. We give ourselves two weeks to build that, and we arranged for the teams to be at the other end to bring the mill in from Folly Mountain.

In the meantime we got this big snowstorm Saturday night. Blow and howl! We had planned to move the mill on Monday. Dad says

Monday morning, "You and Ivan,"—that was my brother—"you better take a shovel and go down. They might need some help." We was in a hollow where we had set up our camp 'cause it was near a run-off from Sutherlands Lake. We took our shovels and come up over the hill. And the snow was so deep, when we come on the main road we had to bend to get under the telephone poles. I looked at Ivan and he looked at me and he says, "Well I guess we won't walk too far today." So anyway, we went and were up to our knees all the way and there were places a lot deeper than that. We decided we wouldn't need the shovels and we wasn't goin' to carry them down Londonderry Mountain.

Finally, we did get down around two o'clock in the afternoon and the teams had come as far as the foot of the mountain and the horses were almost dragged out. They left one sled and doubled up the teams on another that was mostly camp supplies. They started comin' up the mountain and the horses were just floundering all the time because there was two feet of snow and they had to break road all the way. It's a long, six-mile upgrade. They gradually started

Portable saw mill, circa 1900. "In the springtime, you didn't worry. The mill always laid wide open...." (N.S. Museum)

throwin' stuff off to lighten the load. There was no houses along, it was all woods; you dumped it off, it'd be there in the spring. Before they got to what they call the Buckwheat Flat, about halfway up the mountain, they had nothin' but the bare sled, and the horses were still floundering along.

The teamsters were quite concerned because they couldn't leave the horses on the road all night, and they didn't want to wear the horses out so they couldn't get to camp and under shelter, so every once in a while you'd have to rest for about fifteen minutes and let them go again. Finally, the teamster said, "The only way we'll get to camp is leave the sleds." They dropped the sleds right in the middle of the road. We went along about another mile and a half and the horses were still getting draggy. "Drop the harness off 'em." Finally we ended at the camp with just the bridles on the horses and everybody wore out.

The horses were more important than the men those days. You took care of your horses before you ate yourself. We got them all fixed up good and then we went in and had something to eat and settled down for the night. We were just beat and of course we only had a temporary camp. My father says, "We won't move tomorrow, we'll get rested up and head for her the next day." It was such a freak storm come in, comin' on spring then; it come out in lovely days after that. We moved down the mountain two days later and worked our stuff up until finally we got it all up there. But those are some of the experiences you run across.

My father was a great advocator of home remedies. One of the old home remedies if you had asthma, which a lot of people had those days from coal smoke and whatnot, one of the great cures was to take a tablespoon full of paraffine oil and drink it. That oiled all your tissues, your lungs and pipes and whatnot. This Harv Lard, he was a chopper from Pugwash, oh, he wheezed so badly at night it'd keep the men awake. He wheezed somethin' terrible. Dad said, "We can't stand that too long." Those days we used to have paraffine oil lamps, not kerosene. I don't know if you can get paraffine today or not. He give him a tablespoonful and he says, "You drink that now and your asthma will be gone."

Well, he got it in his mouth and he was scared to swallow it and finally it went down the windpipe. Was he in a state! Oh, him wheezin' and tryin' to get his breath was somethin' terrible. We had to make a litter. We just used two poles with a burlap bag and him on that, and four of us had to walk him three miles out of the woods and six miles down the mountain to the Londonderry railroad station as fast as we could go.

We took eight men and we just kept goin', changing over, changing over. You've seen how an Indian will trot, that's the way we went and never stopped until we got him to the station. There was a freight train due there in ten minutes. It used to always stop there because there was a big water tank there. Boys, we got him on the caboose and he was in the hospital here in Amherst for two weeks before they cleared it up. What a time that was.

One time we was up Westchester Mountain and we had Ivan Halliday. He lived just over in a place called Rose; that's up on the other side of Williamsdale. We was working in the woods up there and this Ivan Halliday and, I can't think of the other fella's name, they were choppin'. Course those days, you only wore gum rubbers, lumberman rubbers, just a short boot and all rubber. Well, Ivan was choppin' and the axe cut him right through his toe there. He hobbled to camp. This Garnet somebody that was with him helped him get to camp, and he got out the needle and black thread and he sewed this up, mind you. Put the iodine to it first and then sewed it up. Two days boys, and he was back loggin' again. They thought more about workin' than they did about a sore foot.

I got a bad cut one time. I was putting the planking down in front of the boiler. We had it pretty well boarded in. We had two men on the roof. They double-boarded those days; they didn't put tar paper on because it would burn off anyway because there were sparks flying all the time. That means you put boards on and then you put narrow boards over the cracks. Well, they were puttin' the double boarding on the mill roof and it had a big hole opening around where the smokestack went up. I happened to be down near that, putting the floor down—two-inch floor to walk around the boiler—and I was on my knees putting these plank down. These fellas up above workin' had an axe and it come down through the hole and caught one side of the head. I reached up and pulled down and here was a whole gob of blood and hair. I just put my hand back up and I hollered at Dad, "Come here!" "What's the matter now?" I took my hand down and the blood just rushed down the side. "Oh God," he said, "you cut yourself. Come onto camp."

We got to the camp and I sat down and got the cook out with the creolin. We used to have creolin all the time in the camp for disinfectant. We put three or four drops of that into a basin and it turned the water like milk. He swabbed the blood all off and then he got his razor out, had an old-fashioned razor those days. He shaved all around that cut and got it back about an inch. After he got done shaving, he got me to bend my head down into the pan of creolin. Oh! You talk about sharp! I think that actually cauterized it and stopped the bleeding a lot. He hauled it together and taped it all with this adhesive tape. My head didn't feel too good for two or three days, I'll tell you that. It seems like every once in a while something like that would happen.

In a camp, especially in the wintertime, say you're six miles away from the station or you're three miles in the woods, why you're quite a ways from civilization so you got to make your own fun. Our sawdust pile would cover maybe a hundred square feet and it would be just as level as could be. You'd always have a man haulin' sawdust away from the sawdust chute and every day he'd sprinkle it around and keep it level. We used to go out there and use that for an exercise field at night. We'd do all kinds of juggling and weight lifting, wrestling, and everything else at night, after working ten hours all day.

For something to do Sundays, you'd go down to the mill and see how much lumber you can carry away on your shoulder. One would try to outdo the other. Sometimes, I'll tell you, you'd take some awful loads away from there. The beauty was that you didn't have to pick it up, it was on the skidway and was just the height for your shoulders. You'd just walk under, lift it, and away you'd go. There was a lot you couldn't pick up and carry, but you could carry an awful load. They were thinking up something like that all the time.

One winter we was down there we had about a good half mile all downhill right into the camp and it was twisting around trees and whatnot, so we decided we'd make a toboggan and have some fun there at nights. I got the sawyer to saw me out hardwood, fourteen feet long, tapered, not a knot in it at all. I got it between two trees that was laying down like a log brow and I got a weight on the other end and started bending it. I done it very handy to the boiler so I could soak burlap bags and I kept hot water to it. Every time I put hot water to it, it would sag a little further so then I'd put a little more weight on to bring it down. Finally I got it curled up pretty well. I left it that way until it dried out and it stayed. We used that for a toboggan comin' down this long hill.

There were different men there, they'd go in and build their own little camp and bring the wife and children in. Sometimes you'd have four or five camps in there. They'd only build it about ten by twelve, just big enough to have a stove and a couple of bunks. Never bothered

with any bedrooms; you'd have bunks in one end and your stove and a table in the other end. The men always got their meals at the camp, but the women and children would have to get their own meals. Sometimes there'd be quite a settlement. It so happened this time, one of the kids had one of these little sleds, so we borrowed the sled and put that in front of this great big old toboggan. We laid on the sled and hooked our feet into the rope on the toboggan and we could steer it around the turns. Otherwise, we tried it once or twice, you'd come to a turn and it wouldn't go around the turn, it went right into the embarkment. We'd get as high as eight or ten on that toboggan and that's a lot of weight goin' down that hill. You talk about goin'. You'd only make about two trips a night, but it was all fun.

They used to play in the camp early nights. They'd Indian wrestle, two men would lay down on the floor and hook legs. Then another one, they'd hold onto a broomstick and put your feet against each other and try to pull the other up. Used to do that to the new fellas, get them up on their backsides and let them go. Some liked it and some didn't. You'll always have a prankster in a mill crew and he's always out to make jokes on somebody.

We always had a fiddler in there and a guitar player, and sometimes a banjo player. A couple that stayed with us for years was Fred Chapman and Aubrey Chapman. They were from Chapman Settlement and they were great violin players. Once they got known, the neighbours from outside would come in, especially in the spring cuts when we would be sawing out into a field somewhere. At the same

Two unidentified mill workers duke it out over lunch hour at Lewis Miller's Lumber Yard, Ingramport, circa 1925. Various sporting events were enjoyed by mill and lumber camp crews as a means to relax from the rigours of the day. (PANS)

time, they'd play for dances in the schoolhouses in these little communities. Over the years, we sawed all the way from Moncton to Stewiacke.

Many a night, just for somethin' to do, we'd walk out to the clear, most of us, and that'd be nine miles. We always went out to the post office to see if there was any mail. We knew there wouldn't be any, but we'd go out just for an excuse. Those old country post offices, there's always a lot of people hang around them and it was just to exchange views and get the news. We'd land there; "Come on in for a cup of tea." Lumberjacks, when you go in there for a cup of tea, you want to have lots to eat too. They'd give you a whole plateful of sandwiches and cookies and cakes. About nine o'clock, we'd walk back for camp. No lights, but after awhile you got so you could see pretty well in the dark. You'd be walkin' along, especially after you turned off the main road into the woods, you'd hear crunch, crunch, crunch, right behind you. You'd walk with your head back so you could listen and you'd hear it. As soon as you stopped, it stopped. Well, then, you'd turn around and walk backwards and it'd come again. We smartened up after awhile and took a flashlight with us. Then we'd do the same; we'd go backwards and you'd see these two eyes comin'. They were wildcats. They'd only come so handy the camp.

We had a truck haulin' lumber. We'd haul in the daytime and at night we'd go girlin'. One night, he'd take the truck and the next night, I'd take the truck. I was up on Folly Mountain this night with a girlfriend alongside of the road. My brother had the truck. We always planned on meeting each other at the foot of the mountain to save walkin' all the way up. So this night, I was over four miles on another mountain with a girlfriend and we was gettin' along fine. I heard *wrrr, wrrr, wrrr, wrrr;* I knew that was my brother comin' with the truck for me. He wouldn't wait too long for me, so I said, "Good night," and I ran down that mountain and, you know, you'd just hit the ground about every ten feet. Finally, I did get to the bridge at the foot of the mountain and Ivan wasn't there. It must have been ten or eleven o'clock then. I kind of searched, but I couldn't see if he had come by or not and I listened and listened and couldn't hear a sound.

After I waited there about half an hour, it was gettin' cold, you know, I thought I'd better keep goin'. Well, I started up the mountain, black as the ace of spades. I got way up there walkin' along and you'd hear somethin' behind you and the old hair on your neck would stand on end. No use to run because you had too far to run, you'd be out of breath. You just had to keep listening and walking; a gravel road was crunchy anyway.

While not all that common, some families would spend the winter with their men at the camps. Pictured is a group at Lake Franklin Camp, Digby Co., circa 1910. Most times women and young children stayed home to run the farm through the winter months. (N.S. Museum)

I was goin' along and you can't see your hand before your face, it's so black. My foot hit something soft and I felt and grabbed. I had both hands full of hair and it was gettin' up and I was holdin' on, right in the middle of the road. First thing I thought was a bear. Well, I hung on and it's goin', goin', and I got my legs around underneath the belly of it, holdin' this hair. Boy, it hit the woods and of course the branches struck me right across the face and I went off, ass over kettle. I never did know at that time what it was, but I knew it was goin' one way and I went the other way. I finally found the road and got back to the camp after awhile.

I was tellin' the boys. "Oh, you're dreamin'."

"No," I says, "I'm not dreamin'. Let's go out in the mornin' and we'll see what I jumped on." About six o'clock in the morning, imagine us walkin' out that road and I'd only been in bed about three hours. We walked back and here it was where it had been a steer laying in the middle of the road. See, they used to come in the road and lay down at night; the ground warmed up in the daytime. When I fell on it, it jumped and you could see all the feet tracks around. I'd been on his back for about a hundred yards before the bushes hit me off. I'll tell you, it was scary.

We had a cook, it was my aunt, and we set up camp down at Randy Brook; that's just outside of Truro on the Harmony Road. There was an old, old house been vacant for years; they said it was haunted. My aunt and her husband, they were pretty suspicious. My brother and

I were just young enough to be devilish. So they slept down and we slept upstairs.

Must've been nine o'clock or later when we went to bed. The cook and her husband, they settled down below. We got the flashlight out when we moved up there to go to bed, and we kind of scanned things over to see what was up there. First thing we saw this old chimney, right up through the centre of the hall from down below. You could look down into a back porch and here was a shelf loaded full of old preserve bottles.

Those days the chimneys was only made out of lime and sand, no concrete at all. We scratched out one of the brick. We went over to a hole and held the flashlight down on that shelf and we heaved that brick. Down went the shelf and those bottles crackin'. The cook come to the bottom of the stairs. "Harold! Harold! Did you hear that noise?" I says, "I was nearly asleep. I thought I heard somethin' goin'." "The place is haunted!" she says. God, they got up and walked the roads with a lantern all night. Father come in the next day and he says, "What did you fellas do last night?"

"Nothin', nothin'."

"You did somethin'! The cook's leaving today. She says the place is haunted."

We daresn't tell him 'cause they'd give us the devil if they knew. We had to go down next day and get that brick and put it back in the chimney so they wouldn't notice it.

While we were still at the same place, we used to have an Oliver Murette, he was an old fella in his seventies, a little too old; everybody that age they're pretty well wore out, too old to work. Dad got him a job as night watchman in the mill. Those days, in the summertime, you had to have somebody on because sparks are flying during the daytime and they smolder around and maybe at night they start a fire and burn the mill down. So they had him watchin' the mill.

This night we'd been to town and had it all planned. We knew he was watchman and he'd be down around the mill somewhere. We took the sheet off our bed and Mansel Trenholm—he was workin' with us too—we took his fiddle and bow. We come from town about eleven o'clock. When we come down over the hill, I got the sheet over my head and Ivan got the old fiddle squealin' and I got to hollerin' and goin' on. We seen old Oliver comin' up, walkin' with this lantern. All of a sudden the lantern stopped. The next thing, he just swung that in a circle over the head and run as fast as he could. He never stopped at the camp, just kept goin' right by. We don't know yet where he went or how long he stayed. He wasn't even back in time for breakfast. Dad was suspicious, but he couldn't prove anything. He says, "You give that man an awful scare last night."

I says, "What do you mean? I don't know a thing about it."

"I'll find that out one of these days!" he says.

We used to play some awful tricks not realizing Dad had to go to town to hire another man for night watchman. If he could prove it, he would've given us a damn good thumpin'.

Harry Carter

Harry Carter, 78, has lived all his life in Amherst, Cumberland County. His father, William H., built up a successful business of timber cutting and sawmilling. Harry spent twenty-five years working with his father. "Those days, when you got through, if you had a dollar a thousand, that was good money. If you handled fifteen, twenty thousand a day, that's fifteen or twenty dollars; you paid your men, and by the time you got through, you still had money."

My father, when he first started out, was a carpenter. He built big, two-storey houses and sold them around here—buy the land, build the house, and sell it. He'd build five in one season, he and two other fellas. He'd do the inside finish on the last one around Christmastime—never worked in the winter—and he'd sell them for twelve hundred dollars and make money.

Dad started just after the First World War in '20 or '21 and he logged and sawed almost every year until he died in 1953. We had, one time, over five thousand acres of timberland. Land at that time wasn't worth anything. He bought two thousand acres out here from Rhodes and Curry and he only paid thirty-five hundred dollars for it. They couldn't get rid of it and they had no money. We logged that for years and years and years. If you had a dollar you could buy almost anything, that's about the size of it.

Our land was so extensive we couldn't cut that much in any one place in the winter that would cut it out. A half a million feet was about the limit we'd ever take any one year in any one place. Then we'd move somewhere else and cut maybe two or three hundred thousand, and somewhere else and cut two or three hundred thousand, and that was it. We used to handle just a million or a little more a year. We never operated big.

My old man did things different than anybody else around here in the lumber business. He never operated through the bank; he operated it through himself. He didn't have much money, but he used it all. He bought everything by cash, paid everybody by cash, and he didn't take on any job bigger than he could handle himself. Most of them didn't do that. The bank would finance them all winter and then spring come, they'd saw the lumber and put it to market. They'd get credit back and if they didn't have enough money comin' in, they didn't have anything comin' themselves. These people got in the hole thousands of dollars. The lumber crash came—they call it a crash—the whole thing blew up just overnight. The price of lumber went all to pieces way back around '20, '21, '22 and left these people with extensive money owed to the bank and lumber didn't bring enough to pay it.

Things were very good during the First World War apparently, according to what they told me; I was pretty young then. But after that, lumber went to pieces and there was no demand. The depression just hit that way in the lumber business, it didn't hit in everything apparently; that was before the big depression, the '29 one, come. That's when they were in the hole and couldn't get out because they never got ahead. They never really come out of that first one. Lumber went from thirty-five dollars one night down to ten or twelve the next; you could hardly give it away at ten or twelve dollars a thousand. It was a long while before it come up. The biggest men around here went broke. As you know, when you're financing through the bank, if you can't pay, they take what you've got, that's all.

Dad used to get it all ready to sell before he'd sell it. Others would contract like now for this winter's cut, and next spring you took what the price was comin'. One year he kept part of it over, market prices were too low, and he sold what he could at a good price. That's just before the last war come on. He done that and operated on a smaller scale the next winter. He was that smart he made a success of it. Other people around didn't.

Those days we hauled it mostly all by truck to Pugwash. Most of the stuff, all through the thirties and forties, went to England, practically. There's a wharf right there in the village where they load the salt. That was a big wharf. I've seen millions of feet of lumber piled on that. Before we had trucks big enough, they'd haul it into Amherst here and load it on railway cars and it would go to some shipping point.

Before I got in it, Dad cut a lot of hardwood. He was in Fenwick a couple of winters and his main market at that time was the Amherst Piano Factory. They used clear rock maple for makin' pianos. That was around the twenties, just after the First World War. That's the only place that we ever sold any amount.

Some places we'd go in and just cut pine because we used to sell that to Enamel Heating Products here for pattern work to make moulds for the tubs and like that. Those days you could find places where there was good pine, I mean big pine. They wanted it twelve, fourteen inches wide if they could get it. We cut one place there we had lots of them eighteen, twenty inches wide. Some of the logs were so big they had to cut them in quarters, just cut in one side and then turn them around and cut another side and make it into four pieces. The mills in those days were only a rotary saw, they didn't have band saws like they have today. When they got up over four or five feet in diameter, that's as big as they could go. We had lots of them up in New Brunswick; one place we cut there, they were eight, nine foot because for years nobody wanted pine, so it was left. It didn't blow down because there was always enough other stuff left growing.

You sold a lot of what you could local. Your logs you made into three- or four-inch timber, deal, you'd make a lot of that. We hauled a lot in here because we supplied the Enamel Heating Products. They used to take a million feet of boards a year at the last for crating sinks and toilets and bathtubs.

Dad died in 1953 and I went out in 1955, sold everything, got clear of it. I'll tell you exactly why I went out of it. I could have run on for a long while except that the government had got into it so bad and would not leave us alone. They were after everything they could get. My father didn't believe in giving away money for nothin'. And he always figured that if he had a few men workin', he could take care of that and the bookwork himself because he paid everybody every day. If you had ten dollars comin' or whatever you had comin', he'd pay you and scratch through your name that it was paid. He drew so much money out of the bank and when he got through the week, he showed how much money he had paid out for income tax purposes. In those days you didn't have to pay any income tax because the exemption was way up to over three thousand dollars and nobody here ever made that kind of money hardly at all, not then. If you made five or six hundred clear you had a big year 'cause people were livin' on two hundred and less back in the Depression years before the Second World War.

Just after the war got on they started this unemployment insurance business. Well, I made an agreement with the unemployment insurance officer here that if you were working for me, I paid the whole thing, both sides 'cause it was only a matter of a few cents then, it didn't amount to much. Then later on they come out with the idea that I wasn't paying any income tax for these fellas. First you paid your own income tax, then later on the boss had to take so much off you every week for income tax purposes. I wasn't doin' it and I wasn't goin' to. That meant bookwork and that meant you had to hire a book-keeper to look after your books if you had anybody workin' for you. You could run along with three or four or somethin', but these fellas that are operatin' today with only three or four people, they're half the night doin' their bookwork 'cause they have so many reports and everything. I refused to take money off the men. I owe you so much money, you pay your own bills. They were lookin' for me, so when I found out I just simply up and sold the whole thing and quit. I gave it up completely then.

One thing my old man didn't believe in was waste. When the mill run, he was there every day at the end of the mill and he always had a rule in his hand and a piece of lumber chalk to mark anything that was no good or wrong. A piece of wood come through, he'd check it every once in a while. His eyes would do pretty good checkin', but he'd put the rule on, and if the saw wasn't makin' it right, it was a little bit big or too small, he'd stop the mill and make them correct it immediately. We didn't have a whole lot of waste. Some people, when they got through cuttin', they'd have a great pile. We didn't. You could haul all the stuff we ever left from a cut away in a wheelbarrow. Today is a day of waste, you see it everywhere you go.

My old man was very fussy about the land and about the timber. When he went in a piece of land, he cut what was suitable to cut and everything else had to stay there. And twenty years time, you'd go in and cut again. He didn't do any cutting in the woods personally himself much in the later years. He and I would go through and supervise once a week at least and see what was going on. If a man cut a tree and felled it on another one, a four- or five-inch tree that was no need of, that fella would have his job maybe another day if he didn't let it happen again. But if he saw him do that a couple of times, he'd fire him. Never allowed them to knock anything down if they could help it. The men we had working, he paid a little more money than anybody else and he always had extra good men. A good chopper could land a tree anywhere, but others just cut it off and let it go wherever it went. He didn't believe in that kind of thing, that wasn't his style.

A friend of mine down Stewiacke had a farm and he told me here

"In the old days, you hooked on with a horse; he come up against a tree, he had to stop, he couldn't haul it out. That was it. And through the woods, you'd just see a little trail where they pulled logs out. Now, the whole place is bare." (Ernie Coates)

a few years ago that he was on that farm about seventy years. When they first went, they cut the land. Then they had three cuts after that and when he left it a couple of years ago, the fella that bought it cut again on it. But it'll be another fifty years before there'll be anything, he said, after the way they cut it.

They never used tractors, only horses. See, when they put a tractor in the way they do now, they go in and just push everything over, hook on a tree, and haul it out. It comes up against another tree or ten trees, it takes them right out by the roots. It tears the land all to pieces. In the old days, you hooked on with a horse; he come up against a tree, he had to stop, he couldn't haul it out. That was it. And through the woods, you'd just see a little trail where they pulled logs out. Now, the whole place is bare.

When we sold our land, the companies that bought it went in and had good cuts on it. Every twenty to twenty-five years you can get a cut off the land. A tree, if it's five or six inches in diameter, it's pretty well along in growth. Another ten, fifteen years, that tree's goin' to grow quite a lot. But when you do like they're doin' and plough the whole thing out, you got to start from scratch then. Now that's common sense. For years the Department of Lands and Forests wouldn't allow you to do it. They went around and prosecuted for cuttin' everything. Now it's the other way around.

Any place they start pulping, there's no time, the lumber's gone. We never handled pulp; my father said you just cut the land to pieces.

When they cut pulp they took everything and the old man didn't believe in taking that small stuff. He cut what was good to make a decent piece of lumber and if it didn't, well, let it stand. "Why knock it down?" he said. "It's growin' there. The Lord put it there, let it stay. Another few years, it might be a log, be some good some day." But nowadays, they don't do that. You look from here to Dorchester and through from here to Moncton and see what mess they got. It'll be a hundred years before there's ever anything to look at to cut. It's all over the country. This seems to be stupid, really stupid. He'd turn over in his grave if he saw this stuff.

EPILOGUE

When people talk about the good old days it is because they remember the friendship that was always present. We were not more wealthy, but we were more happy in our families and with each other. There was a lot of sharing, both joys and sorrows, and nobody ever went short of help. Everybody cared.

(Foster E. Hall, *Heritage Remembered: The Story of Bear River*, 1981).

Shipbuilding, fishing, lumbering: in 1867, at Canada's confederation, these three distinguished Nova Scotia as the fledging nation's richest province. The heyday of wooden ships passed a century ago with the coming of steam and iron hulls, and today the plight of the east coast fishery is a separate, sad tale in itself. Lumbering has ridden a cyclic roller coaster for two hundred years, enduring fires, disease, pestilence, embargoes, depressions, recessions and other financial crises. However, the forest industry today may be facing its sternest test.

Canada is still the world's leading exporter of lumber products, pulp, and newsprint, but the entire forest industry from coast to coast is in serious trouble. Softwood lumber exports to the United States are presently centre stage in free-trade disputes over subsidies and export taxes, and the demand for kiln-dried lumber for European markets is making it especially difficult on small operators, a category most of Nova Scotia's approximately 360 sawmills fall under. Coupled with this, for Nova Scotia, are imports of cheap lumber from other provinces and a disheartening public view that all of Canada's forests are being overharvested, with little regard for the future.

At the centre of the controversy is Canada's pulp and paper industry, a $20-billion-a-year megabusiness. Nova Scotia accounts for only a small portion of this business, somewhere around three percent, yet even this means nearly a billion dollars a year to the province and employs thousands. Nova Scotia's three pulp and paper companies—Stora, Scott, and Bowater Mersey—like their counterparts across the country, are the focus of an increasing concern over economic and environmental issues: closures and cutbacks, worker layoffs, low wages, wood marketing boards, poor markets and prices, gluts of newsprint, recycling, spraying, foul air emissions, effluent treatment, environmental regulations, cutting practices, reforestation, pollution controls, technology versus manpower, and recession. So much is spoken and written by both sides that the average person is left with the confusing task of sorting through what he wants to believe as opposed to what he should believe.

Every generation has its faults and it would be idealistic to romanticize the early years in the lumber woods as being free of sin. In fact, the old sawmills polluted rivers, killing trout and salmon with sawdust and waste wood; dams blocked access to spawning grounds; river driving left acidic bark in the waters to poison fish stocks; sparks from sawmills started many forest fires; and, turn of the century game reports blamed lumber camps for killing excessive numbers of moose at a time when their populations were down. Clear cutting was even being advocated by some as early as the 1940s. Yet, for all of this, the environmental consequences of the past were slight compared to the dangers facing us today.

The technological revolution that followed World War Two has reached mind-boggling heights. Today's discoveries are soon yesterday's news as the world rapidly changes. One cannot deny that much of this "progress" has been beneficial and society is better for it. Yet a price has also been paid. We have become artificial and detached from our natural environment, upon which our survival depends. Nowhere perhaps is this more evident than in our forests.

Solutions are not easy at this stage, yet steps, albeit baby ones, are being taken to rectify past mistakes. Much remains to be done, and input is needed from all sides: government, industry, and "consumers." Not to be shrugged off and forgotten are those who are perhaps best suited to speak out, who have seen both sides. As one old-timer put it, "Now, my God, some of these fellas are supposed to be educated and they don't know too much about it. They go to college and learn everything out of a book, but you've got to have some experience too. A lot of these old fellas with experience could tell you more about how to go in the woods and log a piece than some of these fellas has come out of college. Yeah, I'm sure they could. To see these woods all cut down. Gosh! It's goin' to be a long time before another crop grows, isn't it?"

ENDNOTES

HANTS COUNTY

[1] The Brooklyn mill might well have been one of four mills in Hants County owned by T.G. McMullen of Truro. The other three were located at Hartville, Scotch Village and South Maitland. Known as the "Lumber King of Nova Scotia," McMullen came to own 300,000 acres of land and thirteen mills in Nova Scotia. In 1893 alone, he loaded forty ships with more than twenty-two million board feet of lumber at $10 a thousand for Liverpool, England, his major market. Beginning around 1870 as a carriage maker in Truro, his varied interests included lumbering, shipping and railroads. He died a millionaire in 1925 at his Truro home.

LUNENBURG COUNTY

[1] Mersey Paper Company very nearly ended up closing before it opened. During feasibility studies in 1927, it was found that a lifetime guarantee of one hundred thousand cords annually of spruce and fir could not be made within an acceptable radius of the proposed mill in Liverpool. Its founder and financier, the wealthy and influential I.W. Killam of Montreal, was prepared to pull out until the provincial government agreed to provide one million cords of pulpwood from crown lands in Guysborough County and on Cape Breton Island over thirty years. First operational in 1929, Mersey Paper Company not only survived the Depression while many failed, it was also a major employer of woodsmen during the bleak years of the thirties. With huge land acquisitions of its own after the thirty-year agreement with the provincial government expired in 1959, and buying from private contractors and small woodlot owners, Mersey has been an economic mainstay of the provincial economy for more than sixty years. A history of the company, *In the Mersey Woods*, was commissioned in 1989 to mark its sixtieth anniversary.

[2] Lunenburg County was noted for its bell makers. Bells were made from iron with a coat of brass or were cast in solid brass. The shape of the bell identified its maker, and its tone the teamster. It has been said that a teamster could be recognized by the sound of his ox bells long before he was seen.

QUEENS COUNTY

[1] Flumes, or sluiceways, had been used for moving logs and lumber since the 1880s in Nova Scotia. E.D. Davison & Sons of Bridgewater had one on the LaHave River at Gulley Brook in 1892. Archibald McMullen completed a six-

mile sluice the same year at Great Village, Colchester County. His brother T.G. McMullen had built a sluice on Debert Mountain in 1885, and by 1892 they owned twenty-one miles of sluiceway between them. Sluiceways were also used at River Philip, Sand River, and Eatonville in Cumberland County.

2   The book *In the Mersey Woods*, a history of the Bowater Mersey Paper Company, states the term *van* was a shortened version of the Algonquin word *wangan* meaning "container of odds and ends"; it was brought to Nova Scotia by early woods bosses from Ontario.

3   Gold was first mined in Queens County in the 1880s at Whiteburn, and the subsequent "gold rush" that followed soon spread to nearby Molega and Brookfield. It continued until 1905, when the industry collapsed, but was revived again during the early 1930s. It closed for good in 1946 when Colonel S.C. Oland of the Halifax brewery family left Molega for Millipsigate, Lunenburg County, with his ball mill.

4   Ralph Johnson writes that cookstoves were first sold in North America as early as 1830 and they were used in lumber camps in Nova Scotia around 1840.

5   Ralph Johnson, in his book *Forests of Nova Scotia*, is unable to pinpoint exactly when crosscut saws replaced axes for felling and chunking logs. One source he used claims sometime between 1840 and 1880, while another put it at 1897, and still another at 1900. A local source in Johnson's book says the crosscut came into northern Queens County in 1905.

6   Edward Doran Davison was one of the province's largest lumber producers at the turn of the century. Together with his three sons—Henry, Francis, and Edward—he operated E.D. Davison & Sons, with its head office in Bridgewater. They controlled five water-powered gang sawmills in the 1890s: two at Mill Village on the Medway River, two at Bridgewater on the LaHave River, and one at Alpena on the Nictaux River. In 1893 these five mills together produced sixteen million feet of lumber; in 1903 annual production ran between fifteen and seventeen million feet.

SHELBURNE COUNTY

1   Thomas Uriah had moved to Barrington in 1861, according to local historian Hattie Perry.

2   Tom started with gasoline, switched to semi-diesel, changed to full diesel, then to a combination of diesel and electric. With the rise in power rates in 1975, he switched to diesel.

3   A variety of axes have been used in the Nova Scotia lumber woods. The first were the trade axe and broadaxe introduced in the early 1600s. The trade axe was just that, a barter good exchanged with native peoples for fur pelts, and was of poor design and construction. It was replaced around 1750 by the English felling axe, a better performing tool in terms of blade and handle shape and balance. The broadaxe was used for many decades but was an unwieldy beast, weighing as much as thirteen pounds. The single-bitted American "poll axe" was introduced around 1815 in weights between three to five pounds, three and a half being the favoured. It was widely used along with the broadaxe until the double-bitted axe came in around the turn of the century.

4   Shelburne Fruit and Pickle Company was started in 1913 to process the surplus apples being grown along the Roseway waters. They were peeled, sliced, dried and packed for sale in fifty-pound boxes. Seconds were made into apple cider.

Processing fruit became unprofitable about 1917 or 1918, and at a director's meeting on December 19, 1918, the name was changed to Shelburne Woodworkers Ltd. Fred Bower, founder of Shelburne Fruit and Pickle Company, was made managing director/secretary-treasurer of the new company. Shelburne County had an excess of small fir and spruce unsuitable for lumber. As many as fifty ox and horse teams then began hauling wood to the company's mill to make large and small wooden boxes to pack fish in. Most of its business came from the neighbouring fishing villages of Lockeport and Cape Sable Island. Over the years Shelburne Woodworkers expanded their mills, built warehouses, and increased their timber holdings. In 1922 a rotary mill for sawing logs was built. In 1934 the Woodworkers became involved in the bakery business, and in 1936 a sash factory was built. They also operated a portable lath mill at Birchtown from which they sold to fishermen for $2.75 per thousand. The company kept the area alive during the Depression years, paying for wood with much needed groceries and feed. The company was able to buy these supplies with monies received primarily from the large fish companies in Shelburne and Lockeport.

DIGBY COUNTY

[1] The story of the Stehelin family is a most interesting account and forms the basis of Paul H. Stehelin's book, *The Electric City: The Stehelins of New France*. Patriarch Emile Charles Adolph Stehelin was a manufacturer and Major in the French army during the Franco–Prussian War of 1870. Through a series of events, the father of nine sons and three daughters had moved his family by 1896 into the backwoods of Weymouth around Long Tusket and Langford lakes. Having purchased ten thousand acres of timberland and built a water-powered gang sawmill, he established a substantial community, complete with the first electric power plant in Digby County and one of the first in the province. His markets for lumber were Britain and South America. Being twenty miles from Weymouth, he built the New France & Weymouth Railway to increase productivity and efficiency; however, this was to be an economic failure and by 1907 had closed down. The final chapter of the Stehelin odyssey came in 1918 with Emile's death in Weymouth.

[2] Ralph Johnson, a respected forester for half a century, defined silviculture in *Forests of Nova Scotia* as "a branch of forestry dealing with the theory and practise of controlling the establishment, composition, constitution and growth of forests."

[3] This was not an idle boast as evidenced by the following list of 1905 businesses: eleven general stores, meat market, shoemaker, jewelry and repair, harness shop, carriage factories, millinery and dry goods store, four blacksmith shops, Chinese laundry, bakery, photo studio, dentist's office, two doctors' offices, sail loft, hotel, custom's office, post office, bank, drugstore, law office, telegraph and telephone office, sawmill, threshing mill, granite works, and electric light plant.

ANNAPOLIS COUNTY

[1] At the mouth of the Bear River where it empties into the Annapolis Basin were two steel bridges, one of which was a train trestle. Both had to be cranked open manually using a capstan-type mechanism to allow passage of ships, then closed and locked.

[2] Portable steam mills were the cause of many early forest fires. As a preventive

measure, legislation was passed in 1904 making it mandatory for portable mills to have paid watchmen.

3   In 1905, Crossburn consisted of a cookhouse, two dining rooms, bunkhouse, school, four bungalows, commissary, office warehouse, machine shop, and five-stall roundhouse.

GUYSBOROUGH COUNTY

1   Alfred Dickie Lumber Company was in Stewiacke, Colchester County.

2   According to Mr. Anderson, the Norwegian freighters stopped after the out-break of World War Two.

3   Scott Paper Company imported pulpwood from Nova Scotia as early as the First World War and had entertained thoughts of building a mill in the province in the 1920s.

VICTORIA COUNTY

1   Details surrounding the politics of the Big Lease deal can be found in Ralph Johnson's book, *The Forests of Nova Scotia*.

2   The Sydney steel plant started up near the turn of the century. It has been operated under a number of names, most recently Sydney Steel Corporation (Sysco).

3   From 1930 until World War Two, Mersey shipped all their Cape Breton pulp by water. During the war years, when ships were at a premium, it went by rail. Following the war, ships were used again, until 1959 when Mersey's thirty-year crown land lease expired.

COLCHESTER COUNTY

1   In the 1700s, ton timber could be exported round or hewn square. A ton comprised fifty cubic feet of rough, unhewn timber, or forty of hewn. Strict guidelines regarding ton timber were established in 1814. All timber for export had to be symmetrically squared, at least ten inches, straight, and free of marks and rot. Spruce and pine could be no shorter than sixteen feet and hardwood no shorter than ten feet. Anything less than sixteen feet had to be of equal size at both ends.

2   Maggie Graham, 89, lives in Pembroke. She was very matter-of-fact about the incident when asked. "I don't know why I ever undertook to sew anybody's leg, but I did. This was years and years ago. I had forgotten about it. I guess we were the nearest house and he walked over. His moccasin was full of blood. He just came in and asked me if I'd do it and I told him no. He said, yes, I'd have to, so I did. It didn't heal right. Not much wonder. I don't think I took proper precautions."

CUMBERLAND COUNTY

1   According to Layton's brother Arnold, the reason it blew was because the dome on top of the boiler wasn't secured properly. A year or so earlier, while transporting the boiler through Oxford, the dome was knocked off passing under an overhead bridge. The dome was normally bolted, but when it was replaced, it was swelled into position and never rebolted. When the pressure built up, it blew the top off. Although much of the milling equipment on site belonged to the Smiths, the boiler was on loan.

SELECTED
BIBLIOGRAPHY

Adams, Peter. *Early Loggers & the Sawmill*. Toronto: Crabtree, 1981.

Canada and Nova Scotia. *The Trees Around Us: A Manual of Good Forest Practice for Nova Scotia*. 1980.

Coady, Howard. *Sheet Harbour History: From the Notes of an Old Woodsman*. Hantsport: Lancelot Press, 1988.

DesBrisay Museum. *The Ox in Nova Scotia*. Bridgewater: H & B Langille's Print, 1985.

Fowke, Edith. *Canadian Folklore*. Toronto: Oxford University Press, 1988.

Hall, Foster E. *Heritage Remembered: The Story of Bear River*. Bear River New Horizons Centre, 1981.

Johnson, Ralph S. *Forests of Nova Scotia*. Halifax: Four East Publications and N.S. Department of Lands and Forests, 1986.

Kephart, George S. *Campfires Rekindled*. Marion, Mass.: Channing Books, 1977.

Morrison, James, and Lawrence Friend. *"We Have Held Our Own": The Western Interior of Nova Scotia, 1800-1940*. Parks Canada, 1981.

Mullen, Eric, and Millie Evans. *In the Mersey Woods*. Liverpool, N.S.: Bowater Mersey Paper Co., 1989.

Perry, Lillian Scott. *For Old Time's Sake: with pike and peavey on the Barrington River, 1983*. Barrington, N.S.: Cape Sable Historical Society, 1983.

Pike, Robert E. *Tall Trees, Tough Men*. New York: W.W. Norton, 1967.

Robertson, Barbara R. *Sawpower: Making Lumber in the Sawmills of Nova Scotia*. Halifax: Nimbus and the Nova Scotia Museum, 1986.

Saunders, Gary L. *Trees of Nova Scotia: A Guide to the Native & Exotic Species*. Halifax: N.S. Department of Lands and Forests, 1970.

Silver, Arthur P. *Farm-Cottage, Camp & Canoe in Maritime Canada*. London: George Routledge & Sons, 1907.

Stehelin, Paul H. *The Electric City: The Stehelins of New France*. Hantsport: Lancelot Press, 1983.